BEYOND WELL-BEING

THE FASCINATION OF RISK AND OF THE NEW PSYCHOLOGICAL ADDICTIONS

PSYCHOLOGY OF EMOTIONS, MOTIVATIONS AND ACTIONS

Additional books in this series can be found on Nova's website
under the Series tab.

Additional e-books in this series can be found on Nova's website
under the e-book tab.

BEYOND WELL-BEING

THE FASCINATION OF RISK AND OF THE NEW PSYCHOLOGICAL ADDICTIONS

LAURA TAPPATÀ

publishers

New York

NOTICE TO THE READER

The Publisher has taken reasonable care in the preparation of this book, but makes no expressed or implied warranty of any kind and assumes no responsibility for any errors or omissions. No liability is assumed for incidental or consequential damages in connection with or arising out of information contained in this book. The Publisher shall not be liable for any special, consequential, or exemplary damages resulting, in whole or in part, from the readers' use of, or reliance upon, this material. Any parts of this book based on government reports are so indicated and copyright is claimed for those parts to the extent applicable to compilations of such works.

Independent verification should be sought for any data, advice or recommendations contained in this book. In addition, no responsibility is assumed by the publisher for any injury and/or damage to persons or property arising from any methods, products, instructions, ideas or otherwise contained in this publication.

This publication is designed to provide accurate and authoritative information with regard to the subject matter covered herein. It is sold with the clear understanding that the Publisher is not engaged in rendering legal or any other professional services. If legal or any other expert assistance is required, the services of a competent person should be sought. FROM A DECLARATION OF PARTICIPANTS JOINTLY ADOPTED BY A COMMITTEE OF THE AMERICAN BAR ASSOCIATION AND A COMMITTEE OF PUBLISHERS.

Additional color graphics may be available in the e-book version of this book.

Library of Congress Cataloging-in-Publication Data

Library of Congress Cataloging-in-Publication Data

Beyond well-being : the fascination of risk and of the new psychological addictions / editor, Laura Tappat` (Department of Psychology, Catholic University of Sacred Heart, Milan, Italy).
    pages cm
 Includes bibliographical references and index.
 ISBN: 978-1-62417-969-3 (hardcover)
 1. Well-being. 2. Self-esteem. 3. Quality of life. I. Tappat`, Laura.
 BF575.H27B4696 2013
 155.2'5--dc23
                            2013001528

Published by Nova Science Publishers, Inc. †*New York*

CONTENTS

FOREWORD

In this thought-provoking book, Laura Tappatà brilliantly guides the reader from a description of the existential problem of psychological addictions to a possible solution leading to a potentially positive outcome for the individual.

The central theme of the book is anchored in the dismal nature of "postmodern identity" with a focus on searching for meaning in what we are and who we are. This identity is characterized as being narcissistic and fragile, suggesting from the outset that we need to somehow strive for a stronger and more well-defined self in order to, first, survive and, then, possibly thrive emotionally. Living in this postmodern world naturally leads to a superficial existence and the seemingly blind quest of acquiring nonessential and meaningless things designed to bolster our ill-defined, weak and vulnerable self. Although this leads to a false sense of happiness, it does not generate true contentment let alone a sense of well-being. As such, many of us are left to drift with few essential values, certainties and stable points of reference.

The attention we devote to our identity, which is based on the ability to look inward, contributes to the creation of our personal life which is not a constellation of accidental events but the result of the way we look at ourselves. Here lies both the essence of the problem as well as the potential solution. This ability and process of looking at and focusing on ourselves, according to the authoress, becomes "a mental coin to invest carefully." And she argues that "we have to understand how to protect it and how best to spend it, because our resources are not infinite." Not spending this mental coin wisely is exemplified in our quest for immediate gratification and a false sense of happiness, with the risk of falling into the trap of becoming slaves to desires and urges that lead to what she refers to as "the new psychological addictions" such as our obsession with the Internet, technological gadgets, shopping, sex, healthy eating, exercising and the like.

The above condition highlights the need and value of understanding the meaning of our lives and of what and who we are. Moreover, the adeptness and depth of our self-awareness plays an important role in either becoming hooked on the psychological addictions described by the authoress or freeing ourselves from them. Attention, which is essentially looking at and focusing on ourselves and our world, is a valuable human asset, because it impacts motivation that helps us become more engaged in this process in addition to trying to understand these addictions and the risks involved. It empowers us to focus and expands the limits of our mind and mental powers, elevates the spirit and our ability to perceive everyday life with sharpened awareness. Many individuals live a life of spiritual imbalance based on the authoress' message, which impedes our ability to free ourselves from these psychological addictions as well as suggests the need for "spiritual balancing" as described by some. Here lies a possible solution to the problem eloquently described in this book. As such, the solution could be the end result, or ongoing task, of optimally combining, integrating and balancing our belief in what is fundamentally important in life with our mental, emotional, social and moral capabilities. These combined and balanced capabilities help us survive, adapt, do the right things and eventually achieve a sense of stability and true well-being (and not a false sense of happiness and momentary satisfaction) in ourselves, our interpersonal relationships and, hopefully, the ability to go beyond our egotistical selves and do something for the greater good of others, the community and society.

There is often a degree of fascination surrounding this search for balance as well as the fear of the risks involved, and both can become a path for personal growth, a space for self-realization and the expression of one's underlying identity. This also offers a way for people to overcome their fears, demonstrate their courage and prove themselves.

This book attempts to lead the reader on the path from "the postmodern dependence on psychological addictions" to freedom, the expression of one's identity and a true sense of well-being.

Reuven Bar-On
September 30th, 2012

PREFACE

In this thought-provoking book, Laura Tappatà brilliantly guides the reader from a description of the existential problem of psychological addictions to a possible solution leading to a potentially positive outcome for the individual. The central theme of the book is anchored in the dismal nature of "postmodern identity" with a focus on searching for meaning in what we are and who we are. This identity is characterized as being narcissistic and fragile, suggesting from the outset that we need to somehow strive for a stronger and more well-defined self in order to, first, survive and, then, possibly thrive emotionally. Living in this postmodern world naturally leads to a superficial existence and the seemingly blind quest of acquiring nonessential and meaningless things designed to bolster our ill-defined, weak and vulnerable self. Although this leads to a false sense of happiness, it does not generate true contentment let alone a sense of well-being. As such, many of us are left to drift with few essential values, certainties and stable points of reference. This book attempts to lead the reader on the path from "the postmodern dependence on psychological addictions" to freedom, the expression of one's identity and a true sense of well-being.

INTRODUCTION

Italy is a post-modern country: its culture, values, lifestyles, ways, bonds between people, scents, flavours and thoughts are post-modern.

If modern culture was supported by virtues and trust in project-making and progress, in post-modern culture there is a dismantling of traditional values which induces a sense of disorientation and retreating into oneself.

The post-modern personality has abandoned the great ideals of the past and has closed up into itself, into the most immediate present and is totally focused on the instantaneous gratification of desires, incapable of sacrifices and rarely looking towards the future. In this culture of narcissism, man lives by excluding the presence of others because he has lost his vital compass, he can no longer recognize the difference between himself and what surrounds him. Inauthenticity is another key word of post-modernity. The individual can react to the new global set-up with an exaggerated and desperate search for singularity or, exactly the opposite reaction, he can relinquish his cultural roots and his authentic essence, delegating the process of the construction of his identity to external figures, to the various famous people of the time, to the dominant culture: the result is that a false Self emerges.

In this case, the personality of the individual does not develop on the basis of his innate endowment, but in conformity with the expectations and pressures of the outside world.

What the subject ends up by leading is, in the best of cases, an imitative life in a world founded on appearance and not on being.

Man, the victim of the continuous conditioning from the exterior, in particular the mass media, is forced to take on a form and to act wearing a mask (Gatti Pertegato, 1987).

Current lifestyle appears to be oriented towards little control over one's existence; this means little self-discipline and personal skill which will lead to a low level of individual well-being, little balance, non-critical acceptance of rules and behaviour including at risk, in particular at some times of the existence.

Every day, the newspapers and television highlight distress, in particular in the world of the young, which takes on increasingly worrying dimensions. The use of substances and alcohol, the irresponsible exercise of sexuality, violence against persons and things and the obstinate search for risk are signals that forcefully attract the attention and commitment of all adults, parents, teachers, psychologists and social workers.

The impression that there is a lack of a communication code that allows understanding the reasons of the other becomes increasingly clear, but even before that, the need to understand the needs which, in the first person, we have.

The choice of exaggerated behaviour remains a silent and dark language through which young people try to express a profound distress in living and an unconscious, and often desperate, cry for help.

The distress of youth, however, must be interpreted as the sign of a more general distress: today their crises take place, and this is what is new, in a society which is itself in crisis.

The question that we often ask is: what is the disease in today's society?

Our epoch has gone from the myth of the omnipotence of man as the builder of history to another symmetrical and specular myth of his total impotence in the face of the complexity of the world. (Benasayag, Schmit, 2003).

It is precisely this sense of impotency in deciphering reality and in managing complexity that leads many young people to violent actions or to seek refuge in the virtual world where everything becomes real although it is no longer real.

The attraction of risk then becomes a metaphor of human living itself. Risking as daring, taking chances, exposing, venturing and confronting. Taking risks can be understood as a real test of character. Those who decide to take large risks put everything at stake, becoming almost a heroic figure. Risky actions arouse attraction and seduction and suggest, now almost spontaneously, vitality and being at the centre of attention.

The voluntary search for risk focuses its explanation on the fact that exposure to danger can represent a means of personal growth, a place of expression and self-realization of identity, where to show one's courage, defeat fear and prove something to oneself and to the others. In measuring up to risk, people can show off their courage, their spirit of enterprise, their ability and their capacity of resistance (Giddens, 1991).

This book offers a reflection on the subjects of well-being, the search for emotions and sensations, on life choices and on dangerous behaviour, on addiction, on psychopathology and is structured in four chapters.

The first chapter examines the main theoretical models elaborated according to the perspective of Social Cognition: the model of health beliefs, the theory of planned behaviour, the self-regulatory model, the trans-theoretical model and the process of action significant for health, which is followed by an analysis of some lines of research on the concept of well-being, considered in its positive valence, offering three different methods of study; subjective, psychological and social well-being.

The second chapter, after a brief reference to the etymology of the word 'risk', traces its historical evolution and then a distinction between social, environmental and psychological risk is made. The interpretation of the choice of a life at risk is approached looking in particular at the world of young people who consider risk a vital action that becomes a desire to live better, to relive and to be reborn.

For youngsters, breaking rules often becomes important because it corresponds to the need for independence, to the demand for autonomy and also the need to experiment, to go and see and prove whether the rules taken for granted really work, if they make sense and if they have the grounds for existing.

Attention is then placed on the important value that the family and peer group have for adolescents, including in their approach to risk. The role of adults is also important to explain to young people that rules have to be respected and observed.

Identifying with figures that have a strong and positive relationship with rules and nurture a great respect for values is fundamental and the absence of figures of reference to trust is linked, for children and adolescents, to a fundamental problem.

Chapter three is on sensation seekers.

Seeking strong emotions can be translated into various types of behaviour; from alcohol and drug abuse to gambling, reckless driving, extreme sports, unprotected sexual relations and acts of vandalism.

Risk and transgression become synonymous with pleasure, although unfortunately these are often blended into a cocktail of emotions which are too difficult to handle.

Focusing attention on adolescent reality, which is particularly exposed to this type of stimulus, highlights how the adolescent is an individual who falls ill seldom but frequently dies. The causes of death are road accidents and other accidents, suicide, murder and all those types of behaviour which have a great deal to do with taking risks. Death can be traced back more to behaviour than to illness. In the world of the night, there is a widespread risk, which is the use and abuse of substances, with their acute and chronic effects.

Risk is also continuously sought because it is fascinating, attractive and can overcome feelings of fear, insecurity and shame; in many cases, pleasure can be mentioned and it is for this reason that the need to take a risk often appears with particular intensity.

An in-depth analysis is then made of the problem of the use and abuse of alcohol, which is a problem affecting the world of young people not only in the West but, dramatically clearly, in Italy as well. This behaviour is the sign of great dissatisfaction and discouragement which accompanies youngsters at a crucial time in their lives. The need to feel grown-up and to be accepted by the group are only some of the reasons that drive adolescents to drink alcohol. Special attention is given to the phenomenon of binge drinking. This phenomenon is concretized in those subjects who seek a remedy to strong negative emotions, produced by unfavourable situations (for example loneliness or dissatisfaction) and try to find a way out in a total estrangement from reality, precisely in order not to feel the unbearable pain that these cause. However, it appears clear that, as well as failing to achieve the desired effect, alcohol can cause very serious physical, psychological and behavioural damage, which can have repercussions on the correct functioning of the organism and invalidate the relations that will be established in the course of their lifetime.

The fourth and last chapter examines a very topical subject: the new psychological addictions. The rapid and profound changes in culture, social life, the structure and organization of the family, in styles of consumption and in the principle oriented to appearing, in the cultural models and in the management of leisure time, tend to modify the cognitive layout and the regulation of the affective life and take on particular importance as etiological factors of pathological dependencies. For some years, we have seen new forms of psychological disorders emerge but also different presentations of known pathologies which, compared to the past, appear earlier, with greater complexity, in more pervasive ways and, often, in comorbidity with other personality disorders, more frequently of the borderline-narcissistic area.

This is an area of research for which a special need is felt for continuous updating, information and training. The New Addictions, the new non-drug behavioural dependences have a multifactor etiology which includes aspects of a social, cultural and economic type but also factors relative to the neurobiological, psychological and psychopathological dimension. This makes their study engrossing and topical but, at the same time, they outline a particularly complex field of study. It is thus possible to speak of contemporary psychopathology, which shows how social and cultural changes have a strong impact on individual and collective psychic life.

Chapter 1

THEORIES AND METHODS IN HEALTH PSYCHOLOGY. IN SEARCH OF WELL-BEING

ABSTRACT

In Western culture, achieving well-being, happiness and the desire for gratification in life have always been a fundamental objective: philosophers, sociologists and writers have analysed these subjects both at individual and social levels. From its very origins, psychology has also dealt with well-being, but focusing attention on the conditions where well-being was absent, studying and describing only the deficiencies of the individual and maintaining a conception of a passive man, whose behaviour is simplistically regulated by objective facts such as stimuli and reinforcements. A new model then appeared on the scene, the active individual, who experimented, with continuous growth and development, who was capable of accepting challenges to contribute to his psychological well-being. Attention is concentrated on the strong points of the individual, highlighting the role of how people subjectively assess their well-being. Diener (1999) suggests a distinction between the affective component and the cognitive component of subjective well-being: the former refers to the balance between positive affectivity and negative affectivity, i.e. between the frequency and intensity of positive emotions such as joy and desire to live and negative emotions such as anger and sadness, the latter referring to the degree of satisfaction for living conditions according to subjectively defined standards. The sensation of subjective well-being is a complex assessment of one's quality of life that emerges from the integration of the cognitive and emotional aspects of the individual functioning in relation to different environmental situations. The possibility of interpreting the same event as a resource or as an obstacle, feeling capable of meeting difficulties that arise, in a word, the sense of self-efficiency and self-esteem, depend on the way in which the meaning of that specific experience is subjectively constructed.

1. THEORETICAL ASSUMPTIONS IN HEALTH PSYCHOLOGY

Health psychology has deep roots, which go back as far as ancient Greece and perhaps even further, but its history as a scientific subject is short.

The relationship existing between the frequency of physical illness and stressful aspects of life started to be underlined with increasing insistence in the 1950s and 1960s. In particular in the 1970s, the signs of cultural renewal on the themes of health appeared, which highlighted the characteristic of not only individual but also the collective good, the importance of direct and shared commitment by subjects in the phase of prevention as well as of treatment, the need for new relations between individuals, groups and the health service. Since then the institutional development of the subject has taken place at very rapid rates, both in the United States and in Europe.

The first definition of health psychology, by Matarazzo (1980), states that it represents all the specific educational, scientific and professional contributions that psychology can make to fostering and maintaining health, preventing and treating disease and identifying the etiological and diagnostic correlates of health, illness and correlated dysfunctions. Since the 1980s, health psychology has rapidly developed, exploring the individual understanding of the experience of health and illness, the knowledge underlying health practices, the mechanisms and effects of stress on the organism, the efficacy of actions or treatments aimed at improving the psychosocial or behavioural dimensions connected with health, the way in which people interact with the health service, adapt to an illness, cope with rehabilitation and maintain a good quality of life.

Underlying this subject, there is a renewed vision of human health, given in 1946 by the World Health Organization (WHO): a state of complete physical, mental and social well-being, and not only the absence of disease (World Health Organization, 1946).

Rehabilitative medicine quickly adopted the WHO guidelines, appearing immediately, from its institutional development, as the elective field of application of health psychology. Attention for the individual's functionality in relation to his environment represents the nucleus around which rehabilitative medicine and heath psychology can effectively dialogue and be integrated, in order to translate into reality a multidisciplinary model of care.

Over the years, the WHO has drawn up different instruments of classification on the observation and analysis of organic, psychic and behavioural pathologies of the population, in order to improve the quality of the diagnosis of these pathologies.

The first classification drawn up by the WHO, the "International Classification of Disease", (ICD) came about as the result of the sixth revision, in 1946.

The ICD, inserted in the Manual of the International Statistical Classification of Diseases, Injuries, and Causes of Death (1949), meets the need to understand the cause of the pathologies, providing for each syndrome and disorder a description of the main clinical characteristics and the relative diagnostic indications. The ICD is therefore a causal classification, focusing attention on the etiological aspect of the pathology. The diagnosis of illnesses are translated into numerical codes which make it possible to store, search and analyse the data.

The ICD soon revealed various limits of application and this led the WHO to draw up a new manual of classification that could focus attention not only on the cause of the pathologies but also on their consequences: "The International Classification of Impairment, Diseases and Handicap", ICIDH, 1980). The ICIDH does not include the cause of the pathology but the importance and the influence that the environment plays on the state of health of populations. With the ICIDH, the starting point is no longer the concept of illness as impairment, but the concept of health, understood as physical, mental, relational and social well-being that concerns the individual, his totality and interaction with the environment.

The WHO emphasized the importance of using the ICD and the ICIDH in a complementary way (in Italy reference is made to the tenth version of 1992), encouraging the analysis and comprehension of the health conditions of an individual in a wider perspective, as the etiological data is supplemented by the analysis of the impact that that pathology may have on individuals and on their environmental context.

The ICIDH analyses the consequences of the illness highlighting three fundamental components: impairment, as organic and/or functional damage; disability, as loss of operative capacities by the individual due to impairment; handicap, as difficulties that the individual encounters in the surrounding environment as a result of the impairment.

This pattern induces an erroneous interpretation: focusing attention on the illness means running the risk of making the illness coincide with the person, therefore that person tends to be identified as globally ill.

The presence of these conceptual limits in the ICIDH led the WHO to draw up a further tool, "The International Classification of Impairments, Activities and Participation", ICIDH-2, 1999; (Figure 1), which represents the embryo of the conceptual model that will be developed in the most recent classification of the World Health Organization: "The International Classification of Functioning", (ICF, 2001).

The ICF is a classification that aims to describe a person's state of health in relation to their existential environments (social, family, working) in order to see the difficulties that can cause disability in the socio-cultural context of reference.

Through the ICF, the aim is therefore to describe not individuals, but the situations of their daily lives in relation to their environmental context, emphasizing the individual not only as a person who has illnesses or disabilities, but above all highlighting their uniqueness and totality.

The tool describes these situations adopting a standard and unified language, attempting to avoid semantic misunderstandings and facilitating comprehension between different users all over the world.

Browsing through the literature of the sector, in the field of health psychology and going back over the guidelines drawn up by the WHO, the absence of an epistemological reflection that supports the theoretical production and that allows identifying a common object of investigation can be observed.

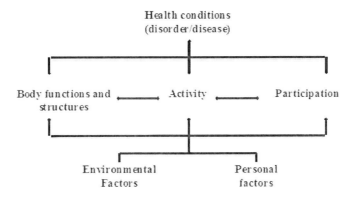

Figure 1. Model ICDH2.

This absence of uniqueness entails two different considerations: the first, is that the areas of application of health psychology vary in relation to the cultural orientations and socio-cultural contexts in which they are generated; the second, that the definition of the disciplinary areas of application is not equivalent to the definition of the discipline itself. In other words, the different articulations of health psychology are constructed defining themes of interest of varying degrees, which meet the demand with regard to where health psychology is applied without having first answered the question on what is meant by health psychology (Turchi, Della Torre, 2007).

It is therefore necessary to describe the main theoretical orientations of this discipline which make it possible to identify the object of study which is to be investigated, i.e. the health-reality.

A renewed vision of human health has been sanctioned by the shift from the so-called bio-medical model to the bio-psychosocial one.

Engel (1977) states that the bio-medical model is based on the following principles: biological principles are separated from the psychosocial ones and are the only ones responsible for the genesis of an illness; the body is like a machine and illness a dysfunction caused by an external agent; attention is focused on the pathological states and on the pathogenic agents. From the bio-psychosocial model, on the other hand, there emerges a general vision of human activity, inclusive of the biological, psychological and social dimensions, both at the level of the factors and systems involved (Bertini, 1988): the well-being or distress of the individual lies not only in the biological organism but also in the quality of his relations with the environment and in the capacity of solving problems in a satisfactory and flexible way in his environment. The dualism is superseded because the body and mind are not considered two separate entities but dynamic and integrated dimensions of the person, both involved in the variations of health and illness. In the new approach, attention is not on the illness but on positive health and on its continuous improvement.

As it is a systemic model, both the importance of the specificity of the levels of analysis relative to the complexity of the organism and the interdependence or integration between these levels is underlined. An epistemological and professional change is therefore taking place and it involves not only the psychologist but also the doctor and other healthcare operators.

It is specific of the bio-psychosocial model to proceed with an in-depth examination of the psychological level identifying the conditions that influence the state of health and illness. They concern the biological changes that can take place before, during or after an emotional reaction of behavioural style. Stress generates an increase in blood pressure, in the heart rate, in the activation of the sympathetic nervous system and is associated with haematic changes that can predispose the subject for the development of cardiovascular diseases or hypertension. Similarly, stress acts on the immune system through a complex intertwining of neural and hormonal pathways and is connected to the onset and development of viral infections, tumours and wounds.

The state of health and illness is also influenced by personal behaviour that can have a significant effect in the short or long term on the health of the subject. If the effect of a type of behaviour is to maintain or improve the state of health, it will be indicated as protective or healthy. Examples are an appropriate diet or physical activity which help the organism reduce the conditions that cause cancer or cardiovascular disease. If, on the other hand, the effect is damaging for the organism it will be indicated as of risk or pathogenic: one example is smoking which causes biological alterations in the lungs and heart such as to predispose them to the development of disease. The relationship between behaviour and health is not unilateral but of the probabilistic type; in addition, a habit practised in certain ways or in certain contexts may be beneficial whilst in other cases it may even be dangerous.

The last condition that influences the state of health of an individual is represented by personal behaviour associated with an illness or the possibility that it occurs. When a health problem arises, the subject implements psychological strategies, such as the tendency to minimize or accentuate symptoms, and behavioural strategies, such as seeking help. A distinction is made between behaviour of the patient to indicate the actions that precede a diagnosis, and the behaviour connected with the role of patient assumed after diagnosis and aimed at improving the psychophysical condition.

There is a complex interdependence and interaction between the three modes of influence. Some types of protective behaviour, such as diet or physical exercise, can improve health by acting directly on the physiological system or indirectly, by reducing the effects of stress on the organism; some risk behaviours, such as the abuse of substances, can have direct effects on pathogenic processes or indirect effects increasing anxiety or worsening the mood. In the opposite direction, stress can activate the start of damaging practices or make it difficult to maintain protective practices in time.

2. GROUPS OF MODELS IN HEALTH PSYCHOLOGY

The Social Cognition approach, which came into being in social psychology in the 1970s, maintains that people develop mental or cognitive representations of reality. These cognitions are constructed and modified through social learning and influence the way people behave.

According to the theoretical models developed in health psychology, there are particular beliefs or individual attitudes at the basis of significant behaviour. The idea is to interpret the human being as an entity that rationally elaborates the information available, calibrates costs and benefits of potential behaviour, evaluates the seriousness of an illness and then decides how to act.

Some of these models have been developed specifically to put forward estimates on healthy behaviour (for example, the model of beliefs on health), others are general models of behaviour (for example the theory of planned behaviour), which have also been applied in the area of health.

The concept of Locus of Control, introduced by Rotter (1966), is perhaps the best-known example of the shift of attention to cognitive variables in the study of health-related behaviour. It refers to the tendency of the individual to perceive the reinforcements as contingent to his own behaviour (internal locus of control) or to consider that facts are determined by external forces, such as fate or other significant persons (external locus of control). It was in 1978 that a questionnaire (Wallston et al., 1978) was developed to identify the locus of control connected with health. A few years later, Wallston and Wallston (1984) provided some support to the idea that subjects with an internal locus of control tend to adopt a greater number of types of health-protective behaviour.

Studies on particular applications of locus on control can be found, through using specific questionnaires for various pathologies such as cancer (Pruyn et al., 1988), diabetes (Bradley et al., 1984; 1990) and hypertension (Stanton, 1987). The subsequent decline of the construct of the locus of control perhaps finds its raison d'être in the difficulty of checking its modifiability and, in the affirmative, being able to identify to what extent and in relation to which aspects connected with the patient's health its modification can optimize management of the illness. A strongly external locus of control can hypothetically expose the patient to the risk of completely delegating the management of his state of health to others, or relying supinely on destiny, with negative results in the long term. It is also probable that patients with a radically internal locus of control relate to the doctor antagonistically, with dysfunctional results in the therapeutic relationship and in the end result of the treatment. The theoretical interest in the concept of locus of control has not corresponded to wide clinical application, and today a progressive reduction in attention to this subject can be seen.

The Health Belief Model, developed by Rosenstock (1966) and subsequently modified by Becker and Maiman (1975) tries to provide an explanation on behavioural choices of a preventive type. The model is structured on the perception of illness as threatening for the subject and on the consequent behaviour of prevention. The probability with which a person adopts significant behaviour for health varies according to the following personal beliefs: the susceptibility perceived, or the personal risk of contracting an illness, or the dangerousness attributed to a pathology or health problem in terms of pain, risk of death or social consequences; the perception of the benefits associated with the preventive behaviour; the perception of the obstacles associated with preventive behaviour.

According to the Theory of Planned Behaviour, developed by Fishbein and Ajzen (1975), behaviour is determined in the first place by the intention to implement it, in its turn predictable on the basis of three orders of factors; the attitude towards preventive behaviour; the subjective norms that refer to the subject's perception of the way his behaviour is evaluated by people in his social environment, such as friends, partner, parents, doctors; the behavioural control which refers to the conviction of being able to put into practice the behaviour in question and which directly influences both behaviour and the intention.

In the Self-Regulatory Model (Leventhal, Cameron, 1987) the individual is seen as an active problem-solver committed to maintaining or restoring a balanced state of health. The richness of contents and the dynamic nature of their interactions represent the qualities of the model, but on the other hand, these make the analysis in statistical terms and verification in an experimental context difficult. The model is based on the assumption that the individual has an active system of acquiring information that leads him to produce both a mental representation of the illness and an emotional response to that illness. Through three stages (representation, coping and verification) the system is organized fluidly and contemplates within it the possibility for the subject to modify his behaviour and coping strategies, if verifications indicate the need for them.

Important developments on the research by Leventhal and colleagues (Leventhal, 1992; Leventhal, Diefenbach, 1991; Leventhal et al., 1980) on the mental representation of illness have thrown light on to a complex and relatively new subject. There are five components on the basis of which we represent illnesses: identity, cause, duration, consequences and controllability (or curability).

The identity refers to the name of the illness, its tangible signs and symptoms. The second dimension (the cause) is based on the ideas of the subject on the ways the illness can be contracted or on its origin. The third (duration) refers to the expectations on the course that the illness will follow and the fact that it is acute, chronic or cyclical. The fourth dimension (the consequences) reflects the perception of the short and long term effects of the illness, and the implications on the social, economic and emotional level. Lastly, the controllability refers to the convictions on the possibilities of cure or of exercising a positive influence on the development of the clinical picture.

The basic assumption of the Transtheoretical Model, developed by Prochaska and Di Clemente (1982), is that a change in health behaviour is not a phenomenon of the "all or nothing" type, but a gradual process that goes through specific stages: pre-contemplation, during which the subject is unaware of the problem or the need to change; contemplation, characterized by emerging doubts and contradictions which lead to a more marked ambivalence with regard to the change; determination, in which the subject is ready to change, defines objectives and a plan of action; action, in which the changes are concretely experimented; maintenance, the phase where the subject actively continues to maintain the change and the new habits are consolidated. This course is not linear but cyclical and at any point along the way there may be a relapse which takes the person back to the previous stages. In this approach, the stages represent both a period and a set of tasks indispensable to the passage to the following phase. The time each individual stays in each stage is variable, but the tasks to be carried out to go to the next one are the same.

The two psychological variables that determine the transaction between the phases are self-efficacy, i.e. the confidence of an individual in his capacities to implement pre-established behaviour, and the decisional balance sheet (or evaluation of the pros and cons) which consists of a comparative evaluation of the positive and negative aspects of a particular type of behaviour.

Prochaska et al. (1988) applied the model to various problems, including giving up smoking, weight control and HIV prevention (1994). Simultaneously with the development of the different models, cognitive-social theory facilitated the knowledge of the processes that govern the promotion of health. Considering behaviour as the result of an interaction between cognitive processes and environmental factors, as for the Theory of Social Learning, means supporting the usefulness of a composite and dynamic vision of the facts, far from static reductionisms and determinisms.

The individual is motivated to obtain the maximum of reinforcement and the minimum of the sanctions by the surrounding environment. Bandura (2000), the greatest representative of this approach, maintains that behaviour is oriented to objectives and motivation and human actions are to a great extent regulated by predictions. Behavioural choices are based on expectations relative to the result, i.e. the degree to which the subjects believe that an action can lead to a particular result, and on expectations relative to personal efficacy, i.e. the degree to which the subjects are convinced of their capacity to carry out the actions necessary to reaching a desired result. The expectations relative to personal efficacy (or self-efficacy) are divided into general and specific types of behaviour. General efficacy (for example, being a self-confident person) is important in particular when the subject is confronted with a new decision, whilst specific expectations may show an inter-individual variability in different types of behaviour (for example, being confident in succeeding in continuing an aerobics course) and as such represent more powerful determinants of behaviour. In both cases, self-efficacy plays a leading role in improving the mental function: those who have high self-efficacy persevere in the attempts to attain an objective, attribute failure to lack of commitment or adverse conditions, are capable of facing up to environmental stressors, have ambitious objectives, low stress levels and are not very vulnerable to depression.

According to Bandura (op. cit.), learning may take place through direct experience (also known as learning by doing) or indirectly, observing and modelling one's actions on those of others in whom one identifies (also known as vicarious learning or modelling).

In socialization processes, the family environment or that of peers, but also the broader one of the mass media, are significant sources of influence and are role models in the adoption of various practices, such as the smoking or the consumption of alcohol. Two dimensions have an impact on vicarious learning of health behaviour: similarity, as the subjects are more inclined to adopt behaviour if the model of reference is similar to themselves and the distribution of power, as people with a higher social status have a greater power of influence on the individual.

Schwarzer (1994) formulated a theoretical model called Health Action Process Approach in which, alongside the action-result expectations (relative to the possibility that modifying a certain type of behaviour can produce a given result), self-efficacy plays a fundamental role as it directly influences the intentions, objectives and action plans that the individual formulates. Coherently with the presuppositions of cognitive-social theory, the model attributes great importance to obstacles and external resources, confirming the need that the environment reinforces or does not hinder maintaining the results reached.

Each of the theoretical models shown has provided a substantial contribution to the comprehension of the processes that start and maintain health-related behaviour. However, each model has characteristics which can be identified as weaknesses if one expects that reality, in all its complexity, is explained in full. We can consider the words of Bloch (1990) enlightening, who said that confusing a model with reality is like going to a restaurant and eating the menu.

3. WELL-BEING AS AN OBJECT OF STUDY

Everyone desires physical, metal, social and spiritual well-being: feeling well is not equivalent to an absence of disorders but refers to an ontological state of full satisfaction with one's existence. This is not an easy objective to attain, on the individual level, and is aggravated by a further aspect: a science of happiness which provides suggestions and scientifically proven indications on how it is possible to reach well-being is not yet widespread (Gardini, Venneri, 2011).

Cloninger (2004, 2006), speaking about attaining psychological well-being, maintains that in general, the sensations of pleasure and satisfaction are confused: in actual fact, the meaning and long-term effects are deeply different. Pleasure is a momentary sensation that is of a brief duration and comes from the exterior, whilst satisfaction is a more lasting sensation that comes from reaching an ultimate good which, for the individual, has a deep and greater importance than the contingent situation. From this point of view, well-being can be achieved gradually, by persevering those behaviours which have an intrinsic value for the person and provide wider satisfaction, although this may require giving up temporary pleasures. The main step to accompany a person to reaching well-being is to act so that he understands what the real objectives of greatest value of his life are; therefore to foster the development of that behaviour of a value type which achieves individual and social well-being such as, for example, giving and receiving respect and love, communicating with others and adopting lifestyles that lead to recognizing fundamental values. According to Cloninger (op. cit.), the state of well-being reached is shown by some aspects that characterize the people that possess them. They show high levels of positive emotions, a coherent and mature personality, a good quality of life and virtues such as courage, patience, moderation and justice; well-being does not depend on the age or level of education, nor is it correlated with the increase of wealth; it is associated with work satisfaction, having meaningful interpersonal relations and a spiritual vision of life. Being determined, cooperative and transcendent allows experiencing a greater level of well-being thanks to reaching greater self-awareness.

Going back over the history of studies in this field, a first indication for research was concentrated on the analysis of the subjective experience of well-being or subjective well-being (Diener, 1984; Andrews and Robinson, 1991). Interest in subjective well-being arises in some specific disciplinary sectors (metal health, gerontology, quality of life) in the attempt to identify more reliable and valid measurements of the quality of life than objective indicators alone.

Psychological research has tried to study in further depth the nature of this component of individual experience and the correlated internal and external variables, conceptualizing well-being as a positive emotional experience (presence of pleasurable effects) and the presence of feelings of satisfaction with one's own life (Diener, op. cit.).

A second direction comes from the declared attempt to overcome the traditional perspectives of well-being as absence of distress, offering a series of criteria of psychological well-being, understood as optimal psychological functioning or positive mental health (Ryff, 1989). In this tradition of research, subjective well-being is considered an indicator of psychological well-being, closely connected to others but in itself not sufficient to define the state of mental health (Diener et al., 1997).

Both the previous perspectives conceive well-being as a strictly individual phenomenon. In recent years, the recognition of the importance of the social context in influencing physical and psychological health has led some authors (Larson, 1993; Keyes, 1998), to propose the construct of social well-being, meaning by this the quality of social relations of an individual in their community and society, as well as their own internal functioning.

3.1. Subjective Well-Being

The first attempts at studying and measuring subjective well-being originate in various disciplinary areas of psychology. From the early 1970s, sociologists began to work on evaluating the living conditions of the general population, for which indicators of the quality of life were developed, firstly economic (like the GDP) and then social (such as living conditions, income and education), that could provide information on the changes in the standard of living due to social reforms (Nuvolati and Zajczyck, 1997). In those years, these instruments were subjected to a series of criticisms and subjective indicators began to be used, like opinions of happiness and life satisfaction or indicators of the perceived quality of life, (Andrews and Withey, 1976; Campbell et al., 1976). These measurements, which since then have been used alongside the more objective indicators, are deemed essential as they reflect the point of view of individuals on their living conditions. Interest in the evaluation of subjective well-being has also emerged in more specific sectors such as gerontology, mental health, medical sciences, rehabilitation and health promotion.

In recent years, some contributions on studying subjective well-being in further depth and the factors that influence it have been provided by social psychology, allowing going beyond the simple conceptualization of well-being as happiness and life satisfaction, to propose more articulated definitions and highlight a variety of cognitive and psychosocial processes that control the subjective experience of well-being.

Subjective well-being refers to the way people evaluate their lives. Three principal and inter-related components of this concept are distinguished: life satisfaction, pleasant affect and unpleasant affect.

Life satisfaction refers to a cognitive process of evaluation of one's life circumstances, referred to specific personal standards (for example expectations, desires and ideals) (Cantril, 1965).

The affective component indicates the emotions that subjects experience during their daily life. Positive affect (which corresponds to the presence of unpleasant affective states such as anger, anxiety and dissatisfaction) and negative affect are deemed conceptually distinct and influenced by variables to varying extents (Bradburn, 1969; Argyle, 1987).

There are numerous variables and processes that have been investigated as antecedents of subjective well-being to explain the stability and change over a period of time. Reflection on the subject has antithetical positions such as the dilemma of well-being as a stable feature (and which therefore cannot be modified) with respect to a changeable and therefore fundamentally relative state influenced by external circumstances.

For reasons of exposition, it can be useful to distinguish the different factors studied depending on whether they focus mainly on the role of the objective conditions of life and socio-demographic and situational factors (approach of sociological derivation), on the role of the psychological and psycho-social processes (for example, the locus of control, the attribution processes, the processes of social confrontation), or on the dynamic interaction between individual and context.

In the sphere of the approach of psychological indicators of the quality of life, research starts from the presupposition that well-being depends both on objective living conditions and the way in which these are experienced and evaluated by the subjects (i.e. the perceived quality of life). For some time now, it has been underlined that the way people perceive and interpret the world has an important role in feelings of well-being. Research carried out in the sphere of Social Cognition has highlighted a series of mechanisms of thought and reasoning which in normal conditions are useful and adaptive, but in other cases, especially if they are used systematically in an improper way, can generate feelings of distress and unhappiness, to the extent of resulting in forms of depression. These include the illusion of control over events, i.e. the conviction of having more control than one effectively has, a belief which can be traced back to an innate motivation to domination, subsequently reinforced by personal experiences and competences acquired in coping with specific situations (Skinner, 1995; Bandura, 2000). Another phenomenon is unrealistic optimism, i.e. the belief of being relatively more invulnerable, with respect to other people, to negative events and circumstances (and more inclined to encountering positive events) (Weinstein, 1980).

Beliefs over one's control of the situation and optimism do not necessarily reflect the objective situation, but on the contrary, it has been seen that these are genuine positive illusions (Taylor and Brown, 1988). People with superior levels of subjective well-being overestimate the control they believe they have over the situation and their actions, they expect from the future more positive events than they attribute to others and underestimate the probability of encountering negative events. These people also nurture exaggeratedly positive opinions about themselves, unlike depressed people, who are more objective. Taylor and Brown (op. cit.) have therefore put forward the hypothesis that these illusions represent an indicator of mental health and well-being.

Beliefs in control and personal efficacy are closely connected to the processes of explaining the causes of events and coping strategies (Skinner, 1995). Those who are convinced of controlling the situation and their lives generally cope better with stress, adopt more effective coping strategies, whilst the loss of control (feeling of impotence) lowers the morale and worsens health.

The roles of styles of attribution in the genesis of unpleasant emotional states, pessimism and depression has been repeatedly emphasized by theoreticians of attribution (Seligman, 1995). Depressed people tend to make internal attributions for negative events (to feel guilty themselves for negative results), to believe that such events also affect other spheres of life (global) and to believe that they will occur again in the future (stable). Happy people, on the other hand, tend to make internal, stable and global attributions for positive events (Argyle and Martin, 1991).

In the context of theories on well-being, it is believed that it is possible to attenuate or extend the emotions through the control of thoughts (Larsen et al., 1987). This principle underlies techniques that aim at correcting explicative depressive styles, for example by teaching positive thought and optimism (Seligman, 1996). Other examples in this direction are represented by having particular beliefs on the world (Myers and Diener, 1995), concentrating on more attainable goals rather than on distant goals that are difficult to attain and trying to be optimistic about the future.

Amongst the cognitive factors, a special role is attributed to the processes of social judgement. Some theories of well-being, also known as theories of judgement (Diener, 1984) or theories of comparison or Gap Theories, underline that the factors that influence subjective well-being vary in time and according to circumstances, and the way in which people evaluate positive and negative life events depends on their effective conditions and on the personal criteria that they adopt in assessing their own life.

Underlying the theory of social comparison there is the assumption that people evaluate their lives by comparing current conditions with a standard determined by the level of other people. This means that the subjects who are favoured in the comparison with the social standard will be satisfied and will feel positive emotions. If the process of comparison gives unfavourable results, unpleasant emotions such as sadness and anxiety can be expected. The nucleus of the theory of social confrontation is represented by the idea that life satisfaction does not only depend on the absolute position of a person (for example whether one is healthy or without illnesses) but also on the position of the other people with whom one is compared, who can be, depending on the cases, the people closest to the subject (friends and family), members of one's group or of other groups, and even imaginary people.

Diener and Fujita (1997) have distinguished two approaches, which differ in the way the targets of comparison are chosen. In the first, defined by imposed social comparisons, the targets of comparison are represented by the people present in the immediate surroundings. The comparisons are imposed by the situation to the extent we look at the other main people, because simply they are close to us. A second approach is that of coping. This model attributes a more active role to the subject in the choice of persons of reference for comparison, and he is more actively involved in the choice of the standards, from a potential list, with the purpose of reaching determined objectives. In some cases, people may even create an imaginary person with whom to compare themselves. The idea at the base of the model is that people can look at others in the attempt to find a motivation to act, improve their mood and obtain specific knowledge. This objective can be reached by observing the people that the subject judges superior to himself in some dimension (for example using them as models) or people in unfavourable conditions (for example to increase their self-esteem).

The Multiple Discrepancy Theory (Michalos, 1985) maintains that people use a variety of criteria when they assess their lives. In particular, satisfaction is believed to depend on the extent of the gap perceived between what the subject has and what he would like to have, what others have, the best experience of the past, the expectations on the future, the personal progress that he believes he deserves and what he thinks he needs. In this perspective, the presence of divergences between present conditions and the various standards of reference is deemed a symptom of dissatisfaction, whilst the correspondence between the various aspects is an index of well-being.

The theme of stability and change in the levels of well-being, and of the factors that are responsible for this, is an important debate. Amongst the positions that underline stability, there are, on the one hand, those that attribute a decisive role to personality factors (as far as making well-being coincide with the possession of specific personality traits) and, on the other, the theories that underline processes of adaptation. Amongst the factors that bring about change, life events occupy a privileged role.

A meta-analysis by DeNeve and Cooper (1998) summarized the results of an impressive amount of research which verified the role of no fewer than 137 personality traits in estimating satisfaction, positive affect and negative affect. The specific characteristics that were most consistently correlated with subjective well-being include the repression of potentially threatening negative emotions, confidence, emotional stability, the locus of control-luck, the desire for control, positive affectivity, hardiness (capacity of individual resistance) and self-esteem. According to the authors, if we consider the way in which these factors operate to produce feelings of well-being, the traits most stably associated with subjective well-being have in common the fact of involving to some extent the experience of emotions (emotional stability, positive affectivity, tension) and the tendency to produce determined explanations for life events.

Cohen (1988) observes that the relationship between life events and psychological well-being is not of a direct nature, but mediated by other variables which, if overlooked, can lead to coming to wrong conclusions and are: environmental characteristics (including those of the event, the availability of social support, the effective living conditions) and those of personality. For example, it has been seen that extrovert people, unlike introverts, possess better social skills and tend to choose pleasant social activities, factors which increase the probability of experiencing positive events (Argyle, Martin, 1991).

According to Headey and Wearing (1991), there is a level of balance in the subjective well-being of people, which is influenced by a series of personal resources, which include characteristics of personality, socio-demographic variables and social networks. Although the levels of subjective well-being may deviate from the average level as a consequence of positive or negative events, the characteristics of personality contribute to restoring it to the normal level of balance.

The meaning of life events for psychological well-being has been shown by Holmes and Rahe (1969). Epidemiological studies have repeatedly indicated that an accumulation of life events can be at the origin of psychological disorders. The critical element according to the authors is the entity of the change and therefore the effort of adaptation that is required by the subject.

There are also other characteristics of the events that play a critical role for well-being. For example, events can vary according to the degree of predictability and controllability (Weistein, 1980). The importance of this characteristic of the events is shown by the results that have examined the effects of dramatic events (for example accidents, disasters, terminal illnesses). It has been found that the experience of such critical events can reduce well-being through the mediation of optimistic beliefs on one's personal control: people who have undergone serious traumas tend to see themselves as more vulnerable and undefended from the future. In these conditions, belief in a stable, foreseeable and controllable world is lost, with serious repercussions for psychological and subjective well-being.

The basic assumption of the Theory of Adaptation is that the occurrence of very positive or very negative events leads to a modification of the expectations and of the personal criteria of a good quality of life (winning a large sum of money can lead to modifying usual habits but which after a certain period of time may be considered normal and no longer extraordinary), with the result that the initially negative (or positive) effect tends to be reduced.

From another point of view, adaptation can be the result of the application of coping strategies (Taylor, 1983). According to Taylor's theory of cognitive adaptation, in the face of very stressful events, such as serious illness, subjects implement a series of coping strategies (aimed at recovering the perception of control over their lives, at reinterpreting the new conditions as without meaning and reinforcing their self-esteem) which would gradually lead to the re-establishment of a condition of relative subjective well-being. The significance of the adaptation to events and to new circumstances underlines the need to consider the dynamic interaction between the individual and his life context.

Some theories state that feelings of subjective well-being depend on reaching determined goals (or life tasks) or on the satisfaction of particular needs. In this perspective, the causes of well-being are not seen as universal, but they are different according to the values and desires of each individual.

The theories of subjective well-being that have placed the accent on the importance of the aims, generally tend to interpret them in individualistic terms. One of these is the theory of personal strivings of Emmons (1986, 1992). Strivings are the characteristic and recurrent aims that a person tries to attain; they are relatively long-lasting personal attributes that integrate the wider whole of aims that a person sets himself. Some properties of the aims, such as for example their degree of ambivalence and conflict, have been associated with a variety of unpleasant states, at physical and psychological level. Another property of the aims that seems to influence well-being is the level of abstractions with which they are structured. It has been seen that those who structure them (cognitively and linguistically) in broad and abstract terms tend to suffer to a greater extent from the symptoms of psychological distress (such as depression), unlike those who structure their aims in concrete, specific and more superficial terms, who suffer from physical illnesses to a greater extent.

There are also aims shared by people who belong to a particular group or who live in a specific culture. These may also include life tasks and the normative tasks of development within a particular group or society (Havighurst, 1953). It is believed that success in meeting the various tasks of development generates greater subjective well-being and increases the probability of effectively solving subsequent tasks as well, whilst failure leads to disapproval by society and difficulty in solving subsequent tasks.

As far as the relationship between goals and well-being is concerned, the importance, depending on the cases, both of having an aim and actively pursuing it and its simple achievement, is underlined. On the one hand, the perception of having a goal to attain and the sensation of making progress in this direction can be in itself a factor that gives significance to life actions in general. On the other hand, attaining a goal is an event that can originate well-being.

Cantor and Harlow (1994) have found that a positive emotional experience depended on the congruence between the objectives of life that the subjects set themselves and the social context. The feelings of well-being are based on the possibility that people use, in pursuing their aims, strategies that are compatible with their personality and with the environment. The progressive tasks and goals are influenced by the phases of development, culture and needs of the individuals. Therefore, although the level of global satisfaction remains stable, the factors that predict it may change in the course of time. It is therefore important to examine the changes in the correlates of subjective well-being during the lifetime, and in particular how personal goals are modified in the different phases of the life cycle and in the presence of critical events.

One conception of well-being that is very close to the previous one is represented by the construct of optimal experience or flow of conscience the Csikszentmihalyi model (1975). It starts from the presupposition that subjective well-being depends on involvement in interesting activities, i.e. those in which there is a condition of balance between the challenges set by the activity and the abilities possessed by the subject to cope with them. The condition of flow is distinguished from boredom (which corresponds to the presence of resources greater than the challenges) and anxiety (represented by the awareness of having greater resources than the challenges), as well as apathy (when there are few challenges and few resources to face them).

The person that is in a condition of optimal experience is totally absorbed by the activity they are carrying out to the point of ignoring the surrounding conditions or the passing of time. The concept was formulated by the author after having observed some artists producing their works. They spent hours painting or sculpting with an enormous level of concentration and without being concerned by anything else.

This theory has been used to explain why certain activities, including work, or leisure time activities, are a source of well-being. For example, it has been found that amongst university students, some activities (such as sports and games, socializing) are associated with levels of optimal experience that are greater than others (such as studying, thinking, watching TV); in addition, subjective well-being is greater when in the company of friends, whilst the lowest levels are referred when the subjects are alone.

Many of the life contexts that were found to be correlated with feelings of well-being can actually be traced back to the experience of the subjects in the context of specific social roles. For example, having a job and being married leads subjects to play particular roles and develop a corresponding identity. In literature it is believed that these aspects take on a fundamental importance for feelings of well-being, and that occupying many roles generally assumes a protective function. For example, in a gerontological context, the loss of social roles (due to retirement or being widowed) is considered a critical factor for the sense of well-being.

Social relations, in particular the closest ones (with the spouse, relations and friends) have a fundamental influence for the subjective well-being and health (physical and psychic). The most important effects of the relations are linked to the possibility that they offer in receiving (and giving) social support. The perception of social support is closely dependent, on the one hand, on the availability of a network of relations in the individual's context of life and the degree of social integration (and therefore of the objective conditions of life) and, on the other hand, on the possession of the social skills necessary to build up and maintain relations.

An interesting distinction in the context of the functions of social relations is that between providing support and simple company (Rook, 1990). The search for social support is often motivated by the desire to receive assistance in coping with personal problems, including obtaining relief in the presence of stressful events and situations; company, on the other hand, is motivated by the intrinsic pleasures that result from having pleasurable interactions (it corresponds to the most expressive function of social relations). Social support and company can be important in different times and contexts: company takes on a central role in the field of everyday relations, whilst support is fundamental at times of stress. According to Rook (op. cit.) they carry out two different functions: company (in particular of friends) is useful in increasing the sense of well-being and positive emotions, through joint participation in recreational activities, humour and expressions of affection. Social support can contribute to restoring the sense of well-being following negative life events, but it cannot necessarily help raising it above the basic level.

3.2. Psychological Well-Being

In psychology a theoretical reflection has developed on the nature of the experience of well-being, understood as positive psychological functioning or positive mental health. In this field, in which a conception of well-being as the absence of symptoms of distress (assessed with instruments that measured symptoms of distress, anxiety and depression), prevailed for a long period, it was also believed that the short-term emotional experience and judgements of satisfaction were too restrictive. One of the limits of these constructs is the fact that they did not come into being with the aim of defining the nature of the optimal experience, and therefore there was no underlying theory (Ryff, 1989). One consequence of the dissatisfaction with these measurements is the adoption, as indicators of well-being, of various socio-psychological constructs, which in literature have generally been studied as antecedents of positive emotions and satisfaction (for example self-esteem, locus of control, optimism, perception of social support) (Grob, 1995). These concepts, whilst undoubtedly picking up important aspects of the experience of being well, arose in the context of theories that did not have the explanation of well-being as the ultimate objective.

In some sectors of psychology there are theories that describe the nature of the optimal psychological experience. For example, in the area of mental health, Jahoda (1958) had proposed a series of criteria of positive mental health, such as nurturing positive attitudes towards oneself (a construct which in part includes self-esteem), the capacity to grow, develop and be self-fulfilled, autonomy, environmental command or control in the field of work and social relations, the capacity to have satisfactory social relations and the integration and accurate perception of reality. Some of these criteria have been stressed and expanded on by other authors, in the areas of clinical and humanistic psychology (Maslow, Jung, Rogers, Allport) and in the psychology of development (Erikson, Neugarten, Buhler). Jourard and Landsman (1980) have proposed very similar criteria; a positive opinion of oneself, ability to take care of others and worry about what is happening in the world, openness to new ideas and experiences, creativity, the capacity to work productively, the capacity to love and have realistic self-perceptions. Taylor and Brown (1988) recognize as criteria of psychological well-being happiness, the capacity to take care of others, the capacity for creative and productive work and positive attitudes towards oneself.

Starting from philosophical perspectives on the concept of happiness, Waterman (1993) has identified two distinct theoretical conceptions: eudemonia (which corresponds to the feelings of personal expressiveness) and hedonism (which places pleasure as the ultimate goal in life). According to the author, these constituent parts of well-being are associated with distinct activities and have different implications for the feelings of self-fulfilment. The activities that originate feelings of personal expressiveness are those in which the subject experiences feelings of self-fulfilment thanks to the possibility of expressing his potential, through the development of personal skills and talents, attaining his goals, or both. They are characterized by an intense involvement in activities, the feeling of being one with them, of being alive, complete and satisfied. They are experiences that are conceptually related with the intrinsic motivation and flow of conscience.

Hedonism, on the other hand, has its origin in a potentially very wide range of activities; it is experienced every time pleasurable emotions are felt as a consequence of the satisfaction of physical, intellectual and social needs. A more articulated perspective on the nature of the experience of psychological well-being has been provided by Ryff (1989). The author has identified in particular six criteria or dimensions of psychological well-being: autonomy, positive relations with others, personal growth, self-acceptance, the life goal and environmental control. Ryff also encountered the presence of differences of gender and age in the criteria of well-being: as age increases, the feelings of autonomy and environmental command increase and the perceptions of personal growth and of having an aim in life decrease, whilst positive relations with other people and self-acceptance continue to be important throughout life.

The criteria of positive relations with others and of personal growth appear to be more central for the female gender. Significant differences (in particular in personal growth and in the aim in life) also emerged according to social class and level of education and culture (in individualistic cultures, the criterion of personal growth is pre-eminent whilst in collectivist ones, the criterion of positive relations with others appears central, but the importance of the well-being of others is also underlined, for example of one's children, in defining one's own well-being).

3.3. Social Well-Being

The social component of health, understood as the influence of the social context and of social factors on health and well-being, has been recognized as a fundamental dimension of overall well-being.

In research literature on subjective well-being, the prevalent trend has been to attribute to social factors the role of antecedents of the condition of well-being. However, it is implicit in the WHO definition of health that the three components of health (physical, mental and social well-being) have to be considered as closely correlated.

The attention paid to the conceptualization and operationalization of social health (or well-being) has been less than that paid to physical health, psychological and subjective well-being. There does not even seem to be agreement on the components of social well-being.

McDowell and Newell (1987) define social health as that dimension of an individual's well-being that concerns his relations with others, how other people react to him and how he interacts with the social institutions and norms of society. The authors define two dimensions of social health or well-being: social adaptation and social support. The first includes satisfaction for relations (the more subjective components which concern happiness and affective well-being), performance in the context of social roles (a more objective component, relative to specific roles and the evaluation of the performance) and adaptation to the environment (a condition of dynamic balance with the environment). Social support refers, according to the authors, to the presence of people the subject trusts, on whom he can rely and who make him feel accepted and loved as a person.

It is obvious, on the one hand, that being included in a social network is a presupposition for building up links with other people and benefiting from relations of help; it also allows having positive experiences and occupying stable and socially recognized and gratifying roles within the community. On the other hand, the possibility of building up social relations is also based on having adequate social skills. The experience of social support also therefore involves both situational and personal factors.

Alongside the concept of social support, which attributes the nature of social well-being to the quality of interpersonal relations, (in particular those with the people closest to the subject, such as relatives, friends or those of a more intimate nature), dimensions of social well-being that refer to relations with the wider community and society in general have been put forward.

In this regard, Keyes (1998) has stressed that, although the existing models of psychological well-being emphasize the personal characteristics of well-being, individuals are enclosed in social structures and communities, in the context of which they have to take on countless social tasks and challenges. To understand the optimal functioning and mental health, social well-being therefore also has to be studied, which is defined by the author as the appraisal of one's living conditions and functioning in society. The author identifies five dimensions of social well-being, parallel to the criteria of psychological well-being: social integration, social acceptance, social contribution, social actualization and social coherence. Social integration consists of the appraisal of the quality of one's relationship with society and the community. Social acceptance refers to the extent to which people feel that they have something in common with others and belong to their community and society. It is opposed to isolation and the feeling of loneliness. People with the characteristic of social acceptance have confidence in others, think that others are capable of kindness; they have a favourable opinion of human nature and feel at ease with others. It is the parallel dimension to self-acceptance (Ryff, 1989). Social contribution consists of the appraisal of one's social value. It includes the belief of being a vital member of society, with something important to offer the world. It is a concept close to that of self-efficacy. Social actualization is the appraisal of the potential and overall trend of society. It corresponds to the belief that society has potentials which are fulfilled through the institutions and citizens. Subjects with higher levels of well-being have confidence in society. It is a parallel criterion to self-fulfilment and personal growth, this time seen in reference to the wider society one belongs to. Lastly, social coherence refers to the perception of the quality of the organization of the social world and includes the desire to know society and its functioning. According to this criterion, people with higher levels of well-being perceive that society is intelligible and has a comprehensible functioning, that there exists an order of things and an underlying meaning. This criterion is related to the perception of a meaning in life and the sense of personal coherence (Antonovsky, 1980).

Another construct that presents various elements of similarity with the components of social well-being is the sense of community (McMillan and Chavis, 1986). Its dimensions include the feeling of belonging (sharing bonds with others), influence (the perception of relying on and being able to influence what happens in the community), integration and the satisfaction of needs and shared emotive connection.

These additional criteria of well-being allow sketching out the condition of well-being in a more articulated way. The subjective and psychological experience of being well appears to be based not only on the experience of positive emotions and of satisfaction, on the possibilities of self-fulfilment, on the quality of the relationship with oneself (acceptance, sense of growth), on one's future (aim in life), on other people (positive relations with others, autonomy), on the environment (command), but also includes the awareness and feeling of belonging to a wider entity in the context of which it is possible to experience positive relations characterized by trust (as well as receiving support in the case of need) and in which belonging has a meaning and a value recognized by others as well, an entity which has potential for development and which is therefore a source of goals, a guarantee of the presence of a meaning in personal life as well and in the actions implemented by individuals to attain their objectives.

Chapter 2

THE FASCINATION OF RISK. A COMPULSORY CHOICE FOR YOUNG PEOPLE?

ABSTRACT

The uncertainty of post-modern society seems to have taken on a dominant, ineliminable and universal position; the projection of the Self into the future appears permeated by the dimension of risk. In such a cultural context, risk accompanies every human experience, whatever the expertise of its protagonist. Starting from this reflection, in time a different orientation to the study of risk has developed, aimed at considering the value that can be attributed to this condition of life (Magrin, 1999). As maintained by Donati (1990), daily co-existence with the dimension of risk leads us to have to evaluate the functional value of this dimension. Positive risk-oriented culture can play an important role, encouraging its members to accept the risk imposed at a social level with competence and skill. In this perspective, we can go so far as to attribute to risk itself the function, indispensable for social co-existence, of introducing diversity and innovation (Altieri, 1991).

The spread of the culture of risk affects the period of adolescence in particular, and it can be considered the time when everything is seen as possible and when everything can be experimented (Sciolla, 1993). Opening up to the category of possibility, typical of this phase of evolution, is a precious element for the development of a positive approach to reality. Concern arises when there are no stable and clear points of reference in the context of uncertainty of adolescents' actions: in this way, the natural inclination to risk could be incapable of going from the phase of experimentation and trial to the successive one of growth.

1. THE CONCEPT OF RISK AND ITS EVOLUTION

Of uncertain etymology, the term 'risk' has been associated since Greek and Latin antiquity with the concepts of danger and opportunity. From the anthropological point of view, it is a purely human phenomenon. The meanings of the term refer to harmful consequences in relation to chance and unforeseeable circumstances. In any case, the concept alludes to probable, but not certain, harm. Risking evokes the possibility of putting something and/or someone at risk. Seeking risk is typically human: it does not have the function of a value, but for the subject is a value in itself; here the value is that of daring and the pleasure of the risk itself is to see how it goes, to try, test and experiment.

This is the attitude of the adolescent who, unlike an adult, runs a risk in full awareness, for the pleasure of doing so. If it is a challenge for the young person, for the adult it becomes a virtue, because it is associated with prudence (Gonzalo Miranda, 2008). From a sociological point of view, its origin could be traced back to the human being's tendency to challenge what he does not know, a characteristic that has been common to man since the origins.

Over the centuries, its meaning has undergone great changes and its use has gradually been extended: today it applies to different situations, attitudes and contexts.

The notion of risk appeared for the first time in the Middle Ages, as a term used in maritime insurance, to indicate the dangers that could have compromised a sea voyage: at that time, it indicated the possibility of an objective danger, caused by a divine act or divine will, a case of force majeure, a storm or some other dangers of the sea that could not be attributed to a man's wrong conduct (Ewald, 1993).

This concept therefore excluded the idea of a mistake or human responsibility. Risk meant a natural event, against which human beings could do very little.

The changes in meaning and in the use of the term are linked to the coming of modernity and, following the Enlightenment, in which the basic idea is that human progress and social order come from an objective knowledge of the world, pursued through scientific enquiry and rational thought. This presupposes that both the natural and the social worlds follow constant laws that can be measured, calculated and, therefore, predicted.

In the 18th century the concept of risk in scientific terms began to be discussed, referring to ideas on the calculation of probability in mathematics.

In the 19th century, the notion of risk was further extended. The factors of risk were no longer exclusively hidden in nature, but "also in human beings, in their behaviour, in their freedom, in their relations, in their associating with one another and in society" (Ewald, op. cit., p. 12). The modernist concept of risk has introduced a new way of seeing the world and its chaotic manifestations, contingencies and uncertainties. The idea that unforeseen results could be the consequences of human action was implicit in its meaning and this sense replaced luck or fate (Giddens, 1990).

By inventing risk, the Moderns had eliminated natural indefiniteness or uncertainty. Thanks to the myth of calculability, they had learned how to transform a radically indefinite cosmos into a manageable one (Reddy 1996). This is how the concept ended up as being used exclusively in reference to events the probabilities of which were known or could be estimated. For the circumstances in which these probabilities could not be known, the term 'uncertainty' was used.

The modernist notions of risk also left room for the distinction between good and bad risks, but today these subtle distinctions tend to be lost. The expression 'good risks' survives exclusively in the esoteric language of economic speculation, where it is used in relation to the accumulation of profit (Luhmann, 1993). As Douglas maintains (1992), recourse to this term does not have much to do with the calculations of probability and, at present, the word means danger and generally is used, exclusively in reference to negative or undesirable results and not to positive outcomes. In everyday language, it tends to be used almost exclusively to indicate threats, hazards, dangers or damage and, in the past few decades, recourse to the use of the term seems to have increased, especially since the early 1970s, with an acceleration in the late 1980s.

According to Beck (1986), the changes undergone by the very nature of risks have increased the interest of the public and experts in this subject. In the last decades of the 20th century, risks were considered to have become globalized and, due to this, their effects would be more difficult to identify and consequently to deal with.

Douglas (1985) emphasizes that opinions on risks and their acceptability vary not only from culture to culture, but also in each culture, from group to group. According to the author, there is a difference between the use of danger in pre-modern societies and the use of risk in modern ones. In pre-modern societies, danger affects single individuals. It is an instrument to reinforce and consolidate the bonds of the community and to support its rules, it does not aim to protect the community but the individual. Being at risk is the equivalent of being victim of a sin, i.e. being exposed to events provoked by others, whilst being in sin means being the cause of the evil. This means that being at risk indicates being in the position of the victim, living under the threat of risks imposed by others, more than taking a risk on one's own initiative.

Following temporal coordinates closer to us, according to some observers, Giddens (1990), Massumi (1993), Lash and Urry (1994), Featherstone (1995), the late or post-modern period is characterized by uncertainty and the ambivalence associated with continuous change, cultural fragmentation and the dissolution of traditional norms.

Time and space have become compressed, the movement of persons and things is getting faster and faster and events and social relations are losing their established meanings. Contemporary Western societies have also been defined as post-traditional, precisely because they have questioned the old traditions, opening up to uncertainty and insecurity (Giddens, 1994).

All these changes lead to a way of understanding the Self and the world in radically different ways compared to the past. People nurture a growing mistrust of the social institutions and traditional authorities and have a more vivid awareness of the threats intrinsic in daily life.

In the past few years, the expression 'risk' has been used as a key word and is interwoven with other terms, such as fear, anxiety and uncertainty, defining a general state of mind of uneasiness and existential disorientation, to the extent that some authors, to describe the condition of post-modern society, have had recourse to the term 'panic' (Kroker, Kroker, 1988).

Each of us identifies the risks from the particular cultural and historical context where we are. Defining something as a risk means recognizing its importance for our subjectivity and our well-being. The phenomena which are the object of anxiety vary from society to society and from period to period.

There are at least six types of risks on which the concerns of citizens and institutions of contemporary Western societies are based today. Environmental risks: caused by pollution, radiations, certain chemical substances, or floods, fires and the dangerous conditions of the roads; lifestyle-related risks: linked to the consumption of certain substances (such as food and drugs), sexual life, the way of driving, stress, health risks: consequences of treatments or medical care (pharmacological treatments, operations, reproductive technologies and diagnostic analyses). Then there are the risks from interpersonal relations: linked to intimate relations, social interactions, love, sexuality, gender roles, friendship, marriage and parenthood; economic risks; linked to unemployment and under-employment, loans, investments, insolvency, distribution of property and failure of an undertaking; the risks of criminality which are concentrated by taking part in illegal activities or being a potential victim.

1.1. The Social Risk

The social sciences have had many different approaches to the question of the perception of risk. The perspective with the greatest following is the realist one, which has been developed and exposed in particular in technical-scientific approaches. One of the most important approaches that adopts this perspective is Cognitivism and one of the main objectives of the representatives of the cognitive approach is to identify the ways in which people react to risk from the cognitive and behavioural point of view: they pursue this objective by constructing various psychological models of human behaviour. In this literature, danger is considered the independent variable, and the reactions of the people the dependent one (Douglas, 1985). The aspiration of many researchers of a Cognitive orientation is to interpret the ways in which ordinary people evaluate and react to risks as they tend to either overestimate or underestimate some categories of risks.

The cognitive approach presents individuals as: "impulsive, impassioned and intrinsically social beings, we humans have been presented in this context as hedonistic calculators shamelessly aimed at pursuing private interests. We are said not to love risk but unfortunately, we are so incapable of manipulating the information that we end up by taking the risk involuntarily" (Douglas 1992, p. 28).

According to some investigations of a quantitative type, women are believed to react to some specific risks in a more anxious way than men, and the same would apply for black individuals compared to white ones.

Flynn (1994) asked a sample of American citizens to order twenty-five types of risk according to the dangerousness of each one for public health. The score attributed to the risks by white men was considerably lower than the scores given by white women and by black citizens, whether male or female. White men are also alleged to be the most dubious, concerning the seriousness of certain risks, for Graham and Clemente (1996), authors of a study which, like Flynn's research, focused on threats to health. Both studies have shown that, amongst white males, the most likely to consider the risks taken into examination as less serious are highly educated individuals with high family incomes and conservative political positions.

1.2. The Environmental Risk

Beck (1994) states that citizens of contemporary Western societies are living in a period of transition and that industrial society is being transformed into a society of risk. In this phase of passage, the production of wealth progresses at the same rate as the production of risks, multiplied following the process of modernization. The main problem of Western societies no longer lies in the production and distribution of goods in a period of poverty, as in early modernity and is still the case in developing countries. The most affluent societies now have to deal with a different problem, which is how to prevent and reduce "evils", i.e. risks.

Citizens, who every day become more aware of the threat of these risks, have to face them in every second of their existence: "in the attempt to avoid the toxic substances to which their lifestyle or dietary habits expose them, each individual fights defensive battles of every type" (Beck, op. cit., p. 66). It is not clear whether it is the risks that have become more acute or whether it is our view of them that has become more attentive (Beck 1986).

Every society has lived under the threat of terrifying dangers: the health and survival of human beings have always been in danger, in every historical period.

The risks of the late modern period are different from those of early modernity from several points of view. In the first place, in contemporary societies, the risks and dangers, in particular of environmental pollution, differ significantly from earlier periods: ionizing radiations and the presence of toxic chemical substances in food, have become real and almost daily.

Since the middle of the 20th century, industrial societies have faced threats to human life. These threats are believed to trigger off effects that we cannot circumscribe in space, in time or in society and our time is witnessing the production of increasingly serious risks. In the society of risk, the dangers of late modern society prove not to be easy to calculate: "although many years have now passed since the catastrophe, the victims of Chernobyl have yet to come to the light" (Beck, 1996, p. 70). With respect to pre-modern societies, both the ways of conceiving the risks and the ways of confronting them have undergone radical change. Greater responsibility and preparation is required. To characterize the reactions to risk, by the citizens of contemporary Western societies, sociological literature often uses the concept of reflexivity, which means the capacity to respond to the situations that arouse fear or anxiety actively rather than passively and the competence in continuously monitoring behaviour and contexts (Giddens 1990).

1.3. The Psychological Risk

When historical buildings are being renovated for their protection, the façades are preserved whilst the interiors are demolished. This society, however, undergoes the dismantling of the load-bearing structures without new ones being designed at the same time, as what were once collective institutions become containers of individuality. In a flourishing society, individual survival has become an end and, in solitary folly, each person continues along their insignificant path. The totalitarianisms of the last century were capable of animating great passions and indicating goals that mapped out the future. Now, however each person is alone with himself: nobody offers them a direction or indicates an objective. Without a utopia, the biography of every single individual remains flat and opaque, a waste land (Francesconi, Zanetti, 2009).

We live in a cancellation of the collective horizon, as though the future were a private matter and each person had to take care of it on their own; a widespread sense of disorientation is the cause of an increasingly anonymous society, where it is difficult to feel someone for someone else.

One example for all which is current, concrete and daily: getting high, which represents a possible, easy and democratic alternative, is at everybody's disposal. In clubs, young people find, waiting for them, the ways to get a buzz: deafening music, promiscuous sex, alcohol and drugs. If they feel the need for all this, it means that they are confused or devastated, if they try to go out of their minds, it means that the mind is not a good container, if they want a high it means that they feel low and suffocated (Francesconi, Zanetti, op. cit.).

Educators denounce in vain the risks of living wildly and the dangers of the night; young people know them but do not pay any attention because, obviously, enjoyment outstrips fear. Fear is an emotion that has always existed because it is part of our instinct, which has the purpose of survival of the individual and the species. As such, it acts, or should act, as an alarm in the face of impending danger or as an activator of reactive energies in the face of an actual danger that is present. From the time we are children, fear is conformed on socially and culturally defined risks.

In the risk experience, the whole process is accompanied by emotional states. The emotion in itself is the inner energy that drives us to carry out an act, this is what gives the act a specific tone and a particular colour. Emotion is a personal psychological condition and, at the same time, a social and cultural one.

Every period, every society and every group has a specific emotive style. In certain families, children grow up in a climate of anxious fear which conditions their attitudes. The same applies to school and in relations between young people of the same age, where emulation, favoured by the activity of mirror neurons which induce the same behaviour as the person opposite, of their emotions, plays a fundamental role.

There are countless cultural repertoires: in our post-modern society, the spectacular ones prevail, in particular the messages that use visual images. Children, well before encountering a real danger, have met a thousand imaginary ones through collection cards, cartoons, adverts and electronic games. When we are faced by a danger, our senses have already incorporated precognitions that orient them, inducing selections and priorities.

The perception and evaluation of a risk proceed together in the interaction between an innate instinctual alarm (such as a fear of heights, thunder or fire), the sedimentation of previous experiences, information and skills.

The evaluation is never separable from perception and perception can easily be conditioned by cultural reinforcements but also, for example, by the use of toxic substances. A small quantity of wine, on average one glass, is sufficient to alter the perception of the dimensions of the road and, consequently, the evaluation of the risk that a driver takes.

The measurement of risk is a probabilistic operation and as such requires a certain intellectual maturity. Under the influence of fear, the outer and inner worlds become narrower whilst time is dilated as though everything were taking place in slow motion.

The emotions, which intervene in every physical and mental process, can act as an incentivizing factor, increasing attention, vigilance, initiative or, negatively, distorting data, inhibiting or disarticulating the response.

Fear can be preventive, present and even in hindsight, aroused by a past danger. An imaginary fear also exists, when the imagination or a virtual scene is frightening.

It is a healthy emotion because, by projecting our aggressive drives outside ourselves, it defends us from the world and from ourselves and our drive for self-destruction. It becomes pathological when it is triggered off too early, too late, excessively or insufficiently, always or never.

Each person has a personal threshold of tolerance to risk, including according to temperament and character. There is a sort of predisposition towards fear. Aggressive personalities are usually the more afraid because they project violent feelings on to the outer world and receive, in return, threatening impressions. In our society, the perception of risk is high and constant. It is mainly an anonymous, widespread, insinuating and faceless risk, which feeds a passive fear, which is equally as vague and fluctuating. Society and individual try to defend themselves from the anxiety and anguish by activating mechanisms of defence, of which the most enigmatic include the search for risk as an end in itself, independently of a purpose to be achieved.

1.4. Risk and Pleasure

In our societies, risk is considered a negative aspect of life and something to be avoided. This is how it is presented by the experts and this is how it tends to be experienced by ordinary people. Much of the scientific literature on risk attributes a state of constant fear to individuals in late modernity. The risks they become aware of arouse a feeling of profound vulnerability in them, fuelling feelings of anxiety and uncertainty.

Taking avoidable risks is considered reckless, thoughtless, irresponsible and even deviant behaviour, a demonstration of ignorance, a sign of the incapacity to control one's Self.

An Australian newspaper (Macken, 1998) devoted an article to the growing fortune of extreme sports, such as sky-diving (doing acrobatic exercises in free fall, postponing opening the parachute as long as possible), rafting, swimming amongst sharks, bungee-jumping, hang-gliding, climbing rock faces or frozen waterfalls or, amongst the more recent, trampoline wall. They are called extreme sports because they are believed to test the resistance of human beings to fear. Those who are attracted to them seek danger, actively taking a risk excites them and makes them feel successful.

For anyone who decides to practise these sports "the dare has been declared. Leave behind the speed limits, the smoke-free zones, tight deadlines, the low fat shopping list, the SPF-15 routine and yell in the face of life" (op. cit., p. 158).

Advertising messages use illustrations of risky ventures, and in particular the messages targeting the market of young people and which advertise sporting goods, SUVs, alcoholic beverages and soft drinks.

In conveying these images, they rely on the desire of potential consumers to be different or out of the ordinary: a desire which is thought to find expression in the willingness to face danger and seek thrills. The growing offer of these cultural products shows an increasingly greater attraction for the pleasures and excitement that feats of risk produce.

Cohen and Taylor (1992) analyse some of the ways in which individuals seek to transcend habits of daily life, to flee or oppose reality. According to the authors, the attempts at escaping always entail some risks: from the marginal risk of offending one's partner or friends, to the risk of losing a limb or even one's life. Going on holiday and using drugs represent "interruptions in the flow of life, distractions, temporary intervals, skirmishes, a glimpse into different realities" (op.cit., p. 158). They are ways to escape the sense of boredom and predictability, to relieve the dissatisfaction that can emerge from this.

Giddens (1990) states that the norm and everyday tranquillity help people to face up to life with a sense of familiarity, stability and certainty. When unexpected events or circumstances arrive, they tend to feel anxiety, fear and hostility. According to the author, other people, however, cultivate risk with the intention of compromising their condition of security. "By facing up to situations of risk, people can display their courage, their enterprising nature, skill and capacity of resistance. They are well aware of the risks that the actions they have taken entail and their objective is indeed to give their life some of that edge that is completely lacking in normal circumstances" (op.cit., p. 159).

It appears that those who really want excitement have to run risks.

Those who have extreme experiences tend to insist on the perfect execution of the risky action, on the ability to keep the situation under control despite the general chaos and in its turn this ability requires firmness and force of resistance to fear. Performing extreme ordeals does not mean completely relinquishing control: doing so would mean attempting suicide or hurting oneself on one's own.

Individuals who have this type of extreme experience tend to consider security as an innate ability, a gift possessed only by a very small elite. In their eyes, those who expose themselves voluntarily to danger do not show recklessness but rather that they have superior qualities that allow them to seek out risk without harming themselves (Lyng, 1990).

The rush of adrenalin produced by risky or dangerous activities allows people to escape the constraints of a rational mind and a controlled body and to experiment, for a certain period of time, the supremacy of the sensations and emotions of the body. The idea is that life becomes more intense, that you approach nature more than culture, that you break the rules imposed on us by society. At the same time, it is possible to attempt the sublime experience that consists of losing one's Self for a second, in transcending the limits of civil behaviour. It is the same type of experience that the Romantics, between the eighteenth and nineteenth centuries, championed: listening to the emotions and feelings was believed to avoid the sterility of modern life, produced by the obsession for rational order and self-mastery. The invitations today to loosen control often refer to neo-Romantic ideals: they exhort a return to the authenticity of nature and putting emotions at the centre of self-expression (Lupton, 1998).

Very strong bonds connect the individuals who take part in dangerous activities, sharing in this common objective. Durkheim (1912) used the definition of collective exaltation to describe the intense emotions that group participation in this sort of feat produces.

Every single individual, taking part in activities such as uprisings, mass conflicts and wars, participation in violent gangs, dangerous feats, excessive drinking and drug-taking with others, is induced to reach the state of collective exaltation which these create, to lose the awareness of their individual identity and be transformed, at least for a certain period of time, into an element of a body or collective Self united by a common or shared objective. It is possible that this merging with others, arouses in some sensations of terror, but as it allows giving up, at least in part, self-control and abandoning oneself to the collective will of the mass, it can also be a source of intense pleasure (Maffesoli, 1988; Mellor, Shilling, 1997).

Exposing oneself to dangers can represent one aspect of a reflective project of the Self, an action to be carried out to reach personal growth. "People who carry out extreme acts of the purest type see themselves as subjects who act instinctively, an experience which produces in them a sensation of purification and exaltation" (Lyng 1990, p. 163).

In this context, risky actions which are intentionally sought are considered an opportunity to show one's courage, to dominate fear, to show something to oneself, a demonstration thanks to which life can be faced with the sensation of having the capacity to modify things: "having defeated the challenge, they feel capable of coping with any risky situation whatsoever" (Lyng, op. cit., p. 163).

Giddens (1991, p. 163), quotes the warning of a self-help book: "If you want to improve yourselves but refuse the idea of intentionally running risks, you will remain trapped in your situation. Or maybe you will take a risk without being ready. In both cases, you will have set a limit on your development, you will have precluded some of the actions necessary to increase your value." Living a life sheltered from every danger means appearing asleep, dying, trapped in habits and ways that are obsolete, and not growing as people.

Discourses that exalt risky actions tend to insist on a revelation of oneself. Running risks would mean giving up controlling one's behaviour in the ways imposed by society, coming out into the open, rejecting expectations, being spontaneous again and seizing the moment.

Those who take risks appear courageous in two ways: not only because they expose themselves to a danger, but because intentionally they go against social norms. There is something extraordinary in those who face danger. People tend to consider those who sail around the world solo or who go round the world in a hot-air balloon by themselves, the mountaineer who conquers an unreachable peak and the audacious entrepreneur who earns a lot of money from risky investments as people who stand out from the crowd. Their courage, their strength of will and determination, their promptness in defying danger and uncertainties are admired.

The capacity to take risks is generally greatly appreciated at work as well. In particular, it is required in those who occupy high level managerial positions and workers from whom creativity is expected: the willingness to take risks is a condition to get ahead in a career.

The choice of exposing oneself to dangers can be considered the other side of modernity, a reaction to the increasing importance given to control and predictability. It is also true that the willingness to run risks goes with some of the most important trends of modernity: "the capacity to undermine the stability of things, to open up untrodden paths, to colonize in this way a segment of the future, is a intrinsic characteristic of modernity and what defines its revolutionary nature" (Giddens 1991, p. 165).

It is possible that individuals in contemporary society need both routine and risk: it is probable that they hanker after both predictability and unpredictability, that they constantly oscillate between one and the other. An excessive insistence on one generates an intense desire for the other. An acute awareness of risks may arouse the desire to expose oneself to their threat. Indeed, even predictability can take on the appearance of a risk.

"We do not want a world in which the guarantee of no longer dying of hunger is exchanged for the risk of dying of boredom," Cohen and Taylor state in a slogan (1992, p. 166).

2. RISK, FEAR AND CHALLENGES

In society people are or feel alone, often not alone out of choice but by necessity, because the containers of identity have been shattered. Bewilderment generates fear and fear, in turn, causes isolation because, without social safety nets, their perception and fear of strangers increase.

Today, we are living in a climate of fear induced by the conviction that we are living in a threatening context, where there is great, widespread and constant danger.

The mass media boost, with increasingly exasperated emotive tones, a sequence of negative pieces of news, often aimed at arousing the fascination of horror, the attraction of mystery and the courage of fear. Sheltered from every risk, it is impossible to grow up.

"The world asks nothing of us", is the lament of the best youngsters, suspended in an immobile time which does not promise a visible and desirable future. Desire, without objectives and strategies, turns into distress, apathy and chronic discontent. To emerge from passivity, from lack of confidence in oneself and in the world, the act of taking a risk for risk's sake appears as a possibility of self-assertion and self-esteem. Going from a passive to an active state, from suffering to acting, arouses a sense of well-being and, at times, a feeling of triumph. This explains the tendency to relive traumas, to replicate failures, up to the constriction of repeating the most frustrating situations of life which Freud calls fate neuroses (Finzi, 2009).

Often those who do extreme sports say: it is a challenge to myself, I wanted to surpass myself, I am my main opponent.

However, there is an important difference between facing up to a dangerous situation, evaluating the probability of being hurt, or facing up to a situation where the alternative is radicalized in living or dying.

In the same way, there is a substantial difference between endangering only oneself and involving others. The excitement induced by danger may be so thrilling as to become a sadomasochist perversion. The eroticization of the risk makes the effectiveness of dissuasive campaigns that use particularly strong messages questionable. They can be so exciting and eroticizing as to fascinate youngsters or so anxiogenic as to induce mechanisms of negation and repression.

Young people who are frightened of fear, who withdraw into themselves, refuse, together with risk, life as well: they do not face dangers because they do not admit losing, they do not accept frustration, they are incapable of managing disappointment, they do not put themselves to the test because they have excluded themselves from every test, as though the prize at stake did not concern them. They feel that life is a competition but they do not enter it because they do not accept the implicit rules. They are so frightened by it that they give up living to survive.

Youngsters who do not understand the positive sense of the challenge implicit in growing up and in becoming an adult, do not believe in themselves or have confidence in their capacities and do not have any self-esteem. They see their peers go ahead whilst they remain at a standstill but they do not question themselves, they avoid every journey of introspection, they prefer to seal off the inner world not to face up to it and they do not ask themselves or others any questions.

When the impossibilities preclude every space for freedom and choice, the subject remains static, closed in himself, apathetic and indifferent because it is not worth taking the risk and, consequently, it is not worth living. During childhood, he has probably not received enough expressions of security and confidence and as a consequence, instead of self-validating himself as the person who challenges himself tries to, he does not enter the arena of life, but stands on the sidelines without taking part in any competition. In the worst case, the desire not to be there or to cease to exist can lead to suicide.

Some youngsters, after school, prefer to remain by themselves, shut up in their room, hypnotized by a video, imprisoned by an unexpressed rancour: without wishing to do so, they have made confidence a suffocating coat of armour. Their vital energies are engaged in stopping time so that nothing happens, in anaesthetizing their emotions not to feel pain, in not loving to avoid being rejected, in blocking out knowledge of themselves and of the world in order not to face up to the unknown.

Medicine has a diagnosis of depression ready for them which justifies and relieves them of responsibilities, confiding in an improbable recovery with medication. More than health, they need salvation, something in which to believe, for which it is worth risking. Life is healed only living it and living means being exposed to the possibility of failure. And the certainty, sooner or later, of dying.

In the face of the fear of the unknown, the anxiety for tomorrow, the most effective drug is hope, the first and last Goddess of our existence (Finzi, op. cit.).

3. THE BIOGRAPHICAL UNCERTAINTY OF YOUNG PEOPLE AND THE PLEASURE OF RISK

Biographical uncertainty is a central question in contemporary sociological thought: in adolescents it concerns not so much the contestation of the early modern certainties by a small group of transgressors, but a condition which is becoming generalized to the extent of becoming a normal element in experience for the young generations.

In addition, it no longer appears as a transitory condition, linked to a particular phase of passage but as a permanent aspect of individual experience, becoming associated with the idea that the construction of one's evolution is a process that continues throughout a lifetime.

Summarizing, the elements that characterize contemporary biographical uncertainty are the following: the reversibility of choices and their distance from consolidated forms of role models in a perspective of growing flexibilization of work and career prospects; the emphasis on the present, compared to an increasingly less predictable future, which follows the acceleration of time of acting, typical of the culture of immediacy. The dilation of times of passage, typical of some phases of life, but which are extended in space and time; and, lastly the progressive centrality of the biographical dimension, associated with the loss of historical memory, the weakening of the limits between public and private which, for some, is resolved in the privatization of all the experiences of life (Rampazi, 2009).

Given these premises, a delicate phase in life can be read and interpreted more precisely, when, with great difficulty, the individual's identity is defined: adolescence, a complex journey marked by the presence of a threatened identity and a significant narcissistic fragility. The adolescent subject presents a psychological condition of particular vulnerability, determined by the need to give up childish bonds with the objects of love and to face the struggle of infantile omnipotence; by aspects of great ambivalence with regard to the parental figures and depression which is variously expressed and connote this phase which, in present-day society, due to a complex of cultural and social factors, tends to extend well beyond the limits which contained it thirty or forty years ago.

In adolescence, a destructuring of the psychic equilibrium previously acquired is necessary, in view of a new structuring which contemplates the integration and overcoming of conflicts. The adolescent's task of development consists of organizing a new feeling of identity, to arrive at being stably identified with his objectives, ambitions and sexuality, both on the individual and collective level and on the social and the ethical level.

It is this constant or recurring awareness of fragility of his existence by the adolescent that shows all his vulnerability, which is moreover specular to his illusion of invulnerability. There is obviously a different degree of vulnerability between adolescents: a different capacity for tolerating the uncertainty of the self, doubts about one's value, the result of the development of the body. Some more than others feel their image threatened and feel their sense of non-value greater with a set of emotions that rotates around them; shame, fear and anger.

The self is mortified by this and the risky action is felt at that point as a vital action, which can have a redeeming value. The affective roots of the conduct at risk emerge in full. The usual defences are no longer enough, they are no longer functional, acts then take over and as a consequence the area of possible risk where conflictual tension is discharged increases.

At-risk conduct improves one's image, with oneself and with others. Adolescents exaggerate to gain value, to show off, to revaluate themselves, not to get hurt. This is an important point, and one which today is often the subject of misunderstanding.

The action at risk is felt as a vital action. The risk and taking it become the expression of a desire not to die, but to live better, to relive and be reborn. If to all this we add, as typical of adolescence, protective mechanisms of dividing parts of the self that can be esteemed and not esteemed, therefore adolescents attribute to the social context (parents, teachers and others) an oppressive and devitalizing power, beyond the specific faults; then escape into at-risk conduct can be combined with an omnipotent dream, which is more as an executioner than a revenge towards a world which is not perfect and against which adolescents are sided. Reckless behaviour is in some way legitimized by the feeling of depression and anger as a consequence of disappointing discoveries.

The adolescent thus finds himself face to face with an affective supplement, an addition which can aggravate at-risk behaviour. All this provides more motivations for so-called normal behaviour of taking risks, although these are known: exploratory curiosity, experimentation, proving oneself and putting oneself to the test, enjoying the sensation of having acquired a greater capacity to control reality, the sensation of excitement and sometimes of thrills.

3.1. Experimenting Risk: A Compulsory Choice?

Adolescents are (or seem so to adults) strange: they go from excessive confidence in their means and certainties to states of depression, anguish and despair: they do not have great confidence in the world they belong to and above all they are mistrustful of adults.

For parents, they are inaccessible, defiant, incomprehensible and seem to be attracted by everything that is prohibited, forbidden and dangerous, bordering on harmful.

On the one hand, parents go from a lifestyle and attitudes aimed at protecting, accompanying and being almost fully responsible to an orientation towards attitudes that revolve around more complex prohibitions and bans that are difficult to manage.

On the other hand, adolescents experience new and accelerated emotions and situations, with a very great desire for autonomy and individual choice; for them, the world is wrong, they think they know how to make it go better, they think they know everything and can do everything. In the abundant existing literature, this is shown as developmental breakdown; it is a phase characterized by emotional, hormonal and situational storms.

Challenges are part of this period: defying everyone and everything, in an attempt to break out of a phase of dependence. With this there is also the attraction for risk. What to adults would seem risky, excessive and dangerous, is experienced by adolescents as appealing, easy and normal.

An adolescence without challenges and risks is deemed suspicious.

At this age, at-risk behaviour often fulfils specific functions and, although it may be harmful from a physical, mental and social point of view, it seems to give the adolescent a way out from the lack of confidence and uncertainties experienced in this period of life.

Though dangerous for oneself and for others, behaviours and emotions linked to risk could be attentively sought because they allow reaching a number of objectives which are above all related to asserting identity and building up new affective social relations. Many adolescents are able to attain these goals through adaptive ways, without excessively endangering their physical, psychological and social well-being.

Other adolescents, on the other hand, do not find any other way to fulfil these objectives except through what is recognized as at-risk behaviour.

One well-known reinforcing element of this situation revolved around the importance of the peer group and the tendency to imitate conduct which is the riskiest: this is the start of gradually moving away from the adults' system of control.

At-risk behaviours can concern the use of substances such as cannabis, synthetic drugs, alcohol (the sporadic use of substances can, on the one hand, facilitate the desire to experiment effects which allow introspection, on the other, exasperate performances, such as listening to music and dancing for prolonged periods of time, having sex, etc.); unprotected sexual intercourse; driving and some particularly risky games. The preventive actions of the use of substances indicate that the qualification of prohibition that accompanies illegal drugs, rather than dissuading their use, encourages it, in a sort of resort to illegal and prohibited behaviour.

Growth towards adulthood, challenges, recourse to at-risk behaviour are elements that are inextricably connected and from this it would appear that recourse to risk is an inevitable part of adolescence. Without recourse to risk, the adolescent does not construct his developmental crisis.

At this age, at-risk behaviour often fulfils very specific functions and, although it is harmful from the physical, mental and social point of view, it seems to give the adolescent an exit route from the insecurity and uncertainties experienced in this period of life.

Jack (1989) has observed that the tendency and experimentation in general of risks, during adolescence, are considered normal behaviour because it helps adolescents reach healthy independence, a stable identity and greater maturity, although taking risks seems to be one of the greatest causes of death amongst adolescents, especially when they are the victims of accidents.

The author reports that young people perceive a sort of personal immunity with respect to the negative consequences of actions, as though accidents, teenage pregnancies, for example, happen only to others, as though they were immune to contagion from diseases such as AIDS, as though the real negative events of life did not concern the adolescent.

There may be adolescents who are able to take their experiences of risk to heart, to emerge with a valid stock of positive instruments and others who may suffer complicated and at times dramatic consequences. The conclusion of this reasoning seems to be paradoxical and worrying: it is not the risk in itself that appears dangerous. "It is not drugs that make the drug addict, but the drug addict that makes drugs," said Olievenstein about substances (1984, p. 18).

3.2. Family, Adolescents and Risk

The importance of the family as a guide and point of reference emerges at the centre of the phase of adolescence.

Some Italian studies (Bonino, 2004; Bacchini, 2004; Marta, 2004; Calandri, 2004; Ingoglia, 2004) have approached the link between family relations and the development of adolescent at-risk behaviour, highlighting the quality of family relations and specific educational practices as protective factors.

As far as the quality of family relations is concerned, it has been seen that a climate of empathy, open to dialogue and support, favours the psycho-social adaptation of the adolescent, unlike an attitude of refusal which is correlated to the development of at-risk behaviour. Psycho-social adaptation is evaluated on the basis of the absence of problems both of externalization (aggressiveness, substance abuse but also lying and disobedience) and internalization (depression and irritability). Feeling rejected leads the adolescent to develop a self-model as a person who is not loved and cannot be loved and a model of others as rejecters; this results in the development of depressive symptoms first and subsequently deviant conditions.

From the point of view of educational practices, on the other hand, the role of parental monitoring has emerged as the factor to protect against deviance. Parental monitoring refers to the knowledge by parents of their children's activities, friendships and the places where they go; it is a form of control, supervision and behaviour which implies a certain degree of involvement and investment by the parents in their relations with their children and therefore of empathy, whilst on the part of the children it requires openness to communication and a certain degree of responsibility.

Recent developments on parental monitoring underline the importance of considering not only the active role of parents in implementing this educational practice but also the influence that the adolescent's behaviour has on the educational and relational practices of the parents themselves.

In parental monitoring, it is important to distinguish between behavioural and psychological control; whilst it is true that monitoring children's activity has been shown to be a protective factor from the development of at-risk behaviour, it is also true that psychological control, implemented through manipulative strategies which act on the children's guilt feelings, has proven to have a contrary effect, fostering the adoption of such behaviour (Trincas, 2001).

The process that leads the adolescent to the definition of the self therefore seems to be more a quality of the relationship than of the individual.

Some relational profiles have been identified based on the levels of autonomy and closeness with respect to parents, with the result that adolescents defined as detached are those that who had to make a clean break with their families to embark on the journey towards individualization; they perceived it as emotively distant and not very welcoming and have more behavioural problems with respect to subjects defined as individualized. The latter group, on the other hand, is made up of those adolescents who have succeeded in finding a balance between the drive for independence and maintaining close relations within the family and who show a psychosocial adaptation (Ingoglia, 2004).

Risk expresses the adolescent's need to put himself to the test, to experiment his limits and learn to know himself and the world outside his family nucleus.

At-risk behaviour is not necessarily negative and the main task of parents (and of adults in general) consists precisely of being able to read the message conveyed by these attitudes. When these attitudes are not understood in their meanings, but ignored or punished, they risk being adopted by the adolescent as the only way to cope with the task of his development; they are transformed into a coaction to be repeated for its own sake, in a world to flee from oneself and not to seek an identity of one's own, thus taking on a strongly maladaptive character (Ingoglia, op.cit.).

The family must appear empathetic and supportive to adolescent changes, recognizing the educational role that it has, without delegating it to third parties, but, if anything, collaborating with other figures and institutions (the school in the first place, the community, a sports club). To do this, it is important that parents are not frightened by the aggressive and provocative behaviour of their children, but that they learn how to read this as a request for help, that they set rules and defined limits, to be provided with an authoritative and not authoritarian attitude, based not only on supervising their children's activities but also on dialogue and communication. It is in this perspective of circularity, where the family climate has its influence on the adolescent but, at the same time, is influenced by his behaviour (Calandri, 2004), that the adolescent can be considered "a joint developmental undertaking by parents and children" (Carrà, Marta 1996, p. 49). Only by taking this into account can the family fulfil a function of containing the fears and confusion of emotions typical of adolescents who are in difficulty and do not always know it.

The task of parents and adults, in general, is to resist attacks by the adolescent, because only time can heal the adolescent and the gradual process of maturation that follows (Esposito, 2003). This process of maturation implies a transformation of the earlier family bonds, a renegotiation not only of the conquests of the previous developmental phases of the adolescent but also of the parent-child relationship, in a perspective which is no longer limited to the family contexts, but extended to the peer group as well.

3.3. The Surrounding World: The Peer Group

The peer group takes on an important role because it is a place of transition and passage from family to society. It is a special stage where, every single subject, in their lifetime, displays their relational skills, their weak points and their strong points. Here we can have confirmation of our worth or not, behind the protective shield of friendship and the solidarity of companions. Within the group we discover diversity, explore, accept opinions, make comparisons and get to know ourselves better and better and grow up. The first group which is formed outside the family is a micro-group. This is the first way through which young people try to separate themselves, to become emancipated and to grow up outside the family. The first outings in the evening take place through this group in miniature, the aim of which is to mutually support one another, be encouraged, reduce anxiety and fear of the outside world. It is a protected place of growth, where the affective component is significant and which is rarely contaminated from the outside. After the micro-group, the next stage is the small group, usually made up of from 4 to 10 or 12 members. This group is formed at secondary school, meeting new contemporaries with the same needs. Youngster like to be with others of their own age. They get on well together they go to the same discotheque, the same café or the same bookshop. In this group they can also meet contemporaries of different origins, but with whom they have things in common: the pleasure of sharing the same taste in singers, bands, a certain type of music or sharing some existential and social conceptions. It is the group in which they share different ways of spending their spare time and even experiment some other transgressive pastimes.

Resemblance is the linking function that prevails to belong to this group, in this case it is not identified with the physical function but more by affinity of needs, interests and lifestyles. What is gratifying is to be with other young people who have similar ideas. Ideas are the element of union.

The next passage is that of entering a larger group: the extended group. This has between 10-12 and 35-30 members. With the passage from the small group to the extended one, personal relations are not as close. It is a heterogeneous group and relations are formed on more anonymous and impersonal temporary grounds. In the end there is the large group, which has from 30 members upwards. In these types of group, interactions are less direct and impersonal. Here the function that unites the youngsters is identification. It is a criterion of belonging relative to the willingness of the youngsters to seek in others their own convictions, ideas and needs. It is possible to belong to the large group even when there is no closeness or resemblance of ideas or needs. Many youngsters aspire to belonging to groups that have a specific identity and which represent a socially desirable status. For youngsters, joining a group is an imaginary way of making their dreams and expectations come true.

However, group life is not always happy and favourable for healthy and interesting proposals. Youngsters may have to deal with proposals that go against their ideas or which entail risks.

Group life is complex and conceals some threats. It is worth seeking them out to avoid them. This is not always easy as there is the risk of being outcast or accused of being a traitor. Being part of any group means having to distinguish what is right from what is wrong, what is morally licit from what is illicit. At times this distinction can be difficult, but it is essential not to completely relinquish one's identity and values.

Every group expresses values of reference: licit and illicit values are at stake.

The licit values are: friendship, honesty, respecting people, helping those in need, appreciating diversity, fun, supporting a team, enthusiasm for a favourite pop star. Illicit values are: violence, taking and selling drugs, self-harm, stealing, doing acts of vandalism, bullying and harassing others.

When there is no dialectic in a group and some take the upper hand, manipulating the choices of all the members, the group risks degenerating and no longer being functional to social growth. A second principle of healthy participation in the group is when it is inclined to always keeping contacts open with the outside. The tendency for any group whatsoever to detach itself from the rest of the community and create barriers that select the entrance of new members, and the circulation of new thoughts and attitudes, is normal. This has the function of conferring stability on the group and protecting its shared values. However, when it is excessively closed and total isolation from the world is created, the group is impoverished, it loses validity and is blocked in its evolution.

Groups are social proposals which are good to belong to, they are opportunities where one can feel part of a project, attention is experienced as is the gratifying sensation of a sense of belonging. Belonging gives confidence, peace of mind, completeness and self-value. Refusal of belonging is greatly feared by young people. Not being accepted with one's human limits is for them a great frustration which often they are not ready to withstand.

Within friendships, consolidated even for some time, there may nestle elements of disturbance which can foster the consumption of substances, dangerous behaviour or the development of other addictions.

If there is the habit of smoking a joint in a group of friends, everybody is responsible and the responsibility cannot be attributed only to those who suggest the idea most often and drag along the others. Then there are other relations with those of the same age, outside of actual friendships, which may foster experimenting with substances. This is the case of extemporary relations in symbolic meeting places: squares, parks, pubs, discotheques, rave parties, beer festivals, a long-awaited concert or at a football match. Here the youngster meets the friend he does not know, with whom he occasionally shares that space of value and meaning. They are places of exchange, formation, identification and cultural closeness in which social integration is worked out and where the search for identity is very open to what is new and possible. Sharing pleasant experiences is often a sufficient reason for a further exchange of experiences.

There are various elements of disturbance that see friendship, bonds between peers and an inclination for deviant or potentially dangerous behaviour as closely connected. One is that the small group is tightly closed off to other friends. The youngster has relations only with the group he belongs to, does not take part in the life of extended and organized groups and accepts, passively and without any sense of criticism, the rules imposed by the group.

Another element of disturbance is exclusion or low acceptance by peers. When a member is cast aside by the group of friends or even excluded, it is easy to acquire substitutive and demonstrative behaviour, especially if it has not yet been adopted by the group.

Yet another one is excessive orientation towards peers, totally giving up any reference to adults and personal inner dialogue: this is typical of insecure young people or those who are in difficult family situations with very negative adult models. The group takes on a vicarious role of the family, without comparison and without possibility of appeal.

The sensation of distress linked to the uncertainty of identity and the sense of existence tends to be camouflaged in the lifestyles of the group. The tendency to conform to the group, giving up one's own personality, is called the gregarious or herd instinct.

Amongst the elements of risk, for the friendship group most at risk for the experimentation of substances, there is the transformation of the group into a gang. This type of deterioration of the group occurs when illicit values prevail within the group. In the gang-group, a subculture of refusal, of contestation of the social and traditional values in an aggressive and depressing climate of aggregation is found: this leads to transgressive behaviour which leads the young person to openly defy adults and the law.

Smoking joints, for example, is frequent behaviour in the gang-group, but transgression is also occasionally experimented in the group of friends with a lighter attitude, without strong aggressive charges, as a moment of opposing adult authority and the community the group belongs to. A joint, the symbol of youth emancipation, lends itself to carrying out this function of making demands and protest. The more it is confined to illegality, the more its transgressive connotation increases and the young person increasingly uses it as a demonstrative act to show his companions his courage and value. The disinhibition effect of the derivatives of cannabis on the psyche foster relations, the exchange of affection and explains the wide diffusion that it is having in the world of young people. In participating in their use, the youngster yields to the dynamics of the group, abandons any responsibility and risks sending his individuality completely "up in smoke" (Riboldi, Magni, 2010).

3.4. Rules and Actions. Understanding Them, Following Them and Breaking Them

Understanding, following and breaking rules are all important actions.

In particular, during adolescence, there is a sort of basic duplicity: on the one hand, the maximum capacity to understand what rules are and what they mean is developed, as abstract intelligence and social intelligence develop and there is an increasingly better understanding of what others expect of us and what has to be done to get on with others but, on the other hand, the greatest motivation to break these same rules is also developed.

Social intelligence is that set of skills that allows understanding what the rules of relationship are within a group, the rules to make a game of interaction, a social game or at times even a game of breaking the rules.

The system of rules of the adolescent type is not easy to manage yet adolescents succeed very well. Breaking the rules is important and, to a certain extent, can be assimilated with a factor of growing up, because it corresponds to the need for independence, a demand for autonomy and also the need to experiment, to go and see and test whether the rules, taken for granted, really work, make sense and whether there are grounds for their existence.

Criticizing rules in adolescence can be done and is done. It represents a finishing point and at the same time a way to go ahead. Adolescents often arouse fear or alarm due to their demands for autonomy, which for them has the meaning of being able to think by themselves, showing and proving that they are no longer children and that they have become capable of evaluating the rules as equals with adults.

In order to be successful, to be someone, to be great men, the rules have to be broken in some way. Understanding the rules and what they are for, means having a social intelligence, but understanding how they work in the real world also means understanding their limits, especially in relation to the contexts in which adolescents live and the pressure and passion to which they are subjected.

The adolescent understands that the rule is followed to be accepted, respected and considered good and smart kids. The idea of being accepted and considered smart is naturally not enough to follow the socially valid rules. It is no secret that even criminals can be accepted and considered smart by others and, sometimes, even to respect oneself for a basic coherence with one's identity when this is an issue.

The individual is always at the crossroads of a group of other people who push him to do different things. Social pressure is an element with a great influence.

The adolescent who breaks the rules always tries to justify himself to himself, to give himself a reason, to construct excuses to maintain that what he did could be right. These are instruments of self-defence of the Ego, which are rather weak from the rational point of view and which on this level can be disputed. Another aspect of possible cognitive weakness in breaking the rules is linked to the poor capacity of correctly foreseeing all the consequences of one's actions. There is an aspect of emotive weakness which leads to breaking the rules: it is linked to the difficulty of identifying with the figures that represent the rules. One of the main protective factors for avoiding getting into trouble, even in the most at-risk or deteriorated situations, is having had figures of reference who have given a positive value to the rules. Identifying with figures that have a strong and positive relationship with rules is fundamental and the absence of figures of reference to trust is linked, for children and adolescents, to a basic problematic situation.

4. SENSATION SEEKING

It therefore appears that the fascination of risk is completely natural when it occurs at a particular time in the construction of one's Self, but there are also other reflections to be made.

Particular sensations or needs may develop in some adolescents which drive them to consume substances. Sensation seeking, i.e. seeking strong sensations is becoming increasingly frequent amongst young people. There is a close relationship between the effects produced by taking substances and the experience of sensation seekers.

Taking substances on the one hand reproduces a particularly gratifying state of excitement (similar to that sensed during dangerous behaviour), on the other hand they induce a sense of omnipotence therefore it is easier to measure up to even more extreme risks.

Seeking strong sensations can be translated into different types of behaviour: from the abuse of alcohol and drugs to gambling, reckless driving, extreme sports, unprotected sexual relations and acts of vandalism.

Seeking new experiences and sensations pulls youngster into increasingly daring choices which are not always made consciously. Risk and transgression become synonymous with pleasure. A way to live more intensely, to increase one's presence in the world, to dilate time, a few seconds that seem to last a few hours. A game that can be exciting but which can also have troubling aspects to it.

The development of sensation seeking recognizes various factors that foster it. One of these is undoubtedly adolescence. Young people are the lovers of risk par excellence. Many of them lose this attraction once they become adults. During adolescence an inclination for risk is developed because all the parts of the brain do not develop uniformly. Whilst the areas of the brain that are involved in emotions (the limbic system) have a rapid development and complete growth during the early phases of adolescence, the areas controlling criticism and judgement (the prefrontal cortex) evolve more slowly, reaching completion only after the age of twenty. This discrepancy between the emotional brain and the rational brain would explain why adolescents show aggressiveness and impulsiveness more easily than adults, why they have less control over their emotions, why they underestimate risk and make decisions differently. Another factor fostering the search for strong sensations is linked to the presence of specific character traits (Riboldi, Magni, 2010) including, in particular, omnipotence, which is an immature aspect of the personality, where the fantasy that everything is possible, everything is due and narcissism reign. The erroneous conviction of being able to do everything, without any limit (the power that can be attributed to a god) is often the result of an ultra-permissive education where the parents are affective slaves of their children and never say no to them. Growing up in omnipotence prevents discovering one's limits and predisposes to risk. Narcissism also predisposes towards risk, but for different reasons. The narcissist is convinced of being superior, special, better than everybody else and does not accept criticism or frustration. In the meantime he feels a constant and profound feeling of emptiness, perhaps due to lack of affection or deep humiliation matured in childhood. The narcissist always needs to amaze, to be at the centre of attention, thus ending up by doing what others fear. Seeking thrills replaces seeking that attention that he has never found in his affective universe. Amongst the factors at the source of sensation seeking, the refusal of authority also takes on particular significance for a young person. Within certain limits, rebellion and transgression are normal demonstrative strategies in adolescence, which express the need for autonomy and emancipation from the family. In some circumstances however, these strategies are converted into risks and express signs of dissatisfaction and demands (mostly towards parents or other adult figures who have played a significant role).

Another factor fostering sensation seeking is an intolerance of boredom. Numerous experimentations have shown how, in conditions of sensory deprivation (the absence of stimuli), not all individuals have the same reactions. Some people do not tolerate monotonous situations well and become restless. This leads them to seek new experiences and thrills, not so much to satisfy a need for exploration as to obtain excitement and make up for their boredom. Boredom is a frequent experience in adolescence. It is a completely normal condition at a time of passage such as this. The youngster's work on identity takes place in a waiting room: waiting and boredom are inevitable. The inability to tolerate boredom, however, is something more, a condition of inner inadequacy, a feeling of emptiness, of total disinterest that is depressing, exasperating and which inevitably leads to seeking new stimuli (Riboldi, Magni, op.cit.).

4.1. Motivations for Risk and Protective Factors for Health

In a culture of fun, excess and disinhibition, the world of the night and the weekend represent a bridge area between normality and deviant temptations, between freely leaving everyday routine and dangerous experimentation in seeking identity and self-assertion. The at-risk behaviour of girls and boys emerges in this bridge area, and around this type of conduct there often revolve a cocktail of emotions that are too difficult to control.

Epidemiology gives us one lesson: the adolescent is an individual who is rarely ill, but who dies often. The causes of death are accidents, road and otherwise, suicides, murders, some infections; death can be attributed more to behaviour than to illnesses.

The often aware underestimation of risks inherent in certain choices and the increase in the frequency of behaviour with the result of self-harm and harming others amongst young people are a fact that is shown by the increase of this culture of risk and the frequency of behaviour which results in harming the self and others (Cavalli and De Lillo, 1993, Buzzi et al., 1997).

Literature on risk is not only alarmist. There are different ways to reach objectives of growth and the construction of identity. Some of these put physical and psychological health at greater risk. In this perspective, at-risk behaviour is considered, even before problematic behaviour, as instruments to reach the developmental aims. It follows on that the elements of risk also represent opportunities for development, therefore they must or can be considered aspects of one continuum rather than opposite poles. The contradiction is internal. Transgression has a developmental face; it comes from a desire for change.

In the world of nightlife there is a widespread risk of the use and abuse of substances with their acute and chronic effects. Beyond the risk of the substance, there are three risks which in part are induced and boosted by the use of the so-called new drugs, and implicit in the way of understanding fun, the night, the weekend. They can be summed up under the heading of the three Vs: violence, velocity and virus.

The epiphenomena of violence are some of the brutalities observed at sporting events, fights in discotheques, a psychopathology of the aggressiveness of the weekend. Episodes in the news and documented research tend to highlight the role of drugs, cocaine in particular, behind such behaviour.

Speed is found in road accidents, the main cause of death amongst young people; road accidents are an expression of banal but very widespread transgressions, such as riding a motorbike without a helmet or the trials by ordeal of driving on the wrong side of the road; the down of drugs and tiredness contribute to reducing attention, the promptness of reflexes and perception of the risk.

In 2010, 211,404 road accidents with casualties were recorded in Italy. There were 3,847 fatal accidents, with 4,090 deaths. On average, every day in 2010 there were 579 road accidents, 11 people died and 829 subjects were injured. However, there is a slight decrease compared to 2009 in the number of accidents (-1.9%) and casualties (-1.5%), together with a substantial drop in the number of deaths (-3.5%). The Italian region with the greatest number of road accidents and deaths is Lombardy with over 39,000 accidents (about 19% of the total) and 565 deaths. This is followed by Lazio, which recorded almost 28,000 accidents (about 13% of the total) and 450 victims (Istat-Aci, 2011). Despite the drop in the number of accidents in almost all the regions of Italy between 2009 and 2010, it is interesting to note how, in some cases, the decrease in the number of accidents did not correspond to a lower number of victims. In July 2010 new rules of the Highway Code were introduced, which tightened the penalties both for speeding and for the use of alcohol and drugs by drivers. There have also been numerous awareness-raising campaigns aimed in particular at young people, as road accidents are the first cause of death of subjects under the age of 40 in all European countries (Ania, 2010).

Thirdly, the virus: this concerns sexually transmitted diseases; some figures show how amongst consumers of cocaine (not intravenously), heterosexuals, involved in nightlife, the percentage in the spread of the HIV virus is significant. The same applies to all sexually transmitted diseases. Nor must unwanted pregnancies be forgotten: today, at the age of 15, one student out of ten has already had sexual relations, at 16 four out of ten. The significant figure is that at least half of them have not had protected intercourse.

The context the adolescent belongs to is important as it appears as a factor of risk and at the same time as a factor of protection in the situations of uncertainty and experimentation which characterize adolescence and which can lead, more easily than in other periods of life, to incurring situations of rick which the adolescent may decide to avoid or in which he can be involved. Various factors can act as protection or, on the contrary, increase the inclination towards risk taking.

In the first place, the family can be considered an important protective factor, on condition that it can have an emotional and at the same time authoritative educational attitude, capable of favouring the acceptance of rules and control and providing the young person with the necessary psychological support (Pietropolli Charmet, 1999). It is certain that, in the current situation, parents sometimes indulge any request of their child, in a vicious circle in which the absolute incapacity of saying no and the absence of precise rules only fuel further requests to be fulfilled, to the extent that the very context of life can be transformed into a factor of risk.

In adolescence however, the element of protection must be sought above all in the peer group; the success of programmes of prevention is often shown by the fact that the protagonists are the youngsters themselves, but the family can also play a role of protection from risk in synergy with the peer group. Agreement between friends and parents and the existence of positive relations with both guarantee an effective promotion of well-being in adolescence. In addition, satisfactory relations with parents and friends tend to improve reciprocally and can form an extensive network of support, creating the most suitable context for adolescent development.

The experience of the group of friends must therefore not always be considered in opposition to the family experience, but as an additional resource to help overcome the developmental tasks of this period, especially as far as development of social skills and definition of the identity are concerned.

It is important to consider the role of peers and adults in starting at-risk behaviour, because many risky actions and more or less dangerous ones are undertaken with others; in this way, it is easier for the adolescent to live his identity in a tangible way, presenting it to the group to obtain recognition, reputation and popularity, as public acceptance and social support are extremely important (Emler, Reichers, 1995).

The actions are undertaken both for the main purpose of becoming visible and to establish a social bond with peers; this bond is reinforced through ritualized gestures (the ritual of the cigarette or joint or of drinking together lend themselves very well to this need). In present-day Western societies, first the child and then the adolescent see as natural the immediate satisfaction of their desires and needs, without the idea that it is necessary to make some efforts to obtain gratification. Where everything is guaranteed, there may not be the awareness that it could perhaps not be worth exposing oneself to great risks to attain the satisfaction of a desire: an example is the widespread diffusion of crime in increasingly lower age groups. Today any intermediate area whatsoever seems to be in crisis; there are no longer any waiting times; in all fields there is a frantic race for change and renewal, wanting to shoot ahead and fulfil desire as soon as it appears. It is as if the young generations had been brought up, more than elaborating absence and deprivation, to accelerate the movement towards the objects or goals of satisfaction. If the Super Ego has to do with the sphere of rules, with the task of preparing areas suitable for coexistence (you can't play without rules!), the ideal Ego imposes on the subject the attainment of grandiose objectives, with the aim of arousing envy and admiration. It is no longer a question of growing up rather than of becoming a great grown-up and quickly, without stopping and before all the others (Di Benedetto, 2003).

Waiting is waiting for the immediate (Sereni 2005, p. 24). The greatest risk is that the dominant feeling is boredom, that dissatisfaction and the sense of emptiness have to be filled at all costs, with whatever instrument that restores to the adolescent the perception of his being here and now, as though in the subjects of the contemporary world there prevailed another form of relationship with themselves and with others where what has been tried predominates over what has been thought, the reality of the object over its representation, the demands of the ideal and of the ideal Ego over those of the Super Ego, recourse to the body that short circuits fantasies or to the action over the external world (Pellai, Boncinelli, 2002).

Another fundamental factor is the regulatory, social, filial and emotive self-efficacy and efficacy of all those contexts that the adolescent considers important in his life. This aspect, amply dealt with by Bandura (1990), is internalized through experiences of mastery, modelling and social persuasion, as well as through physiological and emotional states, so that one can perceive oneself as capable and skilful in the specific contexts of one's own life.

The capacity of self-regulation thus concerns the conviction of one's capacity to provide a certain service, organizing and executing the sequences of actions necessary to adequately control the situations that arise, including those of risk.

Coping, the capacity to activate strategies to cope with and solve a problem through implementing strategies that are functional in varying degrees (from emotive to strategic), that allows handling actions of the at-risk type, including in relation to the type of locus of control characterizing the subject, is also important.

Another significant aspect concerns the self-regulation of moral behaviour, which plays an important part in exercising self-direction. According to the socio-cognitive theory, moral reasoning is translated into actions thanks to mechanisms of self-regulation, like moral standards or internalized sensations, through which the so-called moral agency, i.e. the capacity to act morally, is exercised. Exercising the self-regulatory activity presents two aspects: inhibitory, represented by the power of abstaining from transgression and at-risk behaviour for oneself and for others, and pro-active, expressed by the power of behaving correctly and respectfully.

Chapter 3

THE POST-MODERN IDENTITY AND SENSATION SEEKING. REFLECTIONS ON BINGE DRINKING

ABSTRACT

"He glanced at the other passengers and dried the blood that was trickling from a scratch on his cheek. "If you don't keep quiet," said Filippo, "I'll slap you!" "What do you think," the other man exclaimed, "That would be no skin off my nose. I seek emotions." (Campanile, 1960, p. 57). In 1928, Campanile, a journalist, screenplay writer, playwright and one of the greatest Italian humorists of the 20th century, wrote "Se la luna mi porta fortuna" a story with surprising and unimaginable characters, including the unknown companion in the train compartment in search of strong emotions and, apparently, who desires all kinds of them. Those who live their sensations exasperating them to the utmost have been described not only in literature but also, as is known, in psychology.

Zuckerman (1971) defines sensation seekers those who seek risk, who are always in search of strong sensations. Risk, in behavioural terms (Zani, Cicognani, 2000), is sought because it is fascinating, attractive and can overcome feelings of fear, insecurity and embarrassment; in many cases, even pleasure can be spoken of, and it is for this reason that the need to take risks is often manifested with particular intensity (Salvadori, Rumiati, 1996, 1998).

If in some cases the actions of risk take on a constructive value, in others, on the contrary, they can have destructive meanings, such as the use/abuse of substances, sexual promiscuity and episodes of violence. Defiance, impulsiveness and the sense of invulnerability are functional within certain limits of the construction of identity, but beyond a given threshold, they become factors of risk. The world of youth is continuously characterized by journeys into border territories, where the aware elaboration of the risk is hampered by the almost magnetic attraction that the risk has for youngsters and their conviction (necessary from the unconscious point of view) of being immortal (Beccaria, 2004).

Knowing how to transgress and the ability to face the risk represent choices reinforced by current social and economic reality, which seems to appear as without rules, limits and points of reference, which the youngster also needs to oppose in order to be emancipated from a purely formal respect of the rules (Oliverio Ferraris, 2004). Today, youngsters live in a present in which they are asked to give their utmost (Ingrosso, 2003). Risk ends up by being construed as a real need, as an essential condition to be successful in an increasingly competitive society where there are fewer and fewer guarantees (Buzzi, Cavalli, De Lillo, 1997).

1. CULTURE AND THE POST-MODERN PERSONALITY

· Post-modernity indicates a period which follows, in chronological order, modernity, implicitly decreeing its end. The reflections which tend to sketch out a profile of the features that have characterized the modern age are concordant in highlighting some phenomena which have been well delineated: trust in reason, science, technology and therefore in unlimited progress; the explosion of production and consumption; the hope of being rid of basic needs with great expectations of abundance and happiness; the assertion of great ideological movements which have fascinated and mobilized large masses with their palingenetic illustrations of better and different worlds.

It is possible to state that these cultural trends, as far as lifestyles and personality traits are concerned, have fostered the rise of motivations aimed above all at power and success, material acquisition and self-assertion. More in particular, this basic orientation is expressed in a series of ethical virtues such as constancy in pursuing long-term goals, self-discipline, a sense of duty, the ability to make sacrifices in view of future objectives, the drive to accumulate and save (Dogana, 2002).

The current historical phase takes the name of post-modernity. With modernity entering into crisis, in the early 20th century a completely new age, free of dogmas and the logics of the previous one, came into being. Terms such as post-modernity and post-modernism have entered common use and the birth of this expression is found in various fields: it developed in art and then migrated to architecture, psychology, philosophy and anthropology. The definition adapts to widely differing phenomena: to describe the style of an artist, interior decoration, a new trend, a fashion, the thought of a psychologist or a philosopher. Post-modernism is a strictly cultural fact and a cultural paradigm. It is an anti-Utopian post-industrial perspective, as it opposes what were defined the great myths of the modern age, progress, reason and the revolution. Post-modernity is a social, political, economic and technological condition that is very different and distinct from modernity (Lash, 2000).

Trust in the scientific world and science, as a rational and progressive construction of objective knowledge, disappears with post-modernity. The crisis of confidence in science and progress is also accompanied by the disengagement of ideologies and the great ideals, of which an example is political abstention and the fragility of social commitments.

What characterizes post-modernism is the sense of emptiness and disorientation. The traditional objectives and values of reference have been lost, thus going on to what is defined ethical relativism. Everything is tolerated and everything is allowed: there is an anaesthetized sensitivity and conscience that can no longer distinguish between what is licit and illicit, what is good and what is bad. Everything is in continuous movement, meaning not only movement of the individual but movement as a continuous change of certainties and of stable points of view. Post-modernity is the impossibility to stay still, it is being perennially on the move (Tappatà, 2011).

Everything is at a standstill at today, here and now. Post-modern individuals are glued to the present, attentive to their immediate needs, theirs is a liquid life where goods and results are not transformed into anything lasting (Bauman 2006). Theirs is a precarious life characterized by continuous uncertainty, everything flows implacably and quickly. The individual must keep in step, run fast, continuously throwing himself into new beginnings, continuous modernization and continuous change. Individual freedom is what allows opening oneself up to all the possibilities but it is also what at the same time shatters values into a thousand pieces, strips away all virtues and relativizes everything. Today, any choice made is always less full of value because everyone knows that they can always change it, everyone knows that they have the possibility of modifying their choice, without excessively feeling the weight of responsibility.

As Bauman states (1999), post-modern men and women are affected by uncertainty; the space of individual security is now very limited. Everyone is free to make a determined choice without having the certainty of being fully sure because they know that if they have made the wrong choice they can correct it as often as they like. It is a free man who has lost his confidence in a society which does not need it.

Freedom is seen as a game. In every game that is defined as such, there are winners and losers. The losers today console themselves hoping to be able to win the next time, whilst the winners do not really experience real joy because it is clouded by the presentiment of defeat and the rush to undertake a new challenge.

1.1. The Post-Modern Identity Under Siege

The passage from modernity to post-modernity also determines a change in the conception of identity which, in the post-modern age, is broken into a multiplication of images guided by different models.

One strong signal that characterizes the present time is the constant distress of not being up to situations, the sense of impotence that disheartens the person in the face of the serious problems of the world that seem to elude every possibility of reasonable control by the individual. In such a context, where it becomes much more difficult to build up one's own identity, there is a closure of man into rigidly confined and autonomous identities, often characterized by a degree of omnipotence which, however, conceals the deep fear of one's interior void, fragility and often also a strong fear of otherness (Romano, 2004). On the other hand, however, there is also a process of opening; new identities are being constructed, which are multi-shaped, nomadic, fluid and capable of accepting multiple diversities; it is the possibility of shopping around in the supermarket of identities (Bauman, 2003); it is a fragile identity but certainly more flexible than the previous one.

The post-modern man, precisely to flee the vagueness in which he is immerged, not having the certainty of approval by others, grips on to them in the attempt to construct his own identity. However, this cannot be considered as the result of an individual project, but is imposed by external models; it is never given and defined once and for all, but must continuously be modelled on the "quick-change" act that regulates present-day society. Today, having a stable identity is extremely risky because it is very likely that it will quickly be superseded, unsuitable and out of fashion.

Some authors, including Lipovestsky (1995) and Lasch (1984), state that the post-modern personality is a personality based above all on narcissism.

However, a dissonant meaning is attributed to this characteristic compared to individualism in a utilitarian key which connoted the modern personality; narcissism is not spoken of as a constructive drive based on the spirit of enterprise and self-assertion but a mixture of passiveness and apathy, weakness and dependence, petty hedonism and closing in on the present, the private and the immediate (Dogana, 2002).

Pulcini (1996) speaks of a post-modern narcissistic Ego still anchored in the present, yearning and individualistic, without a glance at the past or the future. The individual is not forward-thinking, incapable of relating and establishing a real confrontation with others and extraneous to public life. The narcissistic ego is completely influenced by the cultural, social and economic aspects of post-modern society from which he strongly absorbs some characteristics and features.

Dogana (op. cit.) uses two metaphors to summarize this state of affairs: the precarious Ego and the light Ego.

When speaking of the precarious Ego, reference is made to an individual who lives in the present-day capitalist phase, characterized by mobility and flexibility where there is a strong need for results and immediate success; there is no permanent employment with a career and the rhythms of life already decided. There are only various forms of flexibility, such as short-term contracts or products soon to expire. People are always in a hurry with a life of continuous changes, pursuing a "bitty" style feeling great anxiety, insecurity, uncertainty and instability in work, in their couple and in their life projects. The other characteristic of post-modern man is his lightness, understood here as attention to what is not essential and superficial needs. As well as observing the productive perspective, we can also try and look at that of consumption and we can note that people live, despite the inevitable areas of backwardness and imbalance, in a condition in which primary material needs are essentially fulfilled and where needs of a second or third level are stated. What is important is not to eat, but to enjoy fine foods; it is not important to dress but the look is; the home is not fundamental but having a holiday home near the sea or in the mountains is; it is not keeping healthy but seeking wellness, perfection or using the so-called lifestyle drugs (Tappatà, 2012). In the final analysis, all this encourages lifestyles and personalities that can be defined as superfluous and frivolous: in this way a new post-modern narcissism is growing up which appears in the frantic pursuit of an egoistic and superficial hedonism, which refuses everything that smacks of duty, commitment and sacrifice.

In the final analysis, the post-modern individual can be read as characterized by countless personalities that are ready to be used whenever they are needed. There is a work personality, a virtual one on a social network, a personality for a certain type of friends and one for the family, with each one presented at the right time. Possessing constellations of personalities can help the individual but can also destabilize him as there are times when controlling them all is difficult or almost impossible.

2. THEORETICAL CONTRIBUTIONS TO SENSATION SEEKING

Transgression appears to be a trend that it is impossible to escape from, like a fashion that is not necessarily the sign of distress or with a risk of evolution (Buzzi, Cavalli, De Lillo, 2002) and adolescent transgression does not seem to come from a lack of knowledge of educational rules, but from the difficulty of development and from relational distress, from the impulsiveness of desires and a poor capacity of control (Pietropolli, Riva, 1995).

The development of the identity is also fulfilled exploring one's limits (physical and psychic) and skills. Thus, adolescents often adopt dangerous behaviour; consumption of alcohol, the use and/or abuse of substances, deviant behaviour, promiscuous or unsafe sexual activity, reckless or careless driving, especially if part of the challenges between peers or in a group. These types of behaviour often perform very precise functions, which seem to give the adolescent a way out of the insecurity and uncertainties experienced in this period of life. Many of them are unable to reach important developmental objectives, such as self-assertion and the construction of effective social and affective relations, except through recourse to at-risk behaviour. One factor that further complicates things concerns specific behaviour that allows identification with the peer group, such as smoking, drinking and having sexual relations in the same way as friends do. These actions allow the subject to feel normal as the same as the others, facilitating acceptance in the peer group (Jessor, Jessor, 1975; Irwin, Millstein, 1986; Tubman, Windle, Windle, 1996).

This behaviour is oriented towards experiences of risk, at times explicitly dangerous and extreme or even potentially self-destructive. For these subjects, less intense experiences related to everyday life appear boring, as they cannot arouse sufficient levels of gratification or even, at times, attention and interest. Boredom, the sense of emptiness, the incapacity to feel pressure and/or simple interest in everyday activities can lead these subjects to seek new stimuli, above all intense and transgressive ones with a high emotional impact.

Zuckermann (1979) has stated that sensation seeking (Sensation Seeking - SS), linked to a very wide variety of behavioural experiences, can be considered a real need and is therefore closely linked to the structure of the individual's personality. According to this interpretation, the SS personality trait is correlated to the inter-individual differences of the arousal system, in particular its base level of functioning and its degree of reactivity to environmental stimuli.

It would be possible to highlight in each subject an optimal level of arousal, corresponding to an optimal level of gratification obtained from environmental stimuli.

An excess of environmental stimuli, but also a lack of them, is believed to cause subjective distress, disorders in the level of arousal, and loss of the gratifying tone connected with the environmental stimulation. The most important aspect of the SS dynamic is alleged to be represented by the intensity of the stimulus rather than the stimulus sought, which is also proportional to the deficit of initial gratification.

Arnett (1992) explains at-risk behaviour of adolescents by pointing the finger at phenomena such as egocentrism and unjustified optimism, understood as the belief in being immune from danger compared to contemporaries put in the same situation, found in studies on driving when under the influence of alcohol.

Slovic, Fischhoff, Lichtenstein (1980) and Slovic (1987) concentrated on the nature of the risks, the knowledge of the people exposed to them and on the effects with which they are faced. They have highlighted how individuals, at the time when they have to assess risks, do not base themselves solely on the frequency with which a negative event occurs, but are more than anything influenced by a subjective perception built up on various characteristics of the risk, such as, for example, its uncontrollability, its knowledge and its sensational effects.

Benthin, Slovic and Severson (1993), analysing the perception of risk in adolescents, have found that there are two aspects that modulate the assessment of riskiness of behaviour: on the one hand, the personal assumption of determined types of behaviour and, on the other, the influence of peers, i.e. the tendency to become uniform with the group.

The perspective of taking a risk (Bell, Bell, 1993), alongside the choice of incurring in behaviour that is inappropriate for health and for social rules, includes the desire to commit oneself to extreme activities (edgework), for example, driving at high speeds or dangerous mountain climbing.

Arnett (1992) has made a major contribution in this field of enquiry. Referring to at-risk behaviour in adolescence, he uses the term irresponsible behaviour to distinguish it from problematic behaviour, not approved by adults, and actual deviant behaviour. These types of behaviour, according to the author, need a multidimensional understanding, as, in the first place they show a high correlation with sensation seeking; secondly because they concern specific factors of adolescent experience characterized by a form of adolescent egocentrism which indicates the sense of invulnerability perceived by the adolescent.

Egocentrism implies the presence of two phenomena: the imaginary audience and the personal fable. The existence of an imaginary audience which listens continuously and which judges his way of acting leads the adolescent to conclude that there is something unrepeatable and unique in his life: it must necessarily be so if all the others observe and worry about his behaviour.

All this makes the young person think that he is invulnerable even though he may behave imprudently. The second phenomenon, the personal fable, is explained through a concept that implies a notion of uniqueness which is so strong as to convince the adolescent that he is invincible, immortal and that the danger of tragic consequences and even death concern others and not him. Adolescents imagine the course of their lives as characterized by security and tranquillity, the future marked by success, power and happiness. The concept of the personal fable consists of the conviction of being completely immune to the consequences which, at times, derive from risky and imprudent actions. A further element implied in the development of irresponsible behaviour depends on the context of the adolescents' socialization. In this regard, Arnett and Jenesen (1992, 1993), elaborated a wide-ranging theory that considers the different contexts for the socialization of adolescents. These contexts can follow two different models of socialization, respectively, broad or narrow (figure 2).

In the case of Narrow Socialization, the social environment in which the adolescent grows up is characterized by a profound respect for the family, the community and traditions; it is marked by education for responsibility, a clear code of conduct and severe punishments with both verbal and physical penalties for every deviation from the accepted standards of behaviour. Broad Socialization, on the other hand, is characterized by fostering autonomy and independence, allows young people to decide and judge what is licit and right from what is not, without offering a precise standard of conduct; clearly, in this dimension, sensation seeking and adolescent egocentrism can be expressed more completely and more frequently.

Narrow Socialization, although being protective of adolescents is limited as regards creativity and independence of thought; in this particular form of socialization, both at-risk behaviour but also new ideas that could tolerate the established order are inhibited. Broad Socialization is typical of highly industrialized societies where, for adolescents, the possibility of taking on at-risk attitudes is greater as is the possibility of creative, experimental and innovative actions.

The model of Narrow and Broad Socialization is applicable both to the culture and to the family context which, in turn, is responsible for the education of young people; it is hypothesized that the families characterized by Narrow Socialization will give their children an education based on strict rules and punishments and that the young people subject to this education will be less willing to undertake reckless and irresponsible actions. Adolescents who have grown up in families characterized by Broad Socialization will more easily experiment with deviant behaviour, as their education is based on greater freedom of thought, free interpretation of reality and are facilitated for new experiences.

	Broad Socialization	Narrow Socialization
Family	Few restrictions, low monitoring of movements, encouragement of independence	High levels of restrictions and monitoring of movements, the sense of responsibility is encouraged with respect to autonomy
Peers	Mutual fostering of irresponsible behaviour, manifestations of esteem and pride for dangerous actions carried out	The peers share an aversion for risky behaviour, reward and reinforce their absence
School	No dress code, low control of attendance, no emphasis on discipline	Precise dress code, compulsory and controlled attendance, strict discipline
Community	Large and differentiated population, autonomy and anti-conformity as a desirable value	Small population with close neighbourhood relations, adherence to standards as value, anti-conformity as a suspicious attitude
Legal system	Minimum legal restrictions on behaviour, light punishments	Definite legal restrictions on behaviour and severe punishments
System of Cultural Beliefs	No specific directive, shared beliefs used as moral base	Children and adolescents are brought up and socialized strictly in the respect of a particular ideology shared by the community
Mass media	Pervasive and unregulated, encourage immediate gratification and self-indulgence	No or few media, close supervision by the state, promotion of self-control and spirit of sacrifice

Figure 2.

2.1. The Perception of Risk: Unrealistic Optimism and Sensation Seeking

From the cognitive point of view, risk is developed precisely from adolescence: "feeling at the centre of the world, feeling the power of the logic abstract which he masters, makes the adolescent unaware or perhaps only inattentive to concrete reality, the limits of which are felt as suffocating but easy to overcome, deluding himself that he is invulnerable to them" (Martini, 1998, p. 42).

The attraction of young people for strong emotions (sensation seeking), risk-taking and challenge (I'm the only one who can succeed), impulsiveness (everything and immediately) and the feeling of omnipotence and invulnerability (I can do everything, nothing will happen to me) if, on the one hand, are functional to the differentiation and construction of personal identity, on the other are an obvious high factor of risk (Zuckerman, 1994; Di Clemente, 1996; Bell, Bell, 1993).

The feeling of invulnerability occupies an important place in these attitudes, and is expressed in what is defined as unrealistic optimism. The phenomenon of unrealistic optimism is also very widespread amongst adults. With this concept, Weinstein (1980, 1982), who spoke for the first time of it in the 1980s, refers to the tendency to underestimate the probability that negative events can happen to oneself, with respect to the assessment of the probability that they happen to a person of the same age (Cicognani, Zani, 1999; Palmonari, Cavazza, Rubini, 2002). This systematic distortion of judgement, accentuated in adolescence, has cognitive and motivational effects.

The perception of risk therefore becomes a fundamental aspect of the adoption of certain types of behaviour, appearing as one of the main variables between the knowledge of determined consequences and the behaviour adopted. Another Italian study (Cicognani, Zani, op. cit.) investigated the phenomenon of unrealistic optimism in the perception of risk during adolescence. The results show that unrealistic optimism seems to be influenced both by the type of risk in question and by some personal characteristics. As far as the type of risk is concerned, the level of controllability that is attributed to an event appears to be important: optimism is the greatest for those types of behaviour that are considered to be under one's own control (driving, consumption of substances, sexual activity) whilst it is the lowest for common and familiar events (such as breaking an arm) or environmental events (such as natural calamities). On the other hand, as far as personal characteristics are concerned, the level of optimism is inversely proportional to the presence of sensation seeking. Unrealistic optimism therefore has an ego-defensive function and can explain how risk is perceived for the majority of adolescents. It is lower in those subjects defined high sensation seekers, who consider an exciting life as a value, with respect to health. These subjects do not need to justify their behaviour to themselves behind the distortion of unrealistic optimism and the false perception of control, but on the contrary behave in a risky way because they need to defy social conventions, showing openly transgressive behaviour, in particular in relation to taking substances, driving habits and sexual behaviour.

2.2. The Sensation Seeking Scale

The theory of sensation seeking has evolved and changed in time. The general Sensation Seeking Scale (SSS) conceived by Zuckerman in 1971 presents four factors useful for understanding and predicting specific behavioural phenomena.

The first phenomenon is Thrill and Adventure Seeking (TAS), through a continuous desire for experiences, including through a non-conventional lifestyle. It indicates the desire to undertake physical activities perceived as moderately risky which offer unusual sensations and experiences, such as, for example, climbing a mountain, skydiving and scuba diving.

The second is Experience Seeking (ES). This factor describes the search for sensations and new experiences reaching a mental and sensory state (music, art and travel) and through a non-conformist lifestyle. In the 1970s it was defined the Hippie factor, whilst in the 1980s this was replaced by the term Punk.

The third, Disinhibition (DIS). For those who accept an established life but find it boring and monotonous, there is the possibility of other ways of evasion; drinking with friends, gambling, partying and having erotic adventures.

This is a search for sensations of an extrovert type. Disinhibited subjects need to be surrounded by people to receive stimuli: they drink to free themselves of any social inhibition. It is an age-old form of seeking socially accepted emotions.

The fourth factor is Boredom Susceptibility (BS). This factor is not another way of seeking sensations, but rather low tolerance for repetitive or constant experiences. Not all the subjects who tend to seek intense sensations are incapable of facing long periods of little external stimulation, but the people who are susceptible to boredom become very restless in these conditions. Individuals with high scores in one of these factors tend to obtain high scores in the others as well. Sometimes however, there are profiles with correspondence to only one factor and values that are only average in others: for example, a person may find all the stimuli he needs in a dangerous sport and otherwise lead a tranquil and completely conventional social life. However, studies on people who have wide sexual experience, who make use of drugs or practise dangerous sports, have generally found high profiles on all the factors that make up the scale.

The need for strong and different sensations makes the person seek out risky activities and experiences, for the charge of excitement they generate.

Not all the activities of sensation seekers are necessarily risky although often the different types of at-risk behaviour are correlated: reckless driving, smoking, abuse of alcohol and/or substances, dangerous sports. At the base there is a biological substratum of great reactivity to stimulation: neurological enzymes and hormonal levels. Like many personality traits, sensation seeking may also have a biological base and however its particular individual expression can depend on a wide range of environmental possibilities.

2.3. At-Risk Behaviour: Phase-Specific Behaviour

Interpretations of a cognitive type refer to the heuristics of willingness: when a person has to assess a probability that a certain type of future event will happen, he does so from the number of examples of events of the same type that have already occurred in the past. For this reason, it is probable that, if he thinks of himself, he ends up by underestimating this probability, unless he has already had many very negative experiences.

Exquisitely motivational interpretations, on the other hand, refer to the need to reduce the anxiety linked to risk and keep a good level of self-esteem thanks to the illusion of being able to control events or, in a more psycho-dynamic sense, phenomena or refusal and/or negation are seen as intervening. Unrealistic optimism, at limited levels, can be considered functional to the individual as it prevents remaining paralysed in relation to the worry caused by the risks inherent in every action. However, if present at a high degree, as it often is in adolescence, it can lead to damaging consequences, because it does not allow an objective evaluation of the possible negative consequences linked to one's actions and the adoption of adequate preventive behaviour.

The perception of risk in adolescence is generally influenced by the fact that these subjects consider themselves immune from the consequences of situations of risk, as they tend to think that they are relatively invulnerable and suppose that only other people are exposed to the undesired consequences of the negative experience. Every adolescent is convinced that he is less at risk than a contemporary involved in the same situation, as shown by the studies on driving under the influence of alcohol (Arnett, 1992), driving in general (Finn, Bragg, 1986), sexual risks (Kalmuss, 1986) and the use of alcohol (Hansen, Raynor, Wolkenstein, 1991).

Sexuality may represent an area potentially exposed to risk. Learning how to relate affectively with a partner and controlling one's sexuality is one of the tasks of development deemed fundamental during adolescence (Coleman, Roker, 1998).

Sexual behaviour cannot be considered in itself behaviour at risk (Bonino, Cattellino, Ciairano, 2003), although it is possible that unprotected sexual relations and the precocious adoption of sexual behaviour make it such.

The former are often associated, equally between males and females, with the use of drugs, alcohol and smoking, and expose the boy/girl to the risk of viral contagion, early pregnancy and parenthood (Bell, Bell, 1993). The judgements are often subject to errors of evaluation and heuristic errors of thinking which lead to underestimating and/or ignoring the probability of the occurrence of a phenomenon or being motivated by false beliefs in this respect, therefore the subject could believe that there is no risk of pregnancy when having sexual intercourse for the first time (Dryfoos, 1990).

In the group, communication on sex tends to encourage at-risk sexual behaviour. In addition, the earlier the age of approaching sexual conduct, the greater the lack of adequate cognitive, affective and social skills necessary to deal with the transition to sexuality, which is more likely to take place in inadequate situational or relational conditions and therefore, conditions of risk (Mitchell, Wellings, 1998).

Gambling is a very exciting activity as it is linked to powerful mechanisms of endogenous reinforcement: the exhilaration of a win and the suspense before the result can in fact be worth the risk of exposure and countless losses. This practice also places the boy/girl face to face with the reality of large economic losses and the need to obtain new money at any cost and with any means, which often represents the premise of the exposure of the subject to new at-risk behaviour in the area of anti-social behaviour. This is behaviour adopted by males and females in different ways and with different frequencies (Zuckerman, 2000).

Impulsiveness is a widespread characteristic amongst gamblers, many of whom experience the incapacity of restraining themselves from gambling and thinking of its possible negative consequences. Gambling is practised insofar as it is a situation that can cause excitement and pleasure due to the element of risk, challenge, unpredictability, surprise and novelty that the sensation seeker is looking for (Zuckerman, 1999).

The presence of depression, anxiety issues, poor control of impulses and personality configurations such as narcissism, borderline and anti-social disorders are conditions that are easily found in many pathological gamblers.

Physical activity is intrinsic both to human beings and to many other species. Zuckerman (1983) classifies sports in three categories: high-, medium- and low-risk sports. The following come under the first category: skydiving, scuba fishing, mountaineering and skiing. Physical contact sports such as football are classified as being of medium risk. Running and gymnastics, on the other hand, are low risk sports.

Gomà-i-Freixanet (2004) has summarized her research following the different sub-categories of SSS and their relations with the levels of risk: the TAS sub-category is high in sports where the level of risk is high; the ES sub-category is high together with the TAS only in sports with a high level of risk (this shows that those who do dangerous sports are seeking something in addition to sensation and adventure); the BS sub-category is high only in the most extreme sports.

All the sub-categories of the SSS and the DIS sub-category are linked to social activities that are developed around the sport, for example the celebrations after a day spent skiing in the mountains.

Zuckerman (op. cit.) adds that amongst high risk athletes, high scores of DIS are found in sky divers but not in climbers. Sky divers find satisfaction in the brief but intense experiences which require little planning. They tend to be more impulsive than climbers as the latter cannot be rushed as all their movements have to be carefully planned. Dangerous sports are classified in: mountaineering, skydiving, skiing and downhill skiing, scuba diving, hang-gliding, paragliding, water skiing; surfing; motor racing and rowing.

For many young people, dangerous driving is an exciting and transgressive experience but which endangers one's own life and the lives of others. This phenomenon is often associated with a state of intoxication and, as this conduct is a criminal offence, it exposes the boy/girl to legal punishment which in turn may lead to the development of deviance. Studying road accidents, the so-called individual factors are explored, referring to the socio-psychological characteristics that contribute to exposure to the risk of an accident. This subject has also been analysed from the psycho-dynamic point of view on a sample of adolescents involved in accidents (Carbone, 2003). According to this perspective, it is not only external factors that come into play but also emotional factors (failure to act, action, self-harm, unconscious suicidal behaviour) or pseudo-aware factors (exhibitionism, challenge, competitions) which contribute to exposing the individual to the risk of an accident.

The youngsters of the sample presented considerable difficulties in relational and affective areas and in carrying out tasks; they also tended to overestimate themselves or to underestimate themselves, oscillating between maniacal behaviour and depression. Although being able to describe in detail the dynamic of the accident, indicating its real causes, they did not assume any responsibility for it, but rather felt they were victims of an unavoidable fatality. It is difficult to say whether so-called introspective illiteracy, where the capacity to read emotions according to a code that deciphers them contributes more to the production of such phenomena or mechanisms of denial and projection of guilt that is unconsciously felt but avoided through these methods.

The use of psychoactive substances amongst adolescents and young people, although it is no longer a recent phenomenon, continues to be an alarming phenomenon, especially in view of the current and increasingly marked precociousness of the first contact (Rosci, 2004). In Italy, in addition, especially amongst young consumers of synthetic substances (Pinamonti, Rossin, 2004), the tendency towards taking multiple substances is on the increase.

The phenomenon is worrying because psychoactive substances increasingly have the function of performance-enhancing drugs, used to feel up to the demands for success and hyperactivity expressed by society (Ingrosso, 2003). We are said to be in the face of a constant increase in very young people starting to use cannabis and other drugs, especially illegal ones, such as ecstasy. In recent years, an increase has been recorded, after a certain downturn in the 1980s and 1990s, in the use of tobacco together with a strong tendency for the consumption of alcohol and drugs, often taken because they are considered the most effective way to reach objectives deemed socially important: gaining the esteem of peers, facilitating socialization overcoming any inhibitions, probing parts of the self that are as yet unknown etc.

Eating disorders can arise following difficulties in the mentalization of the changes, especially of the body, caused by sexual development. Accepting one's body and integrating its image into a more general concept of the self is not always easy because feelings of inadequacy and anxiety relative to the body-self can frequently be generated (Confalonieri, Grazzani, 2002; Bosma, Kunnen, Saskia, 2001). New criteria of assessment on the conditions of acceptability of the subjects as adequate may be developed within the group of friends and new roles and types of behaviour are experimented with, often linked to unhealthy eating behaviour, which can facilitate the onset of fully-fledged pathologies, such as anorexia and bulimia.

3. ALCOHOL AND YOUNG PEOPLE: A HIGH RISK COMBINATION. BINGE DRINKING

Some studies (Griffin et al., 2009) have concentrated their attention on the typical importance exercised by the nocturnal economy of cities and metropolises and the emergence of a culture of fun where alcohol is the element that is always present, with irresistible initiatives, such as happy hours, after-hours and, at the same time, the scarcity of alternative places for socialization by young people. "You can talk about alcohol to talk about young people and talk about young people to talk about alcohol" (Cottino, Prina, 1997, p. 26), because the two phenomena, as shown in the past two decades, are closely linked together.

Society appears alarmed for the alcoholic rate which characterizes the new generations. Alcohol, amongst the various drugs, is in a very particular position. It is a mimetic drug, and not because of its abilities to cause addiction or not, to cause harm or not to the individual, to develop at-risk behaviour or not at personal and social level: it is a mimetic substance principally because alcohol is also food, culture (in particular in Italy) and it is an economic phenomenon.

Young people's drinking is a subject that is often sensationalized on the contemporary scene, in particular some current phenomena such as binge drinking. This is behaviour which strikes the social collective imagination, for the concern that excessive drinking by the young generations may awaken. One of the features characterizing the representation of the relationship between young people and alcohol is that of the consumption of a substance with which a certain degree of risk is connate. It is a risk that takes on multiple aspects and forms (a risk for health, a risk of death, a risk of failed social integration, a risk of moving on to other drugs) and which appears significant because the subjects in question are considered as not having that equilibrium that is usually associated with adulthood. Bonino, Cattelino and Ciariano (2003) divide the functions of at-risk behaviour into two main areas: development of identity and redefinition of social relations. The function most closely linked to the development of identity, which can be fulfilled by alcohol, is feeling grown-up. The consumption of alcohol may represent a significant rite of passage which allows taking on adult social status.

The mass media seem to push young people to the precocious adoption of this consumer behaviour to express their value and show their maturity. Drinking alcohol can be a non-adaptive way to develop a feeling of autonomy that goes through a greater involvement in the peer group and the redefinition of rules and functions in the family context. This behaviour may allow experimenting with new psychological, physical and relational possibilities offered by the specific life cycle being lived, allowing self-assertion and experimentation; transgression and overcoming limits. Drinking alcohol precociously or excessively, going against the rules of the adult world, allows the adolescent to partially assert his autonomy and independence (Crockett, 1997). Transgression is also, in our culture, reinforced by a strong drive to experimentation of what is new and everything that is unusual and the consumption of alcohol may represent an escape from reality and its difficulties.

In a few years, we have seen a rapid transformation in Italy of the styles of using psychoactive substances, in particular amongst the young generations. A number of studies (Scafato, 2004, Doxa-Osservatorio Permanente sui Giovani e l'Alcool (Permanent Observatory on Youth and Alcohol), 2011) show that there is a population of young consumers which is characterized by a use of various substances rather than by actual dependence on one well-defined substance. One characteristic of these young consumers is the way of use which is at regular intervals (in general the weekend or free time between the usual commitments such as school or work), particular rituals and, in these, the substances are taken not only to try out the effects of the substance but also to allow a different and more enjoyable use of free time. In the majority of cases, the experience is shared in the group. This large young population tends to adopt, for periods of varying length, lifestyles characterized by seeking strong sensations. Only a small part of them will develop a real dependence on substances and it is also true that these young experimenters/users of substances are greatly exposed to the risk not only of long-term biological damage but above all immediate damage due to inadequate behaviour following perceptive and cognitive alterations produced by substances. Alcohol occupies a prime position amongst the favourite substances of young Europeans; consumed alone or in association with other substances, it is the lowest common denominator of reckless evenings as an effective remedy which is both disinhibiting and sedative. Until a few years ago, there was a clear difference between the Mediterranean culture of drinking and the Anglo-Saxon one. The former, called "wet" was characterized by the consumption of wine, with a dietary and convivial value of use, whilst the latter is a "dry" culture with prevalent consumptions of beer and spirits, mostly concentrated at the weekend and with intoxication as the value of use.

Today it is commonly observed in Italy that a culture that has been defined "damp" is becoming established, underlining the fact that, alongside the traditional value of use, new styles of consumption, new alcoholic drinks and above all, new values of use, are becoming established, especially amongst the young generations (Cottino, Prina, 1997). This is the scenario in which the consumption of alcohol, in particular in young drinkers, defined contextual drinkers, is located.

The contextual drinker has specific and well delineated characteristics: drinking alcohol does not appear to be activated by an internal physical or psychic driven, but by an extreme situation or an occasion, very often leisure or social. For him, the central pivot around which everything revolves is the social group of reference, the pressure of which determines the choices of the subject: for this reason, the easiest and clearest example of a contextual drinker is that of the adolescent, with the discotheque, the "Saturday night massacres" and so on, although the contextual drinker could also be defined the worker who goes into town to get drunk with his friends at the bar once a week, or at the fair once a year, or the football fan who goes on the rampage on Sundays at the football ground, or even the serious professional man and former soldier in the Alpine regiments who celebrates with solemn booze-ups at the periodic meetings of his brothers in arms (Esposito, 2002).

3.1. The Italians and Alcohol

In Spring 2010, the DOXA Institute carried out, in collaboration with the Permanent Observatory on Youth and Alcohol, the sixth study on the behaviour, opinions and attitudes of adult and young Italians on the consumption of alcohol. The study is based on 2,026 interviews done at home, on a sample representing adults and young people of over 13. The study analysed the behaviour of consumption of alcohol (beer and wine, aperitifs, digestifs and bitters, spirits and liqueurs); what concerns at-risk behaviour; the opinions and attitudes on alcoholic drinks and the socio-demographic characteristics of consumers and non-consumers.

In this edition of the study almost all the subjects considered in the previous editions were taken up again, to assess the changes in recent years and some new aspects were also considered: behaviour in at-risk consumption, behaviour of young people on their first experience of the consumption of alcohol, information and opinion on the punishments for driving after having drunk alcohol.

78.6% of the Italians over 12 drink alcohol at least once in a period of three months. The percentage of consumers of alcohol has remained almost constant: it goes from 74% of individuals of 15 and over in 1993, to 80% in 2000 and in 2005 and 2010. If we consider all Italians of 13 and over, the percentage of consumers has gone from 80.5% in 2005 to 79.6% in 2010.

In the past 3 months, when recording the data of the study, 64.2% of the interviewees had drunk wine, 56% beer, 34% aperitifs, digestifs and other drinks with a medium alcoholic content; 23% distillates and liqueurs and 12% other alcoholic drinks. These percentages, projected on to the population of 52.7 million Italians of 13 and over, correspond to 33.8 million consumers, at least occasional. For wine, 29.7 millions for beer, 18.1 millions for drinks with a medium alcoholic content and 12.1 millions for spirits.

About 70% of young people (13-24) consume alcohol. About 30% of young people do not drink. About 76% of young males drink (24% do not drink); for girls, respectively 63.6% and 36.4%. In the analysis by classes of age within the group of young people, it can be noted how about 61% of pre-adolescents (13-15) do not drink (about 30% drink occasionally, less than 10% drink regularly). From 16 (and up to 19), the number of consumers rises significantly (non-consumers drop to 30%), from 20 to 24 the consumers have the same distribution as the general population: 67% regular consumers, 18% occasional and 15.3% non consumers.

Three-quarters (76%) of the young people interviewed (between 13 and 24) remembered their first experience of consuming beer, 71% the first time they drank wine, 65% the first time they drank an aperitif, bitters or digestifs and 52% the first time they drank spirits or liqueurs. The young people aged between 13 and 24 were asked to remember how old they were when they had their first experience, i.e. they first tasted alcohol, for the different types of drinks. On average the interviewees gave an age of between 14 and 15 both for beer and wine and an average age of 16 for other alcoholic drinks, (aperitifs, digestifs, bitters and also spirits) Very few remembered experiences before the age of 13 (8% for beer, 10.8% for wine, 2% for aperitifs, bitters and digestifs and only 1% for spirits). Many remembered not the first taste but the first repeated experiences, i.e. the effective start of consumption even though with reduced frequencies and quantities.

As far as excessive consumption is concerned, 14.6% of the young people interviewed, aged between 13 and 24, had had recent experiences of a high consumption of alcohol concentrated in a short period of time (at least five glasses in two hours, outside meals, according to the definition of Binge Drinking adopted in the surveys of the Observatory, which differs from that adopted in other studies, where consumption with meals is also considered). 20.4% of males, 8.6% of females (14.6% of males and 6.1% of females in 2005) had had recent experiences of Binge Drinking. 3% of girls and boys between the ages of 13 and 15, 13% between 16 and 19 and 21% between 20 and 24 had also had recent experiences.

29% of young people (35% of males and 22% of females) remembered having been drunk at least once in their lifetime: and almost 15% in the past three months (3% of youngsters aged 13- 15, 13% between 16 and 19 and 21% between 21 and 24).

The average number of experiences of excessive consumption has risen for young people, who remembered excessive consumptions from 1.8 times in three months in the first surveys to 2.5 times in three months in 2010. The percentage of interviewees who say that they have been drunk has also risen, with some oscillations, from 4% in the first surveys, between 1993 and 2000, to 7% in 2005 and 6% in 2010 (with an insignificant drop in the past five years). The percentages of interviewees with at least one experience of states of drunkenness seem to have slightly decreased, but the average number of states of drunkenness recorded has slightly increased, from 1.6 times in 1993, to 2.1 times in 2010. In all the surveys, almost half recorded isolated experiences, with only one state of drunkenness in three months, and another half repeated experiences.

The analysis of behaviour at risk according to age confirms a different structure of the consumption by young people, with respect to adults, with a much lesser importance of wine and a greater importance of beer and other alcoholic drinks for young people, in the first age groups, from 13 to 24. In the experiences of excessive consumption, wine is at the top of the classification in all geographical areas, but with a greater importance in North-Eastern Italy, and a very similar importance to that of spirits in the other geographical areas.

Regarding the experience of driving after drinking, 17.6% of the interviewees admitted having driven at least once in their lives "after having drunk too much". This percentage rises by 8% between 16 and 19 (an age group in which many do not drive or only drive motorcycles), to 21.5 % between 20 and 24, to 25.2% between 25 and 34 and to 24.0% between 45 and 54, dropping to 11.7% for those over 54. Therefore, between the age of 20 and 54, the percentage of adults who have driven at least once in altered states is always over 20% and is closer to 25% in the 25-44 age group. In all the age groups, from half to two-thirds of the interviewees with at-risk driving behaviour, i.e. who have driven several times after having drunk, did so repeatedly (amongst those who drive after having drunk there is a prevalence of those who do so repeatedly).

3.2. The Phenomenon of Binge Drinking

Binge drinking is an English expression used to describe the behaviour of drinking until getting drunk, or going on an alcoholic binge; it refers to rapidly drinking alcohol to produce drunkenness.

Binge drinking, which is increasingly taking on the appearance of a widespread fashion amongst young people, almost as though it were a propitiatory rite to end Saturday nights out as best as possible, unfortunately loses its effects resulting in the sad consequences we all know (including the famous "Saturday night massacres").

From a psychological point of view, the important element is the motivation underlying the behaviour: the subject essentially drinks to get drunk, to lose control and he is, in some way, aware of the results of his behaviour.

The phenomenon of binge drinking was described for the first time by Wechsler in 1992 in an epidemiological study on the alcoholic consumption of college students in the State of Massachusetts (Wechsler, Isaac, 1992). The author defined the episode of binge drinking as having 5 or more alcoholic drinks for men and 4 or more for women in the same evening.

However, not all agree with the amount of alcohol established by Wechsler (op. cit.) to define this behaviour. A study carried out at the Free University of Berlin (Bloomfield, 1999) identifies binge drinking with having at least 10 alcoholic drinks in a short period of time; the Office of National Statistics of London (ONS) on the other hand, takes as a value of reference 8 drinks for men and 7 for women, at least once a week.

The different amounts of alcohol taken into consideration to describe the phenomenon do have in common the indicator of the short period of time within which the alcohol is consumed, which represents its principal risk factor.

The categorizations which make the phenomenon operationalizable do not take into account, however, the individual variables that can influence the effects of alcohol: subjective tolerance to alcohol, the rapidity with which the alcohol is drunk, the amount of food eaten before starting to drink, body weight, the emotional state and the socio-cultural context. These dimensions, both singularly and jointly, can influence the impact of alcohol on individuals. The International Centre for Alcohol Policies of Washington (ICAP, 1999) suggests that the scientific community makes a distinction, in the first place, between responsible and irresponsible attitudes in the consumption of alcohol. From this perspective, an exhaustive definition of binge drinking considers a wide range of behavioural patterns which can be summarized in drinking amounts of alcohol that are sufficient to cause intoxication. For the purposes of research (Bloomfield, op. cit.), to establish the presence of binge drinking, a parameter that is both quantitative, that refers to the amount of alcohol consumed, and temporal, that describes the interval in which the behaviour is implemented, has been used (Oei, Morawska, 2004).

To better understand the phenomenon, a distinction of categories must be made between the different types of drinker.

The non-drinker usually does not drink alcohol or drinks once or twice a year. A binge drinker is someone who has had from 1 to 4 episodes of binge drinking in the past 2 weeks, each time consuming 4 or more drinks if female and 5 or more drinks if male. The binge subjects start to drink outside the family at about 12 and got drunk for the first time at around 16. The social drinker consumes alcohol with a minimum frequency of 3-4 times a year up to a maximum of 3-4 times a week in situations where socialization is of particular significance. Social drinkers, both male and female, start to drink outside the family at between 13 and 14; they started to drink regularly at around 15 and got drunk for the first time at around 16.

Heavy drinkers, if male, drink at least 6-7 times every 2 weeks, consuming 5 drinks at a time. In a study by Morawska and Oei (2005), heavy drinkers represent 7% of the total sample and have an average age of 21. 21.1% of heavy drinkers are women and the remaining 78.9% are men. This figure indicates that heavy drinkers are mainly men, in a percentage that is four times greater than women.

The reasons that drive young heavy drinkers to drink are diverse and concern the social and environmental context, relations with the family, with partners, with friends, the personality traits and even some genetic factors. These aspects, in a complex interweaving, are often dealt with and solved with the abuse of alcohol. A young person who abuses alcohol, first elaborates a favourable orientation on alcohol, considers it positively, appealing and lastly constructs the expectation that drinking can be functional for the satisfaction of his personal needs. Abuse of alcohol in young people is interwoven with the formation of the identity; drinking alcohol can be seen as a way to improve the self-image and regulate emotions. Alcohol can be seen as the way to regulate immediately and simply some unpleasant affective states such as anger or a negative mood; alcohol is appealing because it allows obtaining immediate gratification and a sense of personal control; consuming alcohol can be seen as a new lifestyle to allow the passage from childhood to adulthood. Young heavy drinkers often drink when they are in a bad mood and use alcohol as an instrument to face up to difficult personal and social situations (Christiansen, Vik, Jarchow, 2002). They therefore use alcohol as an instrument to manage and regulate negative emotions. Heavy drinkers drink massively thinking that alcohol can dampen and eliminate the sense of inhibition experienced in relations and above all that it can relieve suffering.

The study by Scafato (2004) shows that, although in the past twenty years in Italy the overall consumption of alcohol has decreased, the percentage of heavy drinkers has increased. This aspect is connected to what has been defined by several fronts as the culture of excess.

A first identikit of the heavy drinker has been sketched out: there is a greater probability that he has a lower level of education compared to those who drink moderately; he has a lower social and professional status; he has problems with education and in finding employment; he cannot easily establish lasting relations and form a family; he also often smokes and consumes other drugs excessively (Rodgers, 2000).

The three groups of drinkers differ according to gender: males are classified more often as binge drinkers and heavy drinkers whilst girls tend to be identified as social drinkers. Heavy drinkers have more positive expectations of alcohol than binge drinkers who, in turn, evaluate more positively than social drinkers the possible effects of alcohol on their lives. Heavy drinkers and binge drinkers describe themselves as less inhibited in social situations, wish more to be involved in new experiences and in risky activities and show a poor appreciation of repetitive activities. Those who use alcohol frequently tend to overestimate the use of alcohol by their friends and the number of friends who drink alcohol as a way to normalize their own behaviour.

Our current social situation, the pervasive sense of crisis and uncertainty, the relational modes it characterizes, the breakdown of systems of values, join an extremized conception of pleasure, of satisfying needs in a compulsive way according to the logic of everything and immediately. The impact and the consequences of alcohol on the young are rather neglected. In the face of the emphasis placed on the consequences of heavy or light drugs, the strong social cost of alcohol, especially on young people, has not been considered. In a study, conducted by Anderson and Baumberg (2006) for the European Commission, it has emerged that 10% of the mortality of young women and about 25% of young men can be attributed to alcohol. The consumption of alcohol and of drugs are similar in certain aspects but alcohol abuse presents special psychological and social characteristics that it is important to know in order to implement effective plans of action and prevention.

In the majority of cases, adolescents choose to get drunk in full awareness for precise aims: to break the ice, to socialize, to pass the time, to have a subject of conversation, to have more fun, to facilitate relations with their contemporaries, to have greater opportunities for intimate relations, to manage stressful situations and to make food tastier (Cox, Klinger, 2004). Girls use alcohol to relate more easily with contemporaries of the opposite sex; boys say that alcohol makes girls more attractive (Presley, Leichliter, Meilman, 1998).

Both Italian girls and boys mainly drink to relieve suffering, then to feel disinhibited and lastly for needs of socialization.

According to Noventa (2004), the suffering of young people is the first risk factor. It could come from a difficult or complex family situation, from quarrels or the divorce of parents, from a difficult economic situation, from failures in the interpersonal and social sphere, from difficulties to fit in with the peer group. According to Cox and Klinger (op. cit.) the behaviour of use and abuse of alcohol is determined by the positive value of the results that the subjects expect to reach. The decision-taking implies the use of emotional processes, the result of which is given by the affective change that people expert to reach through drinking.

The affective change can be determined by both direct and indirect effects. The former concern the chemical effects of alcohol, such as the reduction of tension and stress and the change in mood. The indirect ones, on the other hand, refer to a greater ease in relation to people of the opposite sex and a better acceptance by the peer group. Reduced inhibition and increased sexual relations are highly appreciated effects consequent to the consumption of alcohol. The state of intoxication and associated disinhibition facilitate occasional sexual relations and allow avoiding the responsibilities connected to an intimate and stable sentimental relationship. Parties and evenings in discotheques where the consumption of alcohol reaches very high levels represent the ideal context for this kind of behaviour. Participation in rites of passage is an experience of considerable value: the first beer, for example, makes a subject feel part of the group through sharing the same experience.

The consumption of alcohol represents both an effective strategy to reduce and control anxiety and a way to feel an integral part of the new environment through sharing habits and behavioural models. Greater socialization, however, is an indirect effect of alcohol that produces a change in the affective state because it increases the perception that the subject has of feeling accepted. Morawska and Oei (2005) have suggested a cognitive model that explains the behaviour of binge drinkers. It analyses the expectations, the beliefs in the effects of alcohol and the capacity to resist. The authors (Morawska, Oei, op. cit.) wanted to determine whether the expectations of alcohol could discriminate three profiles of drinkers. Binge drinkers, compared to social drinkers, show higher hopes, a lower capacity of resisting alcohol and binge drinkers are differentiated from heavy drinkers only by the greater resistance to alcohol. Therefore the greater predictor of the behaviour of binge drinking seems to be the expectations from alcohol.

3.3. The Variables to Be Investigated

Binge drinking is an at-risk activity with very many repercussions both on the social level as well as on the psycho-physical well-being of the subject. There are many negative results such as the loss of efficiency in study, progression towards more serious forms of abuse of alcohol or even drugs, road accidents, at-risk sexual activity, violence and vandalism and criminal behaviour.

Numerous variables of personality have been studied in literature with reference to alcohol abuse. Individuals that can be defined as extroverts drink much more than introverts on the same evening and in general show more stable patterns in abuse behaviour, even in adulthood.

Psychic distress, loneliness, depression, anxiety and stress are variables associated with binge drinking. Especially in adolescence, alcohol is frequently used as medicine to heal negative emotions, to fight loneliness and to feel better. Sensation seeking is another personality variable that is particularly significant for the study of many types of at-risk behaviour in adolescence and heavy drinkers seek sensations, independently of their gender or age.

Sensation seeking with alcohol is, in the perception of young people, amply satisfied and is functional to the path of building up an identity, accelerating the mechanisms of exploration of the conducts and strategies of growth.

Alcohol is rightfully considered a means for social integration, to reduce tension and as a reward for an academic or work success. Young people say they drink for fun, to feel good, to be fashionable, to seem more extrovert or simply to fight boredom. Interesting differences of gender have been found: girls drink mainly out of loneliness, to escape problems, to be cured of aspects of depression; boys to conform with the group or to try pleasurable sensations.

The use of alcohol in the group or family is associated with binge drinking behaviour. The peer group can be considered a factor of both risk and protection with respect to the onset of at-risk behaviour and its becoming chronic. One study (Morrongiello, Dawber, 2004) on the factors that influence the decisions of adolescents in adopting at-risk behaviour has shown that the influence of the peer group, and in particular that of the best friend, weighs more heavily than that of the family (Zimmermann, 2004). The study (Morrongiello, Dawber, op. cit.) has shown how there are significant gender differences: for boys, at-risk behaviour is influenced by the hedonistic aspect associated with the behaviour, for girls there is an alleged attempt to synthetize between what the family members think about the at-risk behaviour, what they themselves think and the opinion of their best friend. As far as the use of drugs is concerned, the influence of peers has been universally identified as the single factor that can best predict the use of substances. With respect to parent-children relations, it is now clear that the probability that a youngster shows problematic behaviour, not only with reference to alcohol, is directly connected to the ability of the parents to ensure that their children are not involved in situations of risk. Confirming this, several studies by Barnes (Barnes, Farrell, Banerjee, 1994; Barnes, 1999) show that the most predictive factor of problematic behaviour following the use of alcohol is precisely the degree of parental control, expressed by knowledge of and interest in the children's activities. Parents can limit the exposure to situations of risk or vulnerability to these situations and also exercise their influence on the youngster's social network, for example on the choice of friends. Authors with a systemic-relational approach have stressed the importance of variables such as communication, cohesion, conflict, the degree of differentiation/enmeshment of the family and family myths. These are all significant elements for structuring dependence on alcohol.

Spending many hours outside home or having much free time may seem to significantly predict the adoption of behaviour of alcohol abuse. In addition, the available of financial resources is positively correlated with phenomena of binge drinking: the youngsters of 14 who received a larger amount of money from their parents report a greater number of intoxications from alcohol than others of the same age.

With reference to the Italian context, Di Grande (2000) highlights the presence of two variables which are particularly significant in predicting the behaviour of binge drinking in adolescence: having encountered alcohol for the first time outside the family context and drinking regularly outside the family. Going to certain pubs/bars rather than others is another important variable not only for initiating the behaviour but also for subsequent involvement and for abuse behaviour. The pub/bar, especially during adolescence, takes on the meaning of context that can influence the habits of the subject and the interpretation of his behaviour and that of others.

3.4. Where, When and with Whom

Binge drinkers, both men and women, had their first experience of alcohol outside the home during their pre-adolescence, more or less at the age of 12. It is in this phase of development that the need for autonomy from the family emerges, as well as the desire to start new forms of sociality which allow a gradual re-elaboration of one's personal and social identity (Palmonari, 1997; D'Alessio, Laghi, 2007). The use of alcohol can represent a real rite of passage to the social status of an adult with a specific function for the development of identity. Italian binge drinkers start to drink regularly at the age of 14 and get drunk the first time at about 15. The majority of binge drinkers began to drink alcohol with their friends. A smaller percentage (17% females and 22% males) began to drink alcohol in the family, under the control of an adult relative.

Parental behaviour is particularly significant in making the adolescent understand, both on a cognitive level and the affective level, the difference between the use and abuse of alcohol.

Compared to social drinkers, a larger percentage of binge drinkers started to drink with friends.

Initiation with the peer group, therefore, could be considered a risk factor and, in a multi-factor context, is alleged to contribute to the onset of alcohol abuse. In adolescence, the influence of contemporaries is particularly strong. According to Fishbein (1980) the use and abuse of alcohol depends on the personal intentions of the adolescents, in turn modulated by social pressure and attitudes.

The first element that determines the intention is the social pressure that depends on the normative hypotheses, i.e. the suppositions on what others expect we do and on the motivation to comply with others' desires in order to avoid denigration.

The second factor that acts on intentions is attitude: positive or negative evaluations of an object, constructed on the basis of convictions, beliefs, prejudices and stereotypes. These depend in turn on the expectation of the results of the action to be undertaken which in the case of the consumption of alcohol concern positive changes of the affective state. Another factor which acts on attitudes is the value of the results foreseen.

3.5. Alcohol and the Search for Identity

The abuse of alcohol, as well as threatening personal safety and well-being, can prevent the development of identity and can drive the subject towards a premature block of identity (Marcia, 1993, Bishop, 2005.). Jones and Hartmann (1988) found a greater use of alcohol by youngsters (15-19) in a phase of fragility of the Ego and less experimentation of alcohol in adolescents characterized by a more mature development. Whilst having the habit of drinking, the majority of the subjects defined as drinkers have already identified important objectives to pursue in their lives, have acquired values, embarked on paths and activities that require a certain commitment and that help them in their growth. Alcohol is consumed in a conscious way and is less used than the heavy and binge drinkers to obtain relief from suffering, to feel more disinhibited and sociable (expectations related to the consumption of alcohol). For social drinkers, drinking is not a means to offer a different self-image or to prove being an adult as for heavy drinkers, but it is connected above all to the tradition and culture they belong to.

With respect to satisfying psychological needs (autonomy, competence and relationality) heavy drinkers express the greatest distress for their life. They feel a greater need for autonomy, competence and relationality compared to social drinkers and binge drinkers who are not differentiated.

A profile of an adolescent heavy drinker seems to be outlined and it is characterized by feelings of inadequacy with respect to the perception of his capacities in solving complex tasks and in succeeding in attaining the objectives desired. On the relational level as well, he describes himself as incapable of having profound interpersonal relationships characterized by mutual respect and trust. According to the socio-cognitive theory, the contexts related to social relations are alleged to most provoke anxiety and feelings of inadequacy to which there is a particular reaction in adolescence, through the use of maladaptive coping strategies such as, for example, the consumption of alcohol. Heavy drinkers tend to make greater use of the style of situational coping and avoid the problem compared to social and binge drinkers who are not differentiated.

The positive expectations from alcohol, associated with avoidant coping styles can represent risk factors which predispose some adolescents to make use of alcohol in situations perceived as stressful. As far as the style of emotional coping is concerned, the average scores of social drinkers are lower than those obtained by binge drinkers and the latter have lower scores than the heavy drinkers, who could use alcohol as a way to react to difficulties, as a self-cure for anger and sadness, as a way not to face up to the problem, but to tolerate its effects (Park, Levison, 2002; Park, Armeli, Tennen, 2004).

The social context also expects great things from adolescents: greater maturity, commitment, capacity to see and do things in an adult way. In this situation, young people can have feelings of inadequacy, uncertainty and feel that they do not have self-confidence. Those who feel the burden of this phase of the life cycle as too complex a responsibility could create solutions and instruments that can be used to alleviate and make the difficult journey towards adulthood less difficult.

The use of alcohol can become an aid which at times is essential to reduce negative emotional states of anxiety, anguish and dissatisfaction. Alcohol appears as the prohibited object, the transgression of parental rules and of the world of adults from which the adolescent wishes to escape, to try and build up his own life autonomously and independently.

The adolescent needs to discover himself and have experiences on his own and do so at different times and in different ways, identifying and building differences between himself and others. Using dangerous substances helps the young person undertake a fight with which to create the distances and mark the differences which allow him to mark out the borders of his identity. It is thanks to these *violations* of the rules that the adolescent thinks he can become autonomous and dissolve those affective bonds of dependence on his parents that prevent him from building up his own identity and personal individuality.

3.6. The Coping Strategies of the Binge Drinker

According to the perspective of Social Cognition, the abuse of alcohol by adolescents is linked to the use of maladaptive coping strategies (Baer, 2002). The subjects have great positive expectations from alcohol, such as the possibility of reducing tensions and enhancing social performances and they have more probability of recurring to alcohol in situations perceived as stressful.

The subjects who show shortcomings in coping skills and who have experienced how the abuse of alcohol can help them, at least temporarily, have a greater probability of choosing alcohol to overcome their difficulties. Positive expectations from alcohol and avoidant coping styles can be considered risk factors that predispose certain adolescents to make use of alcohol in situations perceived as stressful. Heavy drinkers are more motivated to drink and they expect that alcohol can reduce negative feelings and appease tensions; in addition they have greater probabilities of recurring to alcohol for the purpose of facing up to stressful situations, with respect to social drinkers, who drink only during social events and do not associate consumption with particular stressful events. Young male binge drinkers use an avoidant coping style to face stressful situations, where the most used is the one, defined in literature as diverse social: in the face of a stressful event, they go out and drink. Girl binge drinkers, compared to the girls in the other two groups, use an emotional coping style characterized by anxiety, anger and guilt feelings with respect to the stressful situation to control.

Young people use a style based on the analysis and evaluation of the problem when they think that the stressful situations can be modified; binge drinkers (and even more so heavy drinkers) consider stressful events as unchangeable and for this reason they often have recourse to alcohol which allows avoiding the problems or often denying them. The evaluation of the situation and of the resources available to face up to the event is of primary importance to understand the emotive quality and the intensity of the negative stress felt by the youngster. As for the resources, they are significant because a negative perception of one's resources makes the subject more vulnerable to stress, whilst a positive perception represents a prognostically favourable factor. Binge drinkers and heavy drinkers have a distorted perception of their resources and in many cases think that they do not have the ability to face up to stressful situations (Armeli, 2004).

3.7. Effects of Alcohol on the Central Nervous System

Alcohol acts as a psychoactive substance, i.e., as well as interacting with every tissue and system of the organism, it manifests its pharmacological effects on the central nervous system in particular.

When alcohol interacts with the nerve cells, it modifies the functioning of the cellular membrane and interferes with the release of neurotransmitters, provoking an alteration in the cerebral and psychic functions in relation to the amount drunk and the time of use. These biochemical modifications are the ones mainly responsible for the psychoactive effects of alcohol. For example, reduction of anxiety, sedation, disinhibition and gratification.

At the subjective level, these effects are perceived in the form of sensations of pleasure, tranquillity, conviviality, comfort, sleepiness, courage, confidence and euphoria. They are, obviously, all gratifying sensations that usually appear at low dosages and justify the reason why people start to consume alcohol and continue to make use of it.

Both the psychoactive substances and behaviour finalized through evolution for the preservation and improvement of the species, such a hunger, thirst, sex, are capable of stimulating the neuronal pathways of pleasure (rewarding system).

Some studies (Gonzales, Job, Dayon, 2004) have shown that the gratifying properties of alcohol, those sensations of well-being, euphoria and relaxation, seem linked to the increased release of a neurotransmitter, dopamine. This neurotransmitter can be defined in some way the neurotransmitter of pleasure and its release causes feelings of satisfaction and euphoria. Dopamine plays a fundamental role in the circuits of gratification. Abuse substances powerfully stimulate the neuronal routes of gratification, producing a false signal in the brain, so that the organism interprets the substance as indispensable for the survival of the individual. At this point, seeking the substance in question becomes essential and replaces the person's primary needs (Di Chiara, 2002). In this way, abuse substances and the relative behaviour aimed at procuring this substance could be considered as surrogates of the primary needs.

Alcohol, in particular, acts on the fluidity of the neuronal membrane, in the case of sporadic consumption, making it hyperfluid. The molecule of alcohol, as well as the dopamine receptors, bind to different types of receptors present on the membrane, such as, for example, the glutamatergic NMDA receptors, which play a fundamental role in the formation of memories, the serotonergic receptors which have a function in regulating mood, nicotinic receptors and GABAergic inhibitory receptors. The effects of this modulation of neurotransmitters consist of a general depression of the central nervous system which on the one hand entails a sensation of relaxation and lowers the levels of anxiety, but at higher levels causes loss of balance, due to the deactivation of the cerebellum, and an excessive behavioural disinhibition.

3.8. Comorbidity and Poly-Dependence

A number of studies (Crum, Pratt, 2001) have shown a relationship between affective disorders and the consumption of alcohol; in particular, they have shown that anxiety disorders and alcohol consumption are often present together.

In a study conducted in Australia, Rodgers (2000) showed a U-shaped curvilinear relationship between the type of alcohol consumption and scores of depression and anxiety. It emerges that those who do not drink at all and those who drink a lot have a much greater probability of incurring in problems of depression and anxiety with respect to moderate drinkers. One heavy drinker out of ten develops a psychological dependence on alcohol (Lukassen, Beaudet, 2005) and one-quarter of heavy drinkers have problems of depression. 32.3% of heavy drinkers who have developed dependence on alcohol are also depressed. According to Costa (2007), subjects with problems of double diagnosis can fit into two distinct groups of psychopathologies. The first group is characterized by problems of severe affective deficiency, a poor capacity of cognitive elaboration, a high degree of impulsiveness and a sense of anguish. Subjects with psychopathic, schizoid and borderline personalities belong to this group. Subjects who suffer from a syndrome of anxiety and/or depression belong to the second group. Clinical and epidemiological studies have highlighted that the consumption of alcohol is associated with the consumption of other substances such as drugs, smoking and medication (Laukkannen, 2001).

The term poly-dependence refers to the presence, amply documented in literature, of various forms of addiction in the same individual (Couyoumdjian, Baiocco, Del Miglio, 2006).

Gossop (2001) in this regard coined the expression "web of addiction" to indicate the interdependence between various forms of addiction.

Other studies (Ingram, Price, 2001) indicate that, with respect to the American context, 72% of adolescents with a diagnosis of dependence on alcohol also use other substances in a problematic way; the most frequent combinations are between alcohol and marijuana and between alcohol and hallucinogenic drugs. A high percentage of alcoholics under treatment report a previous abuse of substances, whilst alcohol abuse is a factor that complicates the treatment of drug addiction. Some adolescents, secondary school pupils with problems of alcohol dependence, have also reported problems of eating disorders (Peluso, Ricciardelli, Williams, 1999). 40% of adults with a diagnosis of anorexia and bulimia also abuse alcohol and drugs, whilst 22% use cocaine in order to relieve their symptoms (Gold, 1987).

A study by Baiocco et al. (2005) shows that in a sample of 1,200 adolescents, about 60% report problems of addiction, of whom only 17% declare a single dependence. 22% declare having two or three forms of dependence, 21% as many as four different types of dependence. These figures show that for young people the norm is poly-dependence.

3.9. Cognitive Behavioural Therapies

As Nizzoli (2004) observes, it is indispensable for the therapist to look not only to the past and the protection of the infantile and reassuring aspects of the Self, but also to look forward, so that he supports the young person in facing up to the tasks of development typical of the age.

The cognitive-behavioural approach is one example of how it is possible to act to help young adolescents solve problems linked to the excessive consumption of alcohol. This approach explains the abuse of alcohol and dependence on substances as a consequence of cognitive and emotional distortions that prevent a non-adaptive interpretation of one's existence. The patient is encouraged to develop skills that can offer them alternative strategies in those situations where normally he would have recourse to at-risk behaviour. In general, this therapy is structured, directive, of a short duration (significant changes are expected within the first six months) and oriented to the present, i.e. aimed at principally solving the current problems of the young person. In alcohol abuse behaviour, the therapy must be focused on the following aspects: developing a greater awareness of the negative consequences of recourse to alcohol and the causes that lead the subject to adopting certain types of behaviour (Couyoumdjian, Baiocco, Del Miglio, 2006). The therapist can help the patient reflect on those situations that generate anxiety and on the alternative strategies of response. Dependent subjects, more or less consciously, attribute a self-curative value to alcohol, which lets them counter the negative affective states. The therapeutic work consists of helping the patient understand why he is using alcohol and establish what he needs to be able to avoid it or to defend himself from any type of encouraging stimulus. This requires, on the part of the therapist, an attentive analysis of the circumstances of each episode, of the capacities and resources available in the patients to improve their self-esteem and social skills. Dependent subjects are characterized by reduced meta-cognitive skills, i.e. they tend to respond according to the requirements of the context and under the drive of their own impulses. The therapy can therefore help the young person develop that meta-cognitive skill which will allow him to adopt behaviour other than massive use of alcohol and other substances and increase his problem-solving abilities. The young person is constantly supported with reference to the perception of his self-efficacy in problem-solving. Some examples can be: giving importance to individual responsibility, encouraging the patient with respect to his successes or those of others, showing the alternative possibilities and the advantages deriving from them.

3.10. The Prevention of Alcohol Abuse in Young People

The objective of prevention is that young people do not make use of alcohol and do not run the risk of suffering damage both at individual and social level. It is clear that this objective must be divided into intermediate and limited objectives that can differentiated into: primary prevention characterized by actions on the whole community, with actions aimed at preventing involvement in the abuse or with activities aimed at fighting use; secondary prevention, to be implemented for those who run greater risks of showing a behaviour of abuse from alcohol; tertiary prevention, which tends to coincide with the treatment, addresses subjects, families, groups or communities in some way characterized by alcohol-related problems.

The most effective preventive actions are those that are integrated into the educational process of the family, the school and the social group. Their structure follows courses in which attention is placed on the cognitive, behavioural and emotional aspects connected to the problematic situation. In this regard, it is possible to speak of actions of direct and indirect prevention.

Direct action is oriented towards the at-risk behaviour of adolescents and the involvement of parents, teachers and significant adults. The actions include information, learning about the meanings and expectations connected to abuse behaviour, the promotion of alternative behaviour, the search for new strategies to achieve similar purposes healthily.

It is known that binge drinkers have very positive expectations linked to the consumption of alcohol. The expectations must be the focus of the prevention actions. Modifying the positive expectations of alcohol abuse behaviour means modifying the culture of intoxication, the culture of leisure and pleasure (Measham, Brain, 2006). It also means focusing on the negative results of at-risk behaviour adopted during the alcoholic binge, promote individual therapies of cognitive restructuring which try to modify the hopes that the young people have about the effects of alcohol, boost their sense of self-efficacy in resisting alcohol and above all modifying the social context of reference. In particular, the role of the mass media and of the Internet represents both a resource and a risk.

A serious and global approach to the prevention of abuse behaviour in young people must contemplate objectives such as offering the young people cultural moments and promoting healthy and health-giving lifestyles. Special attention should be paid to the mass media that often publicize unhealthy models of behaviour and a controlled and positive culture of excesses. It is pointless asking young people simply to refuse at-risk behaviour; they must also be given the possibility to adopt positive and appealing behaviour, giving them correct and scientifically-grounded information that can involve youngsters and arouse their interest. A good informative campaign must be personalized according to age, gender, the social and relational context, the specific situations experienced by the young people in each phase of the life cycle. The local, national and international institutions that deal with the prevention of alcohol in young people should start a technical collaboration and establish a common policy on prevention and the treatment of abuse behaviour. In the same way, there should be a constant exchange between the scientific and/or academic worlds and the political and professional worlds to propose new methodologies of prevention that are based on research data and provide support to operators in terms of documentation and training; to integrate and boost the resources available in the young person, in the peer group, in the family and at school. An adequate work of prevention must involve all the agencies of control, both formal and informal, and generate solidarity in the entire community to develop the full autonomy and responsibility of the person (Baiocco, D'Alessio, Laghi, 2008).

Chapter 4

THE FASCINATION OF THE NEW
NON-DRUG ADDICTIONS

ABSTRACT

Today's post-modern culture shows a tension between two opposing polarities: on the one hand we find an excess of individualism and of particularism, on the other we have the drive towards uniformity and conformism. Individualism/particularism means the drive to recognize and give value to every most negligible need of the subject (this attitude takes the name of culture of diversity); uniformity/conformism refers to the non-critical adhesion to behavioural models and lifestyles offered by the dominant culture (and this is called cultural standardization).

In both cultural orientations, an excess of personalization and an excess of standardization, two opposing forms of lack of authenticity, tend to be promoted (Dogana, 2002). A life lived beyond balance, a condition still far from having been reached, is encouraged.

Our Western culture teaches us not to depend on anyone, that to withstand the delusions and complexity of life, it is essential to prove oneself in strong experiences, that our value depends on the success of our actions, that it is important to be and to feel unique. These are contrasting and severe rules which prevent many from finding a state of real subjective well-being, understood as the essential expression of personal balance and not an exasperated manifestation of exhibition and display.

In such a paradoxical reality, slavery to false values and pre-packed ideals, standardization, the tendency to resemble others and loss of control become attractive and the new addictions are forging ahead.

1. THE CONCEPT OF DEPENDENCE

Dependence is a complex phenomenon and involves the individual at different levels. At the behavioural level it is manifested in the search for a substance or in the reiteration of certain behaviours and, in parallel, at psychological level, it makes the subject who experiences it totally dependent on the object of his dependence to the extent of becoming its prisoner, neglecting everything else, from affective relations to work and commitments in general. The consequences that derive from this situation have a repercussion on the person's whole life, causing a condition of general suffering which also extends to his environment (Guerreschi, 2005).

It can certainly be interesting to focus attention on the relationship that is established between the subject and the object of the dependence: this process appears to be unique and full of meanings.

It is not so much the type of drug or the particular behaviour that causes dependence but the special interaction that takes place between the subject, the object and context in which they are set. Dependence is what comes from the cross between the power that the substance has in itself and the power that the person is willing to attribute to the substance (Rigliano, 1998). Dependence is not a vice or an illness, but a process that is triggered off when a person, in relation to a particular object or behaviour, feels different and interprets this change as more functional and positive.

In this perspective, dependence does not have one or more causes but is built up in a circularity of needs and meanings that restrict the field of possible choices to a single solution: compromising life to the point of satisfying personal needs.

Like every human action, in this case too, we can interpret the special relationship that is established between subject, object of the dependence and context, as an expression of the organization of human interaction, and, as Watzlawick et al. maintain (1971, p. 115), the interaction can be considered a system. The general theory of systems helps us to understand the nature of interactive systems, understood as two or more communicants engaged in a process that implies defining the nature of their relationship.

Once a system has been defined, it is also fundamental to define the environment that is made up of all the objects, the bonds of which are such that a change in their attributes influences the system as a whole.

In a story of dependence, how can the particular relationship between an addict and his most intimate context, i.e. his partner or his family, be forgotten?

Co-dependence is therefore spoken of, which is a form of dysfunctional relationship and represents one of the ways in which the dependence of one of the partners reflects on the entire family system. Anyone who develops a co-dependence completely sacrifices his personal life, his interests and his feelings to dedicate all his attention to the other. His psychological space is totally occupied by the concern for the behaviour of his partner, for whose conduct he feels responsible, developing an attitude of the "I will save you" type. In this complementary relationship, the co-dependent partner takes on the role of saviour, whilst the other is engaged in boycotting his attempts. Both are subjugated by the dependence. It is very difficult to modify these scripts, above all because the couple draws benefits from them: whilst the dependent person behaves irresponsibly, covered by the care and attention of the partner, the other obtains gratification in the role of saviour, with the illusion of controlling the partner's dependence, seeking a sort of security and sense of mission, but which is not attained.

1.1. The New Addictions

The New Addictions form a heterogeneous set of disorders that share common psychological characteristics, such as the progressive loss of control over behaviour linked to the dependence and the endangering of the individual's life at various levels, both socio-relational and regarding the family and work. These are new addictions which do not involve any chemical substances; the object of the dependence is an activity or behaviour that is socially accepted and admitted. We are talking about addiction to pathological gambling, sex, affective relations, shopping, the Internet, work, sport and other more nuanced addictions.

In post-modern culture we have seen these behavioural dependences becoming very widespread and one of the first operations, at the level of a scientific approach, was that of distinguishing between antisocial and illegal dependences and social or legal dependences.

The former include addiction to heavy drugs and all those antisocial and illegal types of behaviour, in part related to them, such as stealing, very aggressive acts etc.

The second include the use of legalized substances such as alcohol, tobacco, medication etc. and activities, which are clearly allowed, such as eating, drinking, personal care, playing, shopping, sport and so on. These are, in part, also determined by changes in the lifestyle of the new civilization and the development of technological innovation. They are concentrated in an individual's life where boredom, emptiness, stress, the search for immediate gratification and personal imbalance are concentrated.

In English there is a distinction between the two terms - dependence and addiction - which in Italian are translated by the same word although it would be useful to underline their difference. Dependence refers to a physical and chemical dependence, therefore the organism needs a certain substance to function and seeks it with every means. Addiction defines a more general condition in which the psychological dependence is pressing and drives the individual towards searching for the object without which his existence becomes void of meaning.

Dependence and addiction do not necessarily appear together, and the recognition of new forms of addiction, for example on activities and not only on substances, confirms the hypothesis that addiction can be developed without dependence: we can have an uncontrollable need to implement behaviour in the absence of an actual physical dependence. Just as there can be a physical dependence without developing a pathological phenomenology which leads to the isolation and self-destruction of the subject. Take smoking, for example: the dependence on nicotine implies that the organism seeks it to maintain a form of balance, just as a psychological dependence is also developed but it is rare that illegal actions or antisocial behaviour are due to smoking (Guerreschi, 2005).

2. NEUROBIOLOGICAL CORRELATES OF THE NEW ADDICTIONS

Studies in biochemistry, functional neuro-imaging and genetics confirm the close relationship, at the neurobiological level, between addictions of a behavioural type and dependence on substances which, with great probability, produce the same functional alterations (Grant, Brewer, Potenza, 2006).

Sex, food and gambling are capable of activating the circuits responsible for gratification in a way similar to the reward produced by psychoactive substances. However, gratification is not the only mechanism that can explain the establishment of the phenomenon of dependence which also implies the functional alteration of the systems regulating affections and the cortical inhibition of dysfunctional behaviour (Goodman, 2008).

From a more general point of view, dependence can be considered as a syndrome with characteristic signs and symptoms that appear in subjects who show a certain vulnerability determined by common biological and psychosocial factors. Clearly, the ways in which each form of dependence appears vary in relation to the specific object of addiction, entailing different psychophysical consequences for the individual.

According to the classic psychobiological perspective, at the basis of dependence on substances and behavioural dependences, there is an alteration of the cerebral mechanisms engaged in gratification, which involve meso-limbic-cortical pathways.

The alteration of the motivation/gratification system causes unpleasant emotions, therefore the subject will tend to adopt behaviour which activates the gratification system more intensely than the primary stimuli (such as food or sex).

The neurotransmitter systems mainly involved in the mechanisms of gratification, are the dopaminergic system, which mediates the motivational drive to search for the substance and the opioid system which mediates the actual gratification. The glutamergic and GABergic systems also exercise a function in the reward processes through the modulation of the release of dopamine. Taking abuse substances (alcohol, heroin, marijuana, benzodiazepine, cocaine, amphetamines) as well as stimulants of various nature such as food, sex and gambling, can stimulate the release of dopamine in the nucleus accumbens shell and this is considered to be the mechanism at the basis of reward and of the effects of reinforcement of the abuse substances (Koob, Bloom, 1998). The abuse substances determine a greater and faster increase in dopamine compared to natural gratifying stimuli and therefore these types of behaviour take on a positive reinforcement which explains the reason why they are continually repeated despite physiological reward behaviour.

The establishment of phenomena of dependence, as well as the reward system also involves complex adaptive neuro-mechanisms that mediate the expectation of the reward, conditioned learning and the motivation that guides behaviour. The greater the gratification produced by a certain type of behaviour, the more probable it is that it is memorized and subsequently repeated.

Other neurobiological theories have been elaborated to explain the mechanisms through which the process of dependence is established. Robinson and Berridge (1993) have proposed the Incentive Sensitization Theory which indicates the psychobiological process through which, after repeated exposure to an abuse substance, there is a hypersensitization of the neurotransmitter circuits which mediate the brain's response to that specific stimulus. Hypersensitization consists of an amplification of the cerebral response to the abuse substance and also a generalization of the response to associated stimuli (such as, for a drug addict, the simple sight of needles, spoons, white powder etc.). This means that salience, i.e. an immense value which drives the subject to uncontrollably seek the substance, is attributed to the substance and stimuli and that it becomes the basis of the motivational drive to take it. The sensitization process is also at the basis of the establishment of the phenomenon of craving, i.e. the uncontainable desire to take the substance or enact the abuse behaviour due to the sensations of pleasure and gratification that it procures.

2.1. Addictions: Cortical and Subcortical Areas

The areas of the brain involved in the development and maintenance of the phenomenon of addiction are those that control impulses (frontal-cortical areas), regulate the emotions (amygdalae), learning and memory (hippocampus).

Thanks to the development of neuro-imaging techniques (fRMI functional Magnetic Resonance Imaging, PET- positron emission tomography, SPECT-single photon emission computed tomography), it is possible to document the functional and neuro-chemical modifications of specific areas of the brain in relation to different phases of the addictive process and different individual behaviours. Studies conducted with PET and SPECT have induced certain researchers to formulate the hypothesis according to which dependent subjects show a reduced availability of the dopamine D_2 receptors at the level of the striatum (Nava, 2004). Dopamine hyperfunctionality is thought to be at the basis of a lower sensitivity to the natural stimuli of reinforcement, therefore seeking and taking the substance would have the function of activating the reward circuits more intensely. Taking substances provokes, as an immediate effect, an increase in dopamine transmission, whilst chronic consumption would be responsible, in the long term, for a dopamine hyperfunctionality of the cortical areas that have an inhibitory control on dysfunctional behaviour.

Reduced dopamine transmission at the level of the orbitofrontal cortex and of the cingulated gyrus would explain the altered functionality of the behaviour control systems and the attribution of salience, which is translated into compulsive searching, typical of dependent subjects.

The cortical frontal regions control the executive functions that allow programming and directing behaviour, foreseeing the consequences of one's actions and exercising control over the behaviour itself. During abstinence from the substance, these areas are hypoactive, whilst activation is recorded when the subject takes the substance and when exposed to stimuli that he associates with it or when he strongly desires it. The cortical activation increases in intensity as the desire for the substance grows. The same areas are activated in subjects suffering from an obsessive compulsive disorder and therefore, it has been hypothesized that they are involved in the compulsive behaviour of dependent subjects who show a deficit in inhibiting compulsive behaviour in searching for the substance (Volkow, Fowler, Wang, 2004).

2.2. Receptors Involved in Addictions

A number of neurotransmitters and neuro-modulators are involved in the addiction process. In subjects who are dependent on substances, there is a reduced availability of dopamine D2 receptors at the striatum level and it can be hypothesized that this condition represents a factor of vulnerability to addiction. Subjects with a reduced receptorial availability, when they are exposed to the abuse substance, show a greater degree of personal pleasure than subjects with a higher number of D_2. It therefore seems that receptorial deficiency is a predisposing condition and prior to abuse, whilst the presence of high levels of D_2 receptors would seem to exercise a protection factor with respect to taking substances.

The reduction of D_2 receptors and dopamine hypofunctionality found in dependent subjects is alleged to be at the basis of a reduced sensitivity to the natural stimuli of reinforcement, therefore these subjects are believed to be more inclined to actively seeking the substances, the reinforcement effect of which is definitely greater than that produced by the natural stimuli.

Amongst the other neurotransmitters involved in the mechanisms of dependence, serotonin plays an important role. It is thought that, at the base of the impulsivity that can be found in some psychiatric disorders including substance dependence, there is a dysfunction of serotonin transmission. This hypothesis is confirmed by studies (Pallanti et al., 2006) which show an alteration of the serotonin functionality in a sample of pathological gamblers and in a group of patients suffering from bulimia who presented episodes of binge eating.

In gamblers, in subjects with sexual addiction and in those who have compulsive eating behaviour, the opioid system can be found to be involved. These types of behaviour effectively stimulate the release of endogenous opioids.

3. DEVELOPMENTAL-RELATIONAL ASPECTS OF PATHOLOGICAL ADDICTIONS

Human behaviour can be interpreted as a phenomenon that involves biological, social and psychological aspects. The study of pathological addictions cannot disregard this interpretation.

Psychoanalysis, for example, started from Freud's drive theory, considering drug addiction as an expression of the fixation at the oral stage, to reach the recent theoretical formulations that have shifted the focus of attention to the psychic processes underlying addictive behaviour.

The great importance of the construct of affect regulation (Taylor, Bagby, Parker, 2000), meaning that process which involves reciprocal interactions between the domains of the systems of emotional, neurophysiological, motor-expressive and cognitive-experiential response, is highlighted. Thanks to this theoretical model, certain psychiatric disorders, including complex ones, are found to be linked to deficits in the cognitive elaboration of the emotions.

It is precisely affect dysregulation that is considered as one of the nuclear factors that seem common to the disorder of substance and other compulsive behaviours such as alcoholism, gambling, eating disorders, sexual addiction and those that are defined affect dependences or object dependences, such as the incessant search for sentimental experiences and states of falling in love.

Pathological dependence is thus defined as a morbid form characterized by the distorted use of a substance, an object or a type of behaviour, which implies a dysfunctional mental state characterized by an uncontrollable desire to behave in a certain and compulsive way (Caretti, La Barbera, 2009).

Despite the evident differences linked to the different object of dependence, addictive behaviour seems to represent a dysfunctional attempt to contrast the uncontrolled emerging of traumatic infantile experiences. The emotive components associated with experiences of emotional neglect, physical, sexual and/or psychological abuse, are at times excluded from the normal flow of conscience and are deposited in a system of implicit trauma memory. If the traumatic emotions tend to re-emerge, they can appear in the form of post-traumatic symptoms (such as hyperactivity, sleep disorders, confused thought, dissociative amnesia) and the subject can try to block them by withdrawing into mental states dissociated from the rest of ordinary conscience. This happens as the psychic development of each individual originates in a primary intersubjective system, where the mental processes of attention, perception and memory are organized, but also the selection of affects and behavioural responses. The reference to Bowlby (1983), who highlighted that mental representations relative to oneself and others are formed during the relationship of the infant with his caregivers and are organized in cognitive-affective patterns that were defined Internal Working Models (IWM), is inevitable. Internal working models of the insecure type (like those characterized by confusion and disorganization) are linked to negligent or negative experiences of care which prevent the development of strategies that are adequate for the affect regulation.

In healthy development, the attention that the figure of reference shows towards the child's emotions is revealed through a process of emotive syntonization. Parents capable of affectively syntonizing themselves with their child have an outstanding sensitivity to its emotive manifestations, pay attention to its behaviour and modify their actions according to what they see in the attitudes of the child. An adequate cognitive and emotive development is thus fostered in the child and a relational world is generated where he can feel he is an individual capable of feeling, thinking and desiring.

Emotively neglected children, on the other hand, develop reduced capacities in representing their mental states and those of other people and this is frequently expressed through the onset of disorders of development and, in adulthood, by the appearance of psychopathological conditions characterized by a strong sense of an affective and cognitive void.

According to this theoretical model, the dependent subject perceives painful emotive experiences both with respect to his own mental states and object relations, but cannot contrast them effectively because he presents a deficit of a developmental nature, with respect to the capacity of identifying and mentalizing the emotions. This makes recourse to forms of pathological dependence more probable, where the object-drug has the function of external regulator of the affective states. One of the main etiopathological factors of addictions would therefore lie in the traumatic relations experienced in childhood, which can cause a recourse to mechanisms of defence of a dissociative type.

3.1. Dissociation in Dependences

Dissociation is a normal function of the mind that excludes from the conscience emotions and sensations characterized by great suffering, both internal and external. It is a mechanism that shelters the ordinary conscience from an excess of painful stimuli and has as its aim, in all the developmental phases, to protect the Ego by altering the state of conscience creating a more favourable parallel reality where refuge can be found. The consolation that is found retreating, momentarily, into this place of shelter is not to be considered pathological but, on the contrary, can be put at the service of the personal energies of the Ego, of creativity and of object relations. It is when retreat is repeated excessively that the risk arises of coactions in isolation and of distortion of the sense of reality and relations with others. It is possible to attain loss of contact with reality fostering the development of forms of pathological dependence up to actual dissociative disorders which have an impact on the capacity of mentalization of the emotive aspects of the experiences. In these cases, the emotive components break away from the cognitive ones, which can be considered one of the factors of vulnerability to stress, implying the non-adaptive use of substances or the perpetuation of pathological behaviour.

3.2. Craving

With respect to the construct of pathological dependence, craving, otherwise described as an incoercible desire, an imperious need, irresistible hunger, takes on a very important role.

The variety of theoretical models on craving shows the complexity linked to this phenomenon and they are evidence of the importance of this factor to understand addictions. Craving seems to be the common denominator of the different expressions through which pathological dependences express themselves.

Janiri et al. (2006) describe craving as an uncontrollable desire for a reinforcement stimulus, which can manifest itself in relation to different objects and/or conducts, showing psychodynamic processes and cognitive elements common to behavioural and substance dependences.

Craving, in the different addictions, assumes characteristics of urgency and compulsivity and the strong attraction for the behaviour of dependence goes well beyond the object-drug per se. If pathological dependence is considered a disorder based on mechanisms of defence of a dissociative nature that derive from childhood traumatic experiences, it is possible to understand how it is not only the physiological effects generated by a substance or by a type of behaviour to induce pathological dependence, but how a psychopathological condition exists, upstream of which craving is the natural epiphenomenon. It is, therefore, present before the subject encounters the object of dependence and belongs more to the sphere of unconscious motivations that have driven the subject to seek behaviour which isolates the traumatic memories and dispels the anguishes of fragmentation.

The dysfunctional mental state of craving is reinforced both by the positive representations associated with the pleasure of the dependence and by the painful and negative representations of abstinence, as well as by the positive representations linked to the possibility of contrasting the dysphoric mood and anxiety that emerge from traumatic emotions through dependent behaviour. At this point, it appears clear that the approaches to treating pathological dependences of an exclusively re-educational or pharmacological type tend to be ineffective. The negative consequences of the dependence behaviour, if not mentalized and elaborated by the person, will always remain in the background with respect to the functions of self-care which are carried out by the behaviour of dependence and sustained by craving (Caretti, La Barbera, 2009, p. 24).

3.3. Psychodynamic Treatment

Given the complexity of addiction, in psychotherapy, attention has to be paid to all the mental processes involved at the present time of the interpersonal relationship between the patient and therapist but also to all the information that concerns the relationship of the subject with his object-drug (whether a psychotropic substance, the Internet, sex etc.). It is fundamental to establish a therapeutic alliance which allows intervening, at the beginning, on the compulsive behaviour and craving and, subsequently, developing adequate coping strategies.

One example of intervention for the treatment of dependences is provided by Marlatt and Gordon (1985) who elaborated the Relapse Prevention Model, which aims to be a psycho-educative action finalized at maintaining the state of abstinence, through avoidance of at-risk situations, the comprehension of the nature of craving, the strategies to resist craving and the questioning of non-adaptive thoughts. The Relapse Prevention Model is structured in a phase of assessment, where the therapist collects information on how, when and in which circumstances the patient began to use the substance-drug, the sensations which he had following its use, how much time he spent in organizing his search. It is also important to be informed of the frequency with which the patient has recourse, in the present, to the object-drug and of symptoms of tolerance, i.e. the progressive decrease of the effects of the substance and of abstinence. In this phase, information on the significant problems that compulsive use of the object-drug has caused in the life of the subject (legality, economic conditions, work, in family relations and friendships) must be collected. It is also useful to assess the presence of two or more disorders that may appear simultaneously (psychiatric comorbidity). This information is necessary to arrive at an accurate diagnosis and plan the treatment to be followed.

Assessment is followed by the treatment which is divided into three phases: the Early Phase, the Middle Phase and the Advanced Phase. The first two are focused on the emotive and relational experiences linked to the relationship between the therapist and patient and on the abuse behaviour.

Work focused on craving is planned in which the patient is helped develop the strategies necessary to limit the exposure to those conditions that can increase the desire for the use of the object-drug; a reflection on apparently irrelevant decisions, an experience which refers to all those decisions which, in the patient's eyes, do not seem to have any relationship with the compulsive desire to make use of a particular object-drug; an exploration of the non-adaptive cognitions such as, for example, those concerning the patient's conviction of having full control over the object-drug and being able to do without it at any time.

Negative affective states are then dealt with, i.e. the patient's substantial incapacity of being able to identify and regulate negative emotions; on the use of empathy, by the therapist, necessary to help the patient interpret and explore unconscious conflicts and, lastly, work is done on resistance, i.e. activating all those mental processes that hinder all understanding of the mechanisms that underlie the compulsive use of the substance or that prevent the recovery of memories which could be of help to the therapist for a better understanding of the patient's mental functioning.

The Relapse Prevention Model can be considered an integrated cognitive-behavioural-psychodynamic model.

3.4. Diagnosis and Assessment

The central aspect, in classic drug addiction, is the pathological use of a substance. In the case of the New Addictions, addictive behaviour concerns habitual and everyday behaviour such as, for example, relaxing in front of the computer with a video game, going shopping, a session at the gym after a difficult day, but which, for some individuals, acquires pathological characteristics and causes consequences which can be serious at the emotive, cognitive relational and economic level.

The absence of specific criteria at times puts the clinician before certain difficulties. If, on the one hand, in the same way as official addictive (use of alcohol and drugs) behaviour, the forms of non-substance dependence are characterized by the presence of compulsivity, abuse, craving, tolerance, abstinence, on the other hand, it is more complicated in these addictions to establish the borderline between normal behaviour and addiction.

The identification of a classification of behavioural dependences shows a series of difficulties of a theoretical (absence of an official nosography) and practical order (lack of psychodiagnostic instruments) which make the diagnostic assessment uncertain and problematic. In general, the characteristics of addicts are held to be narcissistic vulnerability, psychological dependence, a tendency towards depression, intolerance of affective states and compulsivity.

Forms of comorbidity are also present with disorders of psychiatric pertinence and the co-presence, in the same subject, of several forms of dependence. Complications for the diagnosis are due to aspects of our post-modern culture which tend to promote excessive behaviour, becoming, in the final analysis, responsible for forms of psychological distress. Features of addictive psychology are mixed with some aspects of the dominant culture, making the pathological phenomena even more insidious as, apparently, they are legitimized by lifestyles.

The majority of subjects arrive for clinical observation when they have had, a conduct of abuse for several years and, rarely, in the initial phases of the problematic behaviour. When the addict, or more often a family member, asks for helps, the dependence has already had repercussions on the various spheres of his life.

The repeated search for pleasure, abuse, craving, tolerance and the conditions of suffering and distress linked to abstinence, are essential criteria to diagnose addiction. The possibility of having psychometric diagnostic instruments is very useful in orienting operators towards more precise diagnostic formulations that allow an earlier and more correct planning of therapeutic actions. Psychodiagnostic assessment currently uses the classic instruments such as observation, interview and the collection of anamnestic information and giving batteries of tests made up of specific self-report questionnaires for the different addictive conducts.

Amongst the forms of behavioural dependence, the one related to the distorted use of the Web is the one that currently has the most studies in literature. The questionnaire that is most widely used and most widespread is the IAT - Internet Addiction Test, (Young, 2000) which is made up of 20 items that investigate the risks of developing a pathological behaviour related to the use of the Internet, assessing the consequences on working life, social life and family life.

In Italy, the best known instruments are the UADI- Internet Use, Abuse and Addiction questionnaire (Del Miglio, et al., 2001) of 75 items that investigate five factors: Compensation Evasion (EVA) understood as the tendency to use the Internet to evade everyday difficulties; Dissociation (DIS) as the appearance of unusual sensory experiences associated with the tendency to become alienated and escape reality; Impact on Real Life (IMP) defined as the examination of the consequences of the use of the network on habits, on the mood and on interpersonal relationships. Then there is Experimentation (SPE) seen as the tendency to use the Internet to experiment new emotions and, lastly, Dependence (DIP) explained by the presence of tolerance, abstinence and excessive involvement as symptoms of the dependence.

Another questionnaire, again Italian, is the TSB- Tech Style Behaviour, (La Barbera et al., 2006) made up of 32 items which investigate the psychological (cognitive and emotive) and behavioural (frequency and ways of use) correlates connected with the use of new technologies.

Lastly, an innovative diagnostic software called IRP-AS - Internet Related Psychopathology Assessment (Cantelmi, Talli, 2007), which is directly installed in the computer and can warn the user of the dangers connected with abuse of the Web.

For pathological gambling (GAP), there is an official nosographic categorization which allows distinguishing the instruments of assessment of this form of dependence, in instruments based on diagnostic criteria of the DSM.

The most widely used questionnaire is the SOGS- South Oaks Gambling Screen (Lesieur, Blume, 1987), made up of 20 items which investigate the gambler's behaviour and the repercussions of his behaviour on family life. Other instruments based on the DSM are the Diagnostic Interview on Pathological Gambling (Ladoucer et al., 2000) and the Fisher DSM-IV Screen (Fisher, 1999).

Another group of instruments includes the ASI- Addiction Severity Index (Lesieur, Blume, 1992), which is based on a classification of Pathological Gambling as an addiction and allows assessing the possible coexistence with dependence on psychoactive substances.

The Pathological Gambling Yale Brown Obsessive Compulsive Scale (Hollander et al., 1998) refers to the inclusion of pathological gambling as an anxiety disorder and provides information on the gambler's gambling behaviour.

Another instrument frequently used in clinical practice is the Questionnaire of Gamblers Anonymous, (Browne, 1991), made up of 20 items that investigate the conditions underlying the impulse of the gambling subject. Lastly, an instrument which is useful in particular for the psychodiagnostic assessment of adolescents is the MAGS- Massachusetts Gambling Screen, (Shaffer et al., 1994).

As far as sexual addiction is concerned, one of the most widely used instruments is the SAST Sex Addiction Screening Test, (Carnes, 1982) which has two checklists: the W-SAST (Women's Sexual Addiction Screening Test) and the M-SAST (Men's Sexual Addiction Screening Test), both of which have 25 items which explore the at-risk sexual behaviour relative to compulsive disorders and sexual addition, producing a graphic profile.

The other one is Italian, the SAI-2- Sexual Addiction Inventory (Avenia, Pistuddi, 2007), which investigates the tendency to sexual addiction, assessing the gravity of the manifestation. It has two sections:

The first, of 30 questions, seeks the presence of sexual addiction (or the tendency), borderline subjects, the presence of sexual dysfunctions and is given as a screening. The second, with 24 questions, assesses the characteristics and gravity, the self-awareness, the course, the persistence, the tolerance, the psychological responses in abstinence, the level of inhibition etc. and is only given if a tendency to addiction has emerged from the first section. This instrument was used in Italy for the first time in 2004 by the Italian Association for Research into Sexology (AIRS) with a casual sample of 1046 subjects (564 women and 482 men) and recorded sexual addition behaviour in 5.75% of the sample (in particular, men).

As for the other forms of behavioural dependence, it is not easy to reach a precise diagnostic categorization for compulsive shopping, also because, at times this behaviour is considered a symptom of more serious disorders and not as a syndrome per se.

Literature reports some screening instruments such as the Compulsive Buying Measurement Scale, (Valence, D'Astous, Fortier, 1988), made up of 16 items which provide information on four dimensions: tendency for buying, spending in reactive ways, guilt feelings and the shopper's family context. The other instrument is the Compulsive Buying

Scale, (Faber, O'Guinn, 1992) which, with 29 items, investigates the emotive aspects linked
to the compulsive spending.

4. ADDICTION TO COMMUNICATION TECHNOLOGY.
TRAPPED IN THE WEB

The post-modern man can interact increasingly quickly with others similar to him without
necessarily having to be in the same place thanks to the galaxy of social worlds which has
introduced new ways of relating to and meeting others which are far removed from the
traditional ones (Riva, 2004).

With respect to the beginnings of the Web, when surfing the Internet meant visiting static
institutional sites, created and organized by an elite of professionals, without any possibility
of interaction by the average user, there has been a revolutionary rescaling with the advent of
Web 2.0 and social networking.

All users, from the most competent to the least skilful in Information Technology and
media, thus become protagonists of the Web, taking on an active role which allows them to
create, share and comment on texts, images and videos (Various authors, 2010).

It is possible to relate experiences and feelings "not only in the pages of a diary locked in
a drawer but to all the visitors to the Web." (Riva, 2010, p. 15).

A series of recent investigations (Mauri et al., 2012; Cipresso et al., 2012) have shown
the capacity of these technological instruments to produce optimal experiences, defined flow,
which can procure an intrinsic reward for its users. The Internet, the virtual communities that
inhabit it and its consequences on the human psyche and thought have been the object of
investigation by numerous researchers, some fascinated and others indignant about the great
Web.

Rheingold (1993), describing his experience as a member of The Well, one of the first
and most popular online American communities, considers the communities, the virtual
public squares, as real social worlds which are integrated into people's real everyday lives.

In his opinion, modernity has introduced increasingly artificial lifestyles suffocated by
interpersonal relationships characterized by formalism.

The virtual communities, in making up for the absence of sociality in real daily life,
prefigure a new model of social development and emerge "from the web when a certain
number of people carry on public discussions for a sufficiently long period of time, with a
certain level of human emotions, to the extent of forming a network of relations." (Rheingold,
1994, p. 5). In other words, for example, the newsgroups of yesterday and today's social
networks offer a new possibility of interaction that leads to the creation of a network
community, a group of people that share reciprocal social commitments.

Rheingold enthusiastically describes his experience as an online user: "There's always
someone there. It's like being in a bar surrounded by old friends and new, very friendly
people, but instead of putting on my jacket, switching off the computer and going round the
corner, I only have to switch on the modem and they're there. It's a place." (Rheingold, op.
cit., p. 24).

Even when he maintains that in the Web there is a sort of decentralized democracy
making everyone equal, as they are no longer subject to constraints of varying nature, which

can condition communication and discussions in real life, the author's position is characterized by optimism and enthusiasm (Roversi, 2004).

The position of Maldonado (1997) is on a line of thought at the antipodes of the previous one, as he considers virtual communities as mock communities, communities of spectres characterized by strong regressive aspects.

According to the critic, the communities that populate the Web derive from a free and spontaneous confluence on subjects with unanimous views, characterized by a poor internal dynamism.

The enthusiasms on the one hand and the scepticisms on the other reflect the metaphorical image of the Web as a pattern of interwoven threads which supports and saves, but which also captures and ensnares, harming man's freedom and autonomy.

Trying to maintain a wise balance between the two positions and not wanting to pander to an anti-technological perspective, the incredible fragility of the post-modern personality and therefore the identity of the users of the web cannot be forgotten.

Digital technologies are increasingly becoming outlined as psychotechnologies, i.e. instruments that can enter into great affinity with psychic reality, deeply influencing the mind. In the age of new technologies, human experience is oriented towards the search for states of conscience, emotive and affective experiences, mental conditions and cognitive strategies that are increasingly as gratifying as they are disconnected from the material and concrete dimension of reality. The advanced means and technologies of communication can work as extensions of the Ego, or modify the conditions of conscience, or they can become a privileged source of emotions, states of mind and sensations, even though triggered off by a totally virtual and simulated reality (Caretti, La Barbera, 2009).

A fascinating relationship between the human mind and interactive technologies is created but, precisely for this reason, it is important to study what the psychic effects and any psychological and psychopathological risks linked to the use of electronic media there may be. Their irruption into daily life can cause a condition of techno stress and maladaptive use to the extent of reaching forms of abuse and technological addiction.

4.1. The Concept of Tech Abuse

The risk of incurring and falling into the paradox of the Internet is not that far away. Technology develops to a maximum the social potential of globalization but, at the same time, it can drastically reduce the real social involvement of its users (Anolli, 2002).

When a person spends more and more hours online and never feels he has had enough, the tendency to progressively and unconsciously replace the real world by the virtual one becomes increasingly concrete, and the subject can develop conduct of technological abuse.

The concept of tech abuse (La Barbera, 2005) refers to a wide range of techno-media disorders including the Internet Addiction Disorder, video display dissociative trance, technological autism and techno-media deliria.

These cases are characterized by an over-investment in and an excessive and compulsive use of communication technologies that can compromise the individual's psychobiological balance and bring about negative consequences in the functioning of daily life such as, for example, a decline in work or school performance, family and relational problems, to situations of almost total closure and isolation from external social relations.

Virtual experiences can become real refuges for the mind (Steiner, 1996) to retreat to in order to apparently flee a reality experienced as unbearable and distressing.

The importance and the value of the real world can be cancelled, denied or replaced by a dream-like, fantastic and illusionary world.

Increasingly more subjects sit in front of their computer screen, check their email, read and write a message on Facebook or MySpace, follow the lives of others on Twitter, thus remaining in virtual touch with hundreds of people, friends and strangers, without the need to say a word or look into the eyes of the person they are speaking to (Tenzer, 2010).

In the Web, the real body with its emotions disappears from the relationship, leaving room for a virtual one and the subject is deprived of an important point of reference in the process of learning and understanding one's own emotions and those of others, encouraging emotive illiteracy, i.e. the absence of awareness and control of emotions, the lack of awareness of the reasons why a certain emotion is felt and the incapacity to relate to the emotions of others, being unable to recognize them and understand them (Goleman, 1996).

The generation of digital natives is characterized by a high level of emotive illiteracy, linked and consequent to the greater quantity of relations mediated with respect to the direct relations in the daily face to face context (Parsi, Cantelmi, Orlando, 2009).

Another serious problem lies behind the uncontrolled use of time and energy in seeking a virtual life. The incapacity and impossibility of recognizing the other's emotions also prevents understanding one's own, leading to emotive disinterest or, in the worst cases, to psychopathy.

The sensations of power, control and freedom that can be experienced by surfing in cyberspace, distinguished by the possibility of choosing what to see and what to write and even of closing the page, may be revealed as pure illusions.

If a moderate use of online technologies, less than 20% of working time, corresponding to about two hours a day, can produce an increase in productivity, exceeding this limit can conceal a genuine disorder of Internet addiction which has significant and dramatic consequences on individual productivity and on the relational dimension (Coker, 2009).

The first description of Internet addiction goes back to 1995 when the American psychiatrist Ivan Goldberg (1995) provocatively published on the Web the diagnostic criteria of the Internet Addiction Disorder (IAD) with the objective of criticizing the nosological and descriptive approach used by the DSM, the Diagnostic and Statistical Manual of mental disorders published by the American Psychiatric Association (APA, 2000).

IAD is a form of abuse and dependence on the Internet, "as real as alcoholism, it causes like the other dependence pathologies social problems, an uncontrollable desire, abstinence symptoms, social isolation, conjugal and performance problems and economic and work problems." (Cantelmi, D'Andrea, 2000, p. 59).

Kimberly Young (2000a) is considered the pioneer in the scientific field of the study of Internet addiction, having created a self-administered questionnaire to facilitate the recognition of potential subjects at risk.

Eight criteria are stated in the instrument: the subject is exaggeratedly absorbed in cyberspace (for example, he is excessively absorbed in reliving past experiences on the Web, or in considering or planning later online activity). He needs to spend increasing amounts of time in cyberspace to reach the excitement desired. He has repeatedly tried, without success, to control, reduce or interrupt the cyberspace experience. The subject is restless or irritable when he tries to reduce or interrupt the experience of cyberspace. He has spent more time in cyberspace than originally intended. The subject has endangered or lost a significant relationship, work or academic or career opportunities due to cyberspace. The subject lies to the members of his family, the therapist or others to hide the extent of his involvement in cyberspace. He enters cyberspace to escape problems or relieve a dysphoric mood (for example, feelings of impotence, guilt, anxiety, depression).

If the subject replies affirmatively to at least five of the eight items listed, it could be a case of IAD.

The Internet addict progressively increases the amount of time spent online, passing longer periods of time than intended on the Web.

Individuals belonging to the group of addicts in Young's study admitted spending an average of 38.5 hours a week for non-work or non-school activities, about eight times more than that spent by non-addicts who, on average, spend 4.9 hours online.

This temporal data was recorded in 1996, only four years after Cantelmi and D'Andrea (2000) reported clinical cases of subjects who spent up to 70 hours a week on the Web, reaching the observation that 5 or 6 hours a day represents the critical value, with the greater the risk of addiction when this period of time is exceeded.

However, the quantitative factor alone does not explain the presence or not of addiction, as there is no differentiation to arbitrarily separate a normal or acceptable use of the Internet from an addictive habit (Young, 2000b)

Compulsive behaviour in the use of the Internet must be assessed by taking into consideration the significance of the virtual world in the eyes of the subject, to create his hyper-involvement and hyper-investment, which makes it difficult to control his use.

In the assessment, the entwining that is created between the characteristics of the mediated communication and the personal characteristics of the subject using the Internet must be considered (Cannizzaro, La Barbera, La Barbera, 2009).

Online communication, characterized by accessibility and a sensation of excitement, can lead to a condition of omnipotence in the subject who feels free to express himself and with the possibility of concealing his identity, stimulating the wish and need to repeat the virtual experience more and more frequently.

As far as the individual characteristics are concerned, tech abuse is alleged to be prompted by low self-esteem, emotive instability and poor emotional control.

This would concern more subjects with compulsive obsessive personalities, who have a tendency for social retreat and with marked aspects of relational inhibition; in these cases, the IAD could represent avoidant behaviour: the addict seeks refuge in the Internet in order not to face up to his existential problems (Siracusano, Peccarisi, 1997).

In addition, individuals aged between 15 and 40, geographically isolated, who do night work with a high degree of computerization and who are in unfavourable environmental situations such as burn-out, unemployment and marital problems seem to be the most exposed to the development of Internet addiction (Cantelmi, D'Andrea, op. cit.).

IAD becomes even more real when the subject falls increasingly deeper into the web and the reality of the Internet, forgetting and negating daily life and his own emotional distress, experiencing sensations of well-being when he is connected and physical and mental suffering when he is disconnected.

In actual fact, as Cantelmi and colleagues underline (Cantelmi, Toro, Talli, 2010), it is more correct to consider the Internet Addiction Disorder not as a single disorder but as a constellation which includes various types of Cyber Addiction.

More precisely, Cantelmi (2001), underlining the polymorph and complex nature of the Web, introduces the concept of Internet Related Psychopathology (IRP), which includes disorders with similar characteristics, but with different features, such as: Compulsive Online Gambling; Cybersexual Addiction; Muds Addiction; Information Overload Addiction and Cyberrelationship Addiction.

The last one, today, in the age of social networks, takes on the forms of a friendship addiction, the tormented search for friendship requests to collect an increasingly larger number of contacts on one's profile, with about 10% of Facebook users dependent on this (Talarico, 2010).

Many people show increasingly serious signs of addiction on the social networks, with evident signals such as the need to update the contents of their profiles increasingly frequently, abstinence which causes distress at a physical and psychological level in the case when it is not possible to be connected to the Internet for a certain period of time, and symptoms of craving, or the increasingly greater presence of thoughts and strong drives on how and when to be connected.

At the current state of research in Internet addiction, no adequate epidemiological surveys or fully reliable clinical instruments of assessment or criteria that sufficiently discriminate between conditions of use, abuse and addiction are available yet (Cannizzaro, La Barbera, La Barbera, op. cit.)

4.2. Comorbidity in Internet Addiction

In the clinical and research field, it is often possible to observe a pathological and addictive use of the Internet linked to mood disorders (70%), bipolar disorders (60%), anxiety disorders (60%), social phobia (40%), disorders of control and impulses (35%), such as sleep disorders, dissociative symptoms and other forms of dependence on alcohol, gambling, bulimia etc. or personality disorders (Shapira et al. 2003). Kim et al. (2007) have recently observed, in subjects with a problematic use of the Internet, higher levels of depression and suicidal ideas.

In Internet addiction which takes on forms of antisocial behaviour, such as in the case of online fraud or online paedophilia or paedo-pornography, the patients could act completely adequately in real life but behave dysfunctionally only online. Or, they could be patients suffering from an antisocial or borderline personality or from a previous psychiatric disorder, who find both in offline life and in the Internet the ways to behave in a problematic way, as per their disorders, protected by the anonymity, exploiting the speed and accessibility of the contents of the Web as in the case of Cybersex Addiction.

Zanon et al. (2002) have shown that those who spend more than three hours a day connected to the Internet have a more than double frequency of dissociative experiences. Virtualizing one's life can entail an alteration of temporal and spatial dimensions, a distorted perception of the body and of reality and a video display dissociative trance which can be found fairly easily in subjects suffering from that regressive withdrawal typical of dependence on online role games, accompanied by amnesia and transitory identification with the character in the game.

A series of studies (Ko et al., 2008), have analysed the comorbidity of the problematic use of the Internet with ADHD and with depressive and dysthymic disorders.

4.3. Cybersex Addiction

If limited contact with pornography can represent an aid to the discovery of sexuality, excessive resource to it risks turning out to be harmful as, not only can it cause a distorted vision of sexual life, but it can also foster the onset of a pathological dimension of dependence on enjoyment of this type of material.

Virtual sex includes all those activities that can be carried out online and which provoke sexual excitement, such as the use of pornographic material, meetings in erotic chats, virtual sex etc.

Cooper et al. (2000, 2004) have united under the abbreviation Triple A Engine the three powerful factors that, precisely thanks to the virtual reality of the Internet, facilitate sex addiction. They are: Access, i.e. facility of access to online material (the Internet is a practical instrument because connection can be from home, maintaining a certain degree of privacy); Affordability, meaning quantitative availability of the material, with infinite variations on the theme (from chat rooms with an erotic content to films, including amateur); Anonymity, which guarantees that the user is anonymous and lets him externalize sexual fantasies which are normally repressed.

The authors have also drawn up a classification of typologies relative to the use of pornography on the Internet, identifying three groups of cyber-porn users. These are recreational users, who use pornographic material out of curiosity or to relax; those at risk who, if the Internet were not available, could perhaps not have problems connected to online sexuality and lastly, compulsive sex users who, due to an inclination for a pathological expression of sexuality, use the Web as the main reference for their sexual activities.

It is effectively not possible to outline a specific typology of porn-dependent personality but some factors have been associated etiologically with the development of compulsive sexual behaviour. It has been highlighted (Putnam, 2000) how sexual addiction and compulsivity can arise in response to physical, sexual, family and social traumas: behavioural attitudes learnt in the family have been recognized as playing the role of facilitator, as well as personality disorders, mood and anxiety disorders, but also substance abuse and addiction. It emerges that, at least in part, the disorder may be provoked by biological factors such as imbalances in testosterone and serotonin levels.

Subjects considered at risk, i.e. those who may develop a cybersex addiction, may show problems linked to depression and difficulties in facing up to stressing situations. Problems of affective regulation where pornography could be a way to dissociate oneself from the incapacity of elaborating unpleasant and painful emotions, seeking refuge in an alternative and illusory world, are also invoked.

The present post-modern period is defined as being one of "pocket porn", not only because of everything that circulates on the Web but also because of what arrives on mobile phones, which have now become, in particular for the very young, ideal instruments for amateur pornographic videos. Nevertheless, little attention has been given to the subject, and to the potential influence on development processes. Adolescence is a particularly rich terrain and at risk for possible cybersex addiction, also because this particular period of life is, naturally, characterized by the tendency to put oneself at risk in at-risk behaviour. The elaboration of pornographic material by developing subjects is different from that of adults: the adolescents who access cyberpornography exaggeratedly run the risk of falling into the trap of becoming dependent on the whole range of materials of that kind and also of developing a hyper-eroticization, an excessive investment in the sexual sphere, characterized by the priority of satisfying pleasure to the detriment of the relational aspect (Stevani, 2008).

4.4. Media Education. Responsibility of the Parents of Digital Natives

A parenthesis on the educational responsibility of digital natives appears necessary. In the Survey of the Condition of Adolescence in Italy 2011, by Eurispes and Telefono Azzurro in October 2011, 1,266 parents of Italian pupils between 12 and 18 were interviewed. Questioned on the reasons why they use the Internet, the parents gave different answers: looking for information (80.3%), to send or receive emails (64.6%), to read the newspapers online (51.8%), to watch films on YouTube (40.1%). Other activities (often essential for the children) were less known amongst the parents: using Social Networks (35.7%) downloading music/films/games/videos (26.6%) or online shopping (24.6%). Parents are marginally attracted by other possibilities of the Web which, on the contrary, their children like, such as playing with videogames on the Internet (14.6%), reading or writing on a forum (14.3%), reading or writing a Blog (12.4%). 47.6% of the parents know of Facebook, but are not members. About 40% of the adults know it and have a Fb page, but 12.9% of them do not use it although they have it. Despite the fame of this social network, 1.8% of parents do now know what it is.

However, the fact that one parent out of five says they know little or nothing about their children's activities in the virtual world (16.6% of parents are convinced they know a little and 5.4% think they know nothing about it) is worrying. This figure rises with the age of the children: if 3.8% of parents with children aged between 12 and 15 say they know nothing about what they do on the Internet, the percentage is much higher (9.3%) of parents of children aged between 16 and 18. The same trend is found both in the percentage of parents who say they know little (which increases to 14.3% and 21.4%) and in the percentage of parents who say they know a lot (which decreases from 33% to 16%).

It appears that the relationship between the Internet and parents is marked by an oscillating attitude between disconcerting trust and underestimation of the risks. As well as not knowing what their children are doing online, parents also seem to underestimate, at least in part, the risks connected to a use of the Web that offers little protection. Just under half (46.4%) of parents consider that it is almost impossible for their children to come into contact on the Internet with a paedophile, 30.8% consider it possible, but not very probable, whilst 14.2% of parents deem that there is a fairly probable eventuality.

In addition, 88.9% exclude that their children can take their clothes off to send their images or videos online on the Internet, 85.4% exclude that their children make purchases on the Internet using their credit cards, 84% that children spread information/video on the Internet that could make other children of their age suffer (cyberbullying) and 71.5% that they visit sites that praise violence.

25.6% of parents deem that it is fairly probable that their children see violent images when they use the Internet, 17% that they see sexually explicit images, 15.8% that they spend too much time on the Internet, isolating themselves and neglecting other occupations, 14.6% that they illegally download music or videos.

Despite the little knowledge of what their children are doing online, the majority of parents try to tell them of dangerous or potentially dangerous behaviour, coherently with the main anxieties of parents: 79% forbid their children from speaking online with strangers, 78.8% from surfing for too long, 77.8% from meeting in real life people they have met online, 76.9% from revealing personal information on the Internet, 67.7% from making purchases online, 62.6% from accessing some websites and 51.3% from putting their own photos or films online. Lastly, 24.5% prohibit their children from joining a Social Network.

38.9% of parents deem that the best way to protect their children from the dangers of the Internet is to tell them about the risks and help them protect themselves on their own, whilst 18.1% think that regulating the use of the Internet can obtain the desired protective action. The figure of 14.4% of parents convinced that their children are more expert users of the Internet and that they can get by is still too high, whilst only one parent out of ten thinks that it is better to be with their children when online. 3.1% of parents see prohibiting access to the Internet as the best way of protecting their children, whilst 2.9% rely on programmes/systems of parental control.

The real need is to educate on the new media. About 34% of parents deem the commitment of the school (20%) in educating on the new technologies important and a greater knowledge of the Internet by parents themselves (13.9%). Despite the conscious need of implementing new actions of educational co-responsibility, the most significant response for parents is that which indicates the increase of punishments for those who produce online sites/services/contents that are not suitable for children (36.5%). For others, it is necessary to start information campaigns on the dangers connected with the use of the Internet (17.6%) or implement new software that monitors the use of the Web (7.9%).

4.5. Pharmacotherapy of Internet Addiction

Therapeutic action on Internet addiction, to date in Italy, represents a little explored area through studies methodologically oriented to investigating the clinical efficacy, both regarding the psychotherapeutic approach and in relation to the psychopharmacological treatment. There are no controlled trials on psychopharmacological treatment, also because the clinical classification of this condition is still the subject of scientific debate.

A study by Dell'Osso et al. (2006) has shown the efficacy of treatment with escitalopram, an inhibitor of serotonin, in the first phases of the open label trial (reduction of the quantity of time spent online) on a small sample of subjects with compulsive Internet use; however in the second phase of the double blind trial, no statistically significant and important difference was found compared to the placebo.

In one case - report by Bostwick and Bucci (2008), the efficacy of the treatment with naltrexone, used in the therapy of benzodiazepine addiction, was shown in a patient suffering from Cybersex Addiction.

Given that Internet addiction shares a number of clinical characteristics with pathological gambling, the therapies deemed most effective are behavioural-cognitive therapies and support groups.

In Italy, a number of outpatient clinics have started to provide support for those suffering from this addiction such as, amongst the best known, the one in the psychiatric Day Hospital of the Policlinico Gemelli in Rome which has the objective of freeing those ensnared in the web in order to reactivate a real life contact with society and the Istituto Minotauro in Milan.

4.6. The Hikikomori

A tragic but effective example of the dark side of the web is that of the hermits of the third millennium: the hikikomori.

They are aged between 12 and 30, they self-exclude themselves from real life, shutting themselves up in their rooms and plunging into a time which only the present made up of the Internet, videogames and TV makes absolute.

The Japanese term literally means "pulling inward", "being confined": it refers to a form of self-imposed social withdrawal and takes on the appearance of technological autism, limiting interpersonal contacts and contact with the world for months or even for years (Marrazzo, Rumeo, Mulè, 2009). It cannot be assimilated with one of the many adolescent crises. It is a socially invalidating pathology which induces young Japanese, but not only them, to live in a world where access to the other reality is denied.

No official statistics on the phenomenon exist because both families and society conceal the problem in the attempt to solve it by negating it.

The hikikomori syndrome is estimated to concern more than one million youngsters, affecting almost one out of every ten.

A study by the Japanese government in 2002 lasting 12 months, showed 6,151 cases in 697 public health centres. 40% of these involved young people aged between 16 and 25 and 21% were subjects aged between 25 and 30. The majority were male and 8% stayed in their rooms for over ten years (Di Maria, Formica, 2003). They are modern hermits confined to the few square metres of their bedrooms, and begin to live a life in reverse: they sleep during the day and wake up at sunset to spend the night on the Web, made of virtual exchanges and games. They grow apart from the friends, school and family.

A reflection on this pathological phenomenon must also be made in the light of the socio-cultural system of the country where it arose and where cases of it are the most numerous: Japan, a country characterized by very high levels of competitiveness and efficiency, where those who cannot keep up are trodden on and left behind.

The school disciplinary systems are characterized by extreme severity and subject youngsters to excessive pressure and enormous expectations, at times too great for the real capacities of the pupils who are humiliated and stigmatized as incompetent and inadequate.

The value of individuals, their creative and specific dimensions are cancelled by the culture of standardization and by being as required and demanded by society.

The hikikomori is therefore a victim of a normative system which ignores him and to which he reacts by withdrawing from it in a sort of spiritual and private suicide (Jodice, 2005). The Japanese family does not appear to be able to respond to the needs of their child: the family is characterized by an organization where the father is scarcely present, the mother is a continuous and obsessive presence in the children's lives, constantly inciting them to study more, produce more and improve.

Until the children claim the right to refuse and thus escape the game of the "perfect Japanese, perfectly inserted by a perfect mother into the most perfect of societies" (Di Maria, Formica, op. cit., p 25) and lock themselves up in their rooms, the only place where they really feel themselves and free from every obligation is a virtual life, probably less difficult that real life, but by no means authentic.

Watts (2002) notes how the hikikomori syndrome is different from adolescent anxiety and agoraphobia, as it is a unique condition of its kind and found only in Japan. However, this existential epidemic has crossed the borders of Japan, extending to Korea, the United States, Northern Europe and Italy (Ricci, 2008). There are increasing numbers of Italian hikikomori. The parents of more than twenty youngsters, all under 18, have contacted the Istituto Minotauro in Milan; however, as yet there are no statistics on the lost generation in Italy (Mangiarotti, 2009). The invisible world of the Internet, this non-place, without borders and without time, is inhabited by present and absent faces, which can be perceived but not seen, left to the imagination of millions of users who are connected every day (Tappatà, 2011).

5. MOBILE PHONE ADDICTION. IT RINGS, THEREFORE I EXIST

Speaking on a mobile phone, contacting someone, increasingly less for a real emergency, has become a practice with an irresistible attraction, a new form of pleasure, which has subsequently given rise to a new addiction: mobile phone addiction (Di Gregorio, 2003). The 2012 Eurispes Italy Report, in the section on the possession of material goods and consumerism, says that everybody in Italy lives with a mobile phone: 81.4% have at least one basic one. One out of two has a smart phone in their pocket or bag. Referring to mobile phones with basic functions, 35.4% have one, 25.7% have two, 11.5% have three and 8.8% have four or more, against 15.5% who say they do not have one. Almost half of the sample (47%) have a smart phone: 25.4% have one, 14.5% have two, 5% have three and 2.1% have four; the other half (48.2%) do not own one.

Starting from this data, it can be stated that the mobile phone, as well as its function to make communications over a distance easier, has caused many changes in ways of life and interpersonal relations. It offers a sense of freedom, independence and security, it is a constant presence in everyday life, it allows leaner forms of communication, such as via text message and, with its functions, it allows being connected to the Web all the time.

Another change, due to the appearance of this instrument, has come about in the social area: newer and newer models, aesthetically appealing and of the latest generation allow their owners to be in fashion and produce a specific status. Receiving repeated calls, having high volume or original ringing tones and making phone calls are typically post-modern evidence of numerous social contacts and therefore of popularity.

Guerreschi (2005) declares that, together with the Internet, the mobile phone can be considered as a real technological revolution of the last century. The daily relationship that the majority of people have with their mobile phone fuels relational behaviour that could be considered pathological, in the same way as a form of fetishism. We are all, to varying degrees, involved in a direct relationship with a mobile phone, but addiction, pathological use, is, fundamentally, a question of quantity.

In literature, mobile phone addicts are also called fanatics, due to the great importance that they give to their mobile phone and for the extreme difficulty they encounter in facing the events of every day, if they do not have their mobile phone charged (Di Gregorio, 2003). They never abandon it and are in very disagreeable emotional states if they do not have it with them, they use it as a mediator to enter into relation with the other and, in the life of the couple, the mobile phone becomes an instrument to keep the partner under control, continuously checking their movements. These people, to justify their dependence, seek alibis such as the practical nature of the instruments or reasons of security.

There are different categories of addicts: there are the fanatics of text messages who continuously need to send and receive messages. At times they have calluses on the fingers of one hand, generally the thumb, or their keypad is worn out. They use the fast writing system and their mood depends on the number of messages received which, at times, they send to themselves (from the computer to the mobile phone) and on the ones sent which, often, they send to people in their immediate vicinity.

Then there are the addicts of new models, who continuously buy the innovations in the technological field (the frequency of the new purchases, almost always borders on every five months, but this can greatly depend on the social class) and the exhibitionists of the mobile phone who in their choice, pay particular attention to the shapes, colours and design of the cover and price. They always have their mobile phone in their hand so that they can show it to the people close to them; when they phone, they speak loudly or, before answering it, let it ring for a long time in order to capture the attention of those present. They can even simulate a phone call, pretending to be in a conversation, only so that they can show off the model of their phone.

Lastly, the game players whose fanaticism is oriented on games and on the applications in their phone, transforming it into a console and playing for long periods of time until they set a new personal record.

Mobile phone addicts tend to gradually isolate themselves, withdrawing from relations with the real world and real people, spending a lot of time on their own, supporting the loneliness into which they fall, spending increasing periods of time holding their phone, playing and sending text messages continuously. With this behaviour, they run the risk of unlearning how to communicate and convey emotions and states of mind with a language that does not exceed the 160 characters of a text message. In addition, using the cognitive functions only in relation to telephone performance, they run the risk of unlearning how to use the mind to imagine the other and the things of the world. The obligations of technological mediation for affective relations can put people at risk of losing their authenticity and, with it, the capacity to face a direct relationship with emotive resources alone, of losing the habit of establishing spontaneous and original communication which has not in some way been prepared or planned, with a falsely original way of communicating (Di Gregorio, 2003, p. 75).

The world of the very young, obviously, runs the risk of developing a pathological use of the mobile phone, but all of us behave differently with respect to when this instrument was not used. Unwittingly, the systematic use of the mobile phone produces a dependence which is fuelled by itself: whenever its use satisfies a need, whenever we feel less lonely because someone has sent us a message. A person who suffers from this addiction should think that the work of prevention fundamentally starts from themselves. They should self-regulate their dependence on the mobile phone, beginning to think of a form of education on its daily use.

6. WORK ADDICTION. WORKAHOLICS

Present-day society imposes high pressure rhythms of production and the very concept of professionalism increasingly expresses a sense of personal gratification: work becomes an instrument that can build up personal identity. The addiction to work described by Oates

(1971), as a type of obsessive-compulsive behaviour fits into this socio-cultural frame. The central nucleus of this addiction is made up of irrational conditions, completely disconnected from real personal, organizational or professional necessities which drive a person to work without granting himself any respite. It is therefore an obsessive-compulsive behaviour which is shown through an incapacity to regulate habits to the exclusion of the main activities of life (Robinson, 1998a). The workaholic is dominated by his profession, he sees it as an indispensable instrument for personal gratification and works, continuously, as though driven by an inner constriction which does not leave him free to choose and decide otherwise. The APA (2007) describes the workaholic as an individual who feels an excessive drive to work which becomes a cause of stress, interpersonal difficulties and health problems.

The work ethic seems to encourage this phenomenon so that, unlike other addictions, a person who devotes the whole of his life to work does not seem to have any disorder or pathology; on the contrary, his behaviour allows him to receive prestige, recognition, economic affluence and power. The pressure that the world of work exercises on people leads to an emphasis on aspects such as maintaining the organizational role, supervising work spaces, performing beyond expectations, never lowering defences and always being careful of the danger of new competitors. It is also for this reason that this addiction has been described in very unusual ways, such as well-dressed addiction, or as a clean addition, in contrast with the better known and recognized ones as a sign of a diseased and losing way of life (Castiello d'Antonio, 2010a).

Work alcoholism can affect, in differentiated ways, both men and women, of any socio-economic condition, of different ages and in different professional roles. The ideal that the workaholic should be exclusively represented by an executive or manager has been superseded: many of the people that work compulsively are in intermediate professional and technical roles. This is because there is a widespread responsibility at organizational, social and cultural level: a mechanism that, at all levels and in all contexts, incites people towards the infinite self-exploitation, appealing to the ideal of respectability of those who sacrifice their lives for work. It is not surprising that the phrase 'organizational neurosis' (Kets de Vries, Miller, 1984) is used, upheld by styles of leadership and management which, in a clinical-organizational perspective, appear highly pathological and pathologizing (Castiello d'Antonio, 2010b).

6.1. Manifestations of Work Addiction

It is worth emphasizing that there is a difference between the tendency to invest one's energies in work, typical characteristic, for example, of Type A personalities, who show a strong drive to competition, are oriented towards seeking success, aggressiveness and hostility towards others and those who develop an addiction to work. Those who suffer from this addiction are people who have lost control, who cannot give themselves rules, who do not accept their limits and who are not aware of the negative consequences that derive from their attitude. Work is an obsession and any other activity, family, relations, relaxation or entertainment is ensnared in a work approach to life.

As for other addictions and dependences, the workaholic denies having a problem, and justifies his lifestyle by adequate explanations, from responsibility to the work ethic, to the importance of economic peace of mind. Robinson (1998b) identifies some criteria which can suggest whether a person suffers from this type of addiction. Workaholics complete different tasks in the shortest time necessary and check all activities to see whether they have been correctly carried out because, generally, nothing is ever done perfectly; they abandon family and friends declining all responsibility and missing important events; they are restless, impatient and irritable. They show work trances with memory gaps and periods of absence even in conversations with other people, because their mind is busy with thoughts about work; as for other addictions, the experience of tolerance is present and therefore of the progressive need to increase activity and stimuli to reach the same excitement. They have no time for personal care, eat at irregular times and take little physical exercise.

It is also possible to identify some profiles of workaholics such as, for example, the hyper-ambitious worker who is characterized by great energy which he directs to promoting and imposing his professional projects; the competitive worker who needs to attain supremacy over others through good performance and great efforts; the guilty worker, with a masochistic mentality, who experiences the overload of additional work as a reward aimed at reducing his need to receive punishment. There is also the insecure worker who seeks in the approval of others the way to increase his level of self-esteem and self-assertion and, lastly, the isolated and solitary worker who, without family bonds and friendship, seeks, through work relations and during the working day, to have an experience of interaction, in a familiar community with rules that he knows well (Guerreschi, 2005).

6.2. The Origins of the Addiction to Work

The reasons and the causes responsible for this addiction are multiple and difficult to identify. Obviously, it is always necessary to highlight that every person must be treated as a unique individual, with individual personality traits and differences and a particular life story, but it is also true that there are factors that make people more vulnerable to addiction.

From a Cognitive point of view, it appears evident that work addition is developed and maintained according to a rigid system of wrong convictions stabilized in time such as, for example, the thought of perfection and the relative anxiety in the quest for excellent performance; the tendency to absolutize behaviour (typical of the all-or-nothing attitude: either I work for economic affluence or I spend time with my family); orientation to pessimism, the sense of inefficacy; externalization, or the quest for happiness only, and exclusively, in the outside world, in the possession of things and power.

Some key episodes can also be of great importance, experienced in childhood, marked by an educational model where the love and esteem of parents was earned exclusively by getting good marks and excellent results (at school, in sport etc.). Many workaholics do not have a good level of self-efficacy and their working performances could be an unconscious attempt to seek the approval of their parents. They are often people who come from families where work took precedence over every other aspect of life, for real economic reasons or only imaginary ones. Identification with one parent, or with another member of the family, can also be decisive: the workaholic tends to idealize and imitate those who are recognized as being the best, reliable and successful. Through his devotion and fusion with work, he therefore seeks to follow their example in order to be admired in turn. The causes related to the post-modern world of work are also of great significance. Efficiency, availability, flexibility and the capacity of complete dedication can become a trap for those seeking success at all costs. After every achievement, the workaholic increases the difficulty of the task or of the stake, to be able to satisfy himself but, at the same time, he falls into the web of stress, insecurity, anxiety and psychological distress.

Others, on the other hand, try to evade relational distress and interior emptiness precisely through many work engagements. Too occupied by work, they avoid being involved in responsibilities, roles and tasks linked to the family or friendships. Work becomes a guarantee of well-being to survive, it becomes the drug that helps them overcome existential shortcomings and family problems.

6.3. The Health and Relational Life of the Workaholic

Despite the variety of symptomatologies with an anxious and depressive basis that a workaholic may experience, the signals given off by the mind and body are often ignored or dealt with only pharmacologically. In the most complex and serious situations, it is associated with other abusive conduct, such as the consumption of alcohol, psychotropic drugs and tobacco. As far as the relational context is concerned, those who suffer the greatest consequences of this addiction are those who belong to the family and primary relations of the workaholic. The family context is massively affected by his presence/absence: the partner often reports feelings of distance, negative emotions, experiences of a void in marital life; the children grow up with a parent who is perfect from the point of view of attaining economic peace of mind and the willingness to have experience, but completely absent throughout their growth. At times, however, devoting one's existence to work can represent an acceptable way of solving conjugal and/or family tensions, feelings of personal and social inadequacy, states of shyness or inferiority.

It is certain that, in some particularly stressing situations, the workaholic can be isolated from the family nucleus because he is no longer considered an active subject of the family dynamics.

It is not easy to help a person who suffers from this addiction because, more often than not, he is not even aware of needing help or that he is suffering, and making others suffer for the problem, but he actively defends his existential state as fully functional to maintaining his personal balance, his gratification and the affluence of his family.

Prevention in the workplace should be the starting point, with the aim of limiting all situations of organizational distress but, as is obvious, prevention has yet to be carried out in Italy.

6.4. Comorbidity in Work Addiction

Comorbidity with the obsessive-compulsive disorder is clear: it appears through ritualizing patterns of thoughts and behaviour, in life and in work, poor interpersonal relationships, and at times a poor work performance, despite all the energy and time devoted to work, due to the self-invalidating and recursive aspect of the obsessive-compulsive personality or a symptomatic obsessive-compulsive disorder.

This addiction has a tendency to deny one's limits, complete centring on oneself, little control over impulsivity, the difficulty in accepting and facing criticism and failure, the need for success and the search for power in common with the narcissistic personality disorder, where excessive investment in the professional sphere fills the void of depression.

Comorbidity with eating disorders such as anorexia, bulimia or obesity as well as compulsive buying is also often found.

In the case of comorbidity with the dependent personality disorder, the clinical case is characterized by an incessant and continuous need for approval and the inability to refuse onerous requests, from the point of view of commitment and risks, in work.

Comorbidity with adult ADHD has also been hypothesized (Robinson, Kelly, 1998), characterized by a continuous quest for stimuli, easily bored, incapable of relaxing and with difficulties in completing a job due to the rush to start another one. Work becomes the place where the charges of energy that are difficult to contain can be engaged.

7. PATHOLOGICAL GAMBLING. GAMBLING AWAY ONE'S BALANCE AT DICE

Gambling appears so deeply entrenched in human nature that archaeological and anthropological research has found its presence in every period, social condition and culture. In recent years, all over the world, gambling has become an activity of enormous economic importance and considerable social proportions and gambling and/or betting in general (horse races, lotteries etc.) also represents a greatly expanding practice in Italy as well. The prevalence of gambling amongst adolescents, in particular males, appears to be growing, and the characteristics typical of this phase of life, such as sensation seeking and impulsivity, make youngsters particularly vulnerable to the risk of falling into the vortex of Pathological Gambling (PG), in particular in its technological variations (Croce, 2001). According to some studies (Smart, Ferris, 1996; Griffiths, Wood, 2000), men, who are more exposed to the risk of becoming pathological gamblers, are driven by the desire to feel the excitement of the stake, the desire for fast and easy gain and seem to prefer highly competitive gambling or with immediate payment. Women, on the other hand, invest in gambling as an alternative to situations of distress, frustration and loneliness: they prefer to stake on luck, prefer games like bingo, lotteries and scratch cards. These games with immediate payment seem to be more at risk of addiction because the phase of excitement linked to waiting for the result is short but very intense, therefore it predisposes the gambler to try the same thing instantly.

A further difference between genders concerns the age of onset: it seems that pathological gamblers who develop the disorder at a later age generally belong to the female gender whilst pathological gambling is started at a younger age, between 19 and 30, by men. The prevalence in the adult population of pathological gambling appears to be commoner amongst relatives of gamblers and in subjects with a lower standard of education compared to the general population (Raylu, Oei, 2002).

Amongst those who have worked on gambling, one difficulty found has been to give an exhaustive definition of what a gambler is and when gambling becomes a disease; in literature, gamblers who bet frequently and lose large sums of money have been classified in various ways. They have been called pathological gamblers, compulsive gamblers, dependent gamblers and, more recently, the DSM-IV (2004) defined pathological gambling as persistent and recurrent maladaptive gambling behaviour, which compromises personal, family or work activities, whilst the ICD-10 (1992) included it in the habit and impulse disorders (Savron et al., 2001). Over the years, PG has been variously labelled with terms such as compulsive, pathological, problematic and this last one is the most used as it avoids the stigmatizing label given by the definition of pathological gambling, allows including a greater number of gambling experiences and, lastly, allows evaluating the problematic nature of the behaviour in general and of the gambler in particular, without stopping at the study of the symptoms of the disorder (Caretti, La Barbera, 2009).

7.1. Psychological and Psychopathological Features of Pathological Gambling

Guerreschi (1998) suggests a classification of gamblers in six clearly defined types: compulsive gamblers with a dependence syndrome; inadequate gamblers without a syndrome of dependence; constant social gamblers; adequate social gamblers; antisocial gamblers; non-pathological professional gamblers.

It is not possible to outline a single psychological profile of the gambler, because the variables that contribute to the onset and continuation of this addiction are different and can assume differing degrees of importance in each person: what is certain is that some personality traits and some psychological and psychopathological states seem to be particularly present in subjects affected by problematic gambling. Impulsivity is a widespread characteristic amongst gamblers, whether they are occasional, problematic or pathological, and many of them are incapable of resisting gambling, even though aware of the negative consequences of their behaviour. Sensation Seeking is common to many of them, precisely because gambling is practised as a source of excitement and pleasure, in particular for the element of challenge, risk, unpredictability and surprise that the sensation seeker avidly searches. This trait appears to be present in gamblers who prefer fast gambling and where the person plays an active role, such as for example horse racing, rather than those where the gambler is at the mercy of chance as in repetitive and static games such as slot machines, where the very gesture linked to gambling is monotonous.

The tendency to dissociation is frequent in those gamblers who like solitary games. The dimension of gambling is seen as a protected oasis where reassurance and refuge can be found, an alternative to the chaos of daily life with all its frustrations (Steiner, 1996).

In addition to the characteristics that can be present in the population at large, there are psychopathological configurations that expose the subject to a greater risk of developing a problematic relationship with gambling. For example, the presence of depression, anxiety disorders, impulse control and personality characteristics such as narcissistic, borderline and antisocial disorders, which represent conditions found in many pathological gamblers.

7.2. Models of Classification of Pathological Gambling

Over the years, the contributions of etiology, clinical research and treatment of PG have differentiated, privileging either a medical approach or a psychological one: currently there is a tendency to integrate the contributions by the different disciplines, following the awareness that, behind gambling, there may hide many different configurations, from biological to purely psychological and social.

The medical model considers gambling a disease: this orientation entails an absolutist interpretation, i.e. the problem either exists and therefore causes a disease which is expressed with symptoms and signs, phases of evolution, or it does not exist, therefore there is no disease. In this way, PG, understood as the inexorable impulse to gamble, is a disorder that has many points in common with substance dependence, such as craving, tolerance, symptoms of abstinence with dysphoria and irritability, compulsion and investment in gambling as a self-therapeutic instrument. Traces of the contributions of the Psychological Model are already found in Freudian thought which saw gambling as an unconscious substitute for the need for love and attention mortified by parents and therefore gambling as a motivation for gratification. In the 1980s, gambling started to be included amongst the non-drug addictions and Custer (1984) conducted the first research on the subject, identifying the presence of structures of personality, motivations for gambling and clinical characteristics present in various gamblers. He identified six types of gamblers, qualified by different levels of gravity, highlighting how the development of the pathological gambler's career, which starts from the winning phase to the losing one to reach a phase of despair, characterizes in particular one type of gambler. We find the professional gambler, the antisocial one, the casual social gambler, the neurotic gambler (and so far, these are non-pathological profiles), and finally the compulsive gambler who is addicted to gambling, who gambles heedless of the economic damage and repercussions on the family and social context, i.e. for whom gambling has become the sole reason for living.

More recently (Raylu, Oei, 2002) have divided problematic gamblers into two categories: the first includes the profile of the gambler characterized by a strong internal motivation, who seeks the excitement and confirmation of his skills through gambling and therefore prefers games of skill or with a high degree of involvement; the second includes that type of gambler in search of gratification from the exterior, who seeks low personal involvement and who tends to rely on external factors independent of his own abilities and skills, such as, for example, lottery gamblers.

From another psychological point of view, however, the theoreticians of Learning interpret gambling as behaviour that is learnt, on the one hand due to the factors of positive reinforcements obtained, such as learning the mechanisms of gambling, the wins and the excitement of gambling, and on the other, due to the reduction of the stress guaranteed by fleeing from difficult situations, daily life and the focus of attention on gambling with the consequent exclusion of the surrounding world (Diskin, Hodgins, 1997).

The contribution of Cognitivism, on the other hand, greatly enriches the theories on PG, bringing to the attention of scholars the role that the perceptions, convictions, dysfunctional motivations, physiological hyper-activation have in the onset of pathological gambling, the maintenance of which is due to the poor coping skills of the subjects, fuelled by the consequences of gambling, like family and social pressure, substance abuse, lowering of self-esteem and legal problems (Sharpe, Tarrier, 1993).

The Bio-Psycho-Social Model outlines the presence of three distinct typologies of gambling distinguished by a level of growing gravity, characterized by precise biological, personological configurations and particular life stories. The first type, the least serious one, can arise at any age and occur, according to the mechanism of condition from the exterior, following exposure to gambling, not necessarily directly, for example, by seeing a family member or friend gamble. These are subjects in search of winning and who can easily develop symptoms of anxiety and/or depression.

The second typology is more problematic and has a less favourable prognosis, compared to the first type, due to the personality characteristics that characterize the gamblers. They show poor coping and problem-solving skills, associated with symptoms of anxiety and depression, linked to difficult life and family stories. The third type is that of impulsive-antisocial gamblers who see a precocious onset, a fast escalation and a worse prognosis both due to the seriousness of their behaviour and the lack of support for any form of action, which depends on a precise neurobiological configuration, the presence of antisocial traits and the lack of control of impulses, attention disorders, the poverty of interpersonal relations and the presence of a history of gambling in the family.

Lastly, the theoretical contribution of the Sociological Model interprets gambling as a response by the subject to his inability to fit into society and belong to it in a constructive, effective and gratifying fashion. In this perspective, gambling helps create a subculture and a less complex microcosm, triggering off a negative reinforcement. The gambler, increasingly engrossed in the dimension of gambling, will be less and less skilful on the social level, from which he will receive continuous negative reinforcements, inducing him to increasingly seek refuge in gambling.

7.3. Comorbidity in Pathological Gambling

In subjects with PG, mood disorders and a history of attempted suicide, ADHD with marked expressions of irritability and facility for boredom, substance abuse and dependence, antisocial personality disorder, narcissistic disorder and borderline, Sex Addiction and compulsive shopping can frequently be observed (Fernandez Montalvo, Echeburua, 2006), whilst Kruedelbach et al. (2006), found in 61% of their sample a personality disorder more frequently belonging to cluster B (dramatic or erratic), followed by C (anxious) and lastly by A (odd or eccentric). The investigation into the personality of gamblers has defined some of the most recent research, in the Italian scientific field.

A study by Cocci et al. (2006), at the Gambling and New Addictions outpatients' clinic of the Department of Addiction of the Local Health Authority no. 8 of Arezzo, aims at analysing the characteristic personality traits of gamblers. The researchers have presented some characteristics of the gamblers that show: antisocial traits; borderline traits and the presence of a fragile Ego to whom gambling seems to act as a support to gain value and power, just as the substance does with the drug addict; alterations of the mood with oscillations between hypo-maniacal excitement and depressive sadness. And also: a component of anxiety linked to emotively traumatic experiences; a tendency to somatise anxiety through hypochondriac symptoms.

The researchers dwell in particular on some points that have emerged from their work. First of all, on the hypochondriac component that emerges as a recurring trait in the sample of gamblers. Starting from this data, it can be useful to investigate the extent to which the hypochondriac symptom becomes a way for the gambler to react to the environmental requests that he perceives as stressful. The evaluation of narcissistic traits and the prevalence of operatory thought as a signal, in the gambler, of a poor mentalization, present as in psychosomatic personalities and the presence of alexithymic traits. The decision to gamble in the sample examined seems to be accompanied by a borderline functioning and antisocial forms of relating to the other which are also very frequent in substance addicts.

Lastly, Sacco et al. (2008) indicate a significant correlation with the borderline personality disorder suggesting, from the analyses carried out, a complex relationship between borderline disorder, PG and symptoms of depression.

7.4. Pharmacotherapy of PG

The pharmacological treatment of gambling contemplates a targeted action on the typical symptoms of the disorder and on any psychopathological condition in comorbidity such as mood or anxiety disorders etc. The reason why SSRI, selective serotonin re-uptake inhibitors, are chosen is given by the neurobiological hypotheses which maintain that, underlying impulsive behaviour, there is a dysfunction of the serotoninergic system.

The use of fluvoxamine would appear to be effective at doses between 100 and 200 mg/day (Hollander, et al., 2000) although in a placebo-controlled double blind trial, the effect was not any greater than that of the placebo, in controlling the symptomatology, except in a subgroup of male patients (Blanco et al., 2000).

Two open label trials evaluated the efficacy of citalopram (Zimmermann et al., 2002) and of escitelopram (Black et al., 2007a), in reducing the symptoms in subjects suffering from PG.

The use of mood stabilizers is justified by the analogies between the clinical manifestations of pathological gambling and some characteristic elements of the maniacal phase of the bipolar disorder, such as impulsivity and the tendency to spend large sums of money. The studies in this field are still limited but a possible efficacy of treatment with lithium, valproate (Pallanti et al., 2002) and topiramate (Dannon et al., 2005) has been shown.

Amongst the antagonists of the opioids, naltrexone seems to be effective in controlling impulsivity (Kim et al., 2001). More recently, the adequacy of nalmefene in the treatment of PG has been investigated (Grant, Brewer, Potenza, 2006). Atypical antipsychotics can be useful in the treatment of gambling addiction in comorbidity with psychotic spectrum disorders; in addition, thanks to their capacity to modulate the serotoninergic and dopaminergic systems, they could be effective in the therapy of PG. However, further studies are necessary to confirm this hypothesis (Caretti, La Barbera, 2009).

8. AFFECTIVE ADDICTION. LOVESICK

Affective addiction is a mental condition which is typical of our time and, for some people, represents an important source of security, substituting the eclipse of values and securities that characterize post-modern culture. The instability and the precariousness which are also found in interpersonal relations tend to select ambivalent or conflictual styles of attachment and to foster the formation of inconstant and weak bonds (Guerreschi, 2005).

Love, for affective addicts, is obsessive, suffocating and inhibited; it has to be preserved and protected from any change; it is parasitical, stagnant and requires absolute devotion of the partner. Affective addicts are led to think that, by acting in favour of their partner, they will put their relationship in a safe place. According to Giddens (1992), affective addiction is characterized by some particularities. In the first place by inebriation, a sensation which the addict effectively feels when close to the partner and which is essential to feel well, then by the exaggerated need for the presence of the partner. The affectively dependent subject tries to spend increasingly larger amounts of time with the object of his love; he exists only when and if the other person is there and reassurance and proof of love is not enough but he needs continuous and tangible evidence of the other's devotion. Time spent together often excludes time spent with the rest of the world and if the addiction is reciprocal, the couple feeds on itself: the other is seen as the only form of gratification in life. When the other person is absent, the dependent subject feels he does not exist and is unable to think of a life on his own: in actual fact, this model of thought reveals a low level of self-esteem.

Lastly, in love addiction, there is a loss of the Ego as there exists a high degree of loss of the Self, the critical capacity and a good examination of reality.

Dependence is present in almost all relations characterized by psychic distress. It appears from literature (Miller, 1997), that the majority of affective dependents are women, in different age groups: from post-adolescent to adults, even with children. They are fragile women, continuously seeking a gratifying, unique and deep love; women who feel inadequate and have little awareness of the right, indefeasible for every human being, to live in psychological well-being and balance; women who beg attention and depend on continuous requests for confirmation.

Many of those who are affectively dependent, have undergone physical and emotive abuse and have a symptomatological history that is very similar to the victims of Post Traumatic Stress Disorder. The symptom of a profound negation of the self, which characterizes love addicts is comparable to the post traumatic stress disorder. This hypothesis is in relation to the fact that physical and emotive abuse have conditioned the person, producing attitudes of submission and passiveness.

In affective addicts, a great devaluation of feelings and a great fear of losing love and being abandoned are found; an addict fears separation, distance and loneliness.

The objective of a possible therapeutic process is represented by the acquisition of awareness that also includes the discovery that interior fragility can coexist with strength and gaining a realistic vision oriented to improving one's life.

8.1. Comorbidity in Affective Addiction

In this addiction, the person sacrifices every developmental drive and every desire, in favour of keeping love, even though it is a suffocating and passive love and that this hides a great deficit of self-esteem.

In addition to the comorbidity with Post Traumatic Stress Disorder, a connection is found with the personality dependent disorder, the obsessive-compulsive disorder and all the cluster C disorders (anxiety) (Miller, 1997).

Often types of addiction such as those to food, sex, gambling, physical exercise and substances are present; a dysthymic disorder, or a mood disorder which refers to a clinical condition in which the depressive symptomatology presents a lesser gravity than the greater depressive disorder, but which follows a more chronic course and with symptoms lasting at least two years; and anxiety disorders.

It is possible to find comorbidity with cluster B dramatic and borderline disorders (Albano, Gulimanoska, 2006).

9. Sexual Dependence. Let's Not Call It Love

Sexuality is relationship, play, communication and a privileged exchange of intimacy: some people, however, experience it obsessively and become dependent on it.

It is compulsive sex when the natural inclination to experience sexuality, as the fundamental expression of a relationship, is transformed into a frantic activity, characterized by an uncontrollable crescendo of desire which absolutely has to be satisfied.

Carnes (1991), maintains that the sex addict establishes a distorted relationship with people or things that can modify his mood. He gradually passes through phases in which he withdraws from friends, family and work. His private and secret life becomes more concrete than his public one, he creates a mental prison inside of which ideas, fantasies and sensations all revolve around the sexual act; due to this sort of double identity, he has feelings of guilt and shame. Cantelmi et al. (2004) define sexual dependence as a diseased relationship with sex, through which the person relieves stress, flees from negative or painful feelings and moves away from the intimate relations that he cannot control. The sexual relationship becomes the fundamental need in respect of which everything else is sacrificed, including people, who become objects to be used.

From the clinical point of view, sexual addiction appears through a series of manifestations such as compulsive masturbation, prolonged promiscuousness (heterosexual, homosexual and bisexual), excessive sexual requests to the partner to the point of making the couple's relationship problematic. Performing sexual activity and intensification of pleasure can also be sought through consuming visual and multimedia pornographic material, telephone and erotic chat services, the use of pornographic objects and taking stimulating or hallucinogenic substances.

Goodman (1998) and Mick and Hollander (2006) observe that, in sexual addiction, impulsive aspects coexist along with compulsive ones. In particular, the dimension of impulsivity seems to be involved in the initial phases of addiction, being expressed as the irresistible need for pleasure or immediate activation, whilst that of compulsivity emerges in the advanced phases of the process, in terms of inner conflict and painful experiences of guilt and shame, which the subject is able to placate only thanks to abusive conduct.

Liggio (2007a), on the other hand, highlights the psychophysio-pathological component of sexual addiction or orgasmic reaction, which can be understood as a condition of alteration of the cerebral system of gratification and its sensitivity to β-endorphins, endogenous hallucinatory substances released during sexual intercourse.

9.1. Diagnostic Criteria and Etiopathogenetic Models

There is no precise official nosographic classification of sexual addiction. Some Italian researchers (Cantelmi, Lambiase, Sessa, 2004) propose observing six diagnostic criteria, such as persistent maladaptive sexual behaviour which leads to a clinically significant distress, caused by obsessive thoughts, images, impulsivity, compulsivity, present for a period of time of not less than 16 months; the presence of sexual behaviour which engages the subject for most of the time of his day and which significantly interferes with his habits, his school or work performance, with social relations or other usual activities.

Subsequently, the incapacity to have affective intimacy with the partner and the consequent presence of a picture of multiple, instable and intense relations; the appearance of untruthful communication with family members or therapist or friends, precisely to hide the entity of sexual activity and its consequences; and lastly, that the persistence of these fantasies or activities is not the symptom of another somatic or psychic disorder such as bipolar disorders, obsessive-compulsive disorder, various organic situations and paraphilia. According to Guerreschi (2011), in the latter, the object under examination is sexual behaviour (exhibitionism, fetishism, voyeurism etc.), whilst in addiction what is really of interest is how the model of sexual behaviour interferes with the life and decision-making capacities of the addict.

A number of models are proposed to understand the factors and processes that specify dependence and the dynamics through which it evolves.

The cognitive-behavioural model proposed by Carnes (1991) and Coleman (1992) attributes a fundamental role to the genesis of the disorder, to the family history, to the presence of pathological dynamics characterized by the constant disavowal of the child's needs, by the lack of emotive closeness and excessive and inadequate expectations. Within these relational contexts, the person develops a self-image marked by shame and elaborates a system of inexact beliefs which express feelings of self-devaluation and lack of confidence in interpersonal relations, with the conviction of not deserving being loved, of being a bad person etc. and the belief that sex can be the only source of response to his fundamental needs.

Schwartz (1989) presents a cognitive-behavioural treatment that implies six stages. The first requires blocking the unwanted sexual behaviour, including by using techniques of behaviour modification and, if necessary, pharmacological therapy to modify the sex drive; the second stage is that of the patient's admission of accepting the existence of a problem and promises to start out on a well-defined and sincere journey with the therapist. Then techniques of reducing anxiety are applied, such as progressive relaxation, so that the patient does not have to have recourse to sex to relieve the anxiety accumulated; there is a cognitive therapy for the purpose of modifying irrational convictions, those that are at the basis of the sex addiction. Lastly, the patient is trained in skills such as assertion, problem-solving for the aim of facilitating their use in an adaptive social functioning, and, the last stage, the solution of the remaining problems in the individual, establishing a primary sexual relationship and attaining this level often implies couple therapy with the involvement of the sexual partner of the period prior to the treatment.

Within the same model, Lambiase (2001), underlines how, due to the repeated infantile experiences of a lack of affective harmonization with the caregiver, the sexual addict has been unable to develop an adequate theory of the mind thanks to which he can regulate his behaviour and emotions, experiencing a sense of personal adequacy oriented to having a significant life. Ritualized sexual behaviour represents the powerful means through which the addict believes he can overcome all the problems. However, the more frequent and intense the sexual activity becomes, the greater the feelings and experiences of humiliation and in this way, the dysfunctional beliefs are reinforced, triggering off a vicious circle where sex becomes an object of increasingly unrealistic expectations and investments.

The Bio-psycho-social model proposed by Goodman (1998) combines the cognitive-behavioural theory with the psychoanalytical one and that of attachment, hypothesizes that addiction disorders are characterized by an underlying psychobiological process, i.e. a very strong and persistent tendency to adopt behaviour which produces pleasure, relieve pain and regulate self-esteem. Due to a combination of genetic and environmental factors, some people show a compromise of the regulation system of the Self, the internal psychobiological system which regulates internal subjective states and the behavioural states of the individual and which make them particularly vulnerable, suffering from states such as depression, anxiety, loneliness and anger.

Genetic, temperamental, personality and learning factors orient the addict towards his choice: in particular, that of sexual addiction, is believed to develop in predisposed individuals, who have had experiences of hidden or manifest infantile seduction, or a relationship with figures of attachment that promoted sexuality as a defence mechanism.

From a clinical point of view, it should be borne in mind that subjects who suffer from sex addiction experience a strong confusion of languages (Ferenczi, 1933), and, in particular, seem to confuse that of affectivity with that of impulsivity and the fullness of love with the aridity of the sexual drive. In the sphere of psychoanalytical contributions, Fenichel (1951) identifies in a pathological and obsessive need for love, the most significant expression of non-drug addiction, assimilating this condition to that of drug addicts, alcoholics, and pathological gamblers. More recently, McDougall (1990) introduced the term sexual addiction to describe those forms of non-perverse sexual relationship in which it is the sexual act itself, and not the interpersonal relationship that is repeatedly sought in order to relieve painful mental states and constantly repeated to reduce aggressiveness towards oneself or towards the interiorized representations of the parents.

Due to these characteristics, the addictive sexual relationship is never a function of desire but rather of the stereotyped need of the other, experienced only as an instrument which, instead of gratifying, simply reduces the search for pleasure (Di Maria, Falgares, 2004).

A recent interpretation (Reid et al., 2008), proposes considering sexual addiction as an expression of the deficit of affective regulation and of the attempt to make up for this deficit with a dissociative defence. In this sense, the consumption of psychoactive substances, fasting and binging, intense physical and sexual activity can facilitate the control of the negative effects, generating hypnotic states that are self-induced or similar to trances.

9.2. Therapeutic Perspectives and Prevention of Relapses

The sexual addict has a clinically significant distress and also resources that he does not know of or is not capable of using on his own. To define a therapeutic project, it is necessary to understand the subject's personality, his resources and the motivation to start the treatment.

For the diagnostic evaluation, it is fundamental to start with a systematic interview which can help the patient to open up to a concrete comprehension of his problem and highlight the presence of paraphilia, sexual dysfunctions and present or past clinically significant psychiatric disorders. It is also extremely useful to analyse the development of the subject, the dysfunction of the sexual identity and that of the relationship between the couple or the lack of an intimate partner, the presence of organic diseases and, last but not least, plan a laboratory screening for the evaluation of sexually transmitted diseases.

The treatment of sexual addiction requires a multimodal approach, i.e. an integrated therapy that includes the use of psycho-education, psychotherapy (cognitive-behavioural, psychodynamic, couple and group therapy), pharmacological therapy and self-help groups, all variously combined with one another, following a course marked by short-, medium- and long-term objectives.

Many times these addicts come for treatment for problems linked to other addictions or because they have been convinced by someone or due to legal measures that oblige them to follow treatment. The process starts with an indispensable passage: motivating the individual to change, a key element in order to increase the patient's awareness and make him able to face the difficulties of the journey towards balance. The next point is that of breaking the isolation to which he has confined himself and, one of the most suitable instruments for this is self-help groups, based on the 12-step method borrowed from Alcoholics Anonymous (Nerenberg, 2000).

It is then necessary to live soberly, learning to control and overcome crises of abstinence (in the first phases of the therapy the patient must abstain from any sexual activity for at least ninety days), solve the situations of crisis (work, financial, health, legal), learning to elaborate feelings of guilt and shame.

Good results can be obtained with cognitive-behavioural therapy which suggests shifting the focus from the sexual sphere through techniques of aversive conditioning and systematic desensitization through images. Then, subsequently, family or couple therapy is useful to restore communication and trust and foster intimacy through sharing feelings (Bird, 2006).

The strategies of preventing relapses which help sexual addicts to recognize factors and situations that are associated with a greater risk of sexual acting out, to more effectively oppose sexual drives and to rapidly recover from episodes of symptomatic behaviour are also of great importance (Guerreschi, 2011).

The fundamental point of the complexity of the approach to this addiction lies in the fact that, unlike drug addiction, where the objective is to attain definitive abstinence from the use of the substance, in sexual addiction the objective is to return to a healthy sexuality and therefore to attain a complete equilibrium of the person.

9.3. Comorbidity in Sexual Addiction

In Sexual Addiction, the erotic act is experienced as a means to relieve stress, fleeing negative feelings and emotions that are impossible to control. This set of aspects makes it close to other forms of latent depression and is accompanied by low self-esteem and levels of impulsivity, aggressiveness and obsessive behaviour, present at higher levels compared to the average population.

Frequent comorbidities are drug abuse (42%), work addiction (28%), compulsive shopping (26%), pathological gambling (5%), eating disorders (32-38%), cybersex addiction (6-8%), anxiety disorders (46%), social phobia (47%), mood disorders (62%) and depression (62%).

Sexual addiction can also be secondary to other disorders such as schizophrenia, neurological lesions or a bipolar disorder. It is not infrequently associated with antisocial conduct such as sexual violence and paraphilia. Comorbidity can also be found with some borderline personality disorders, narcissistic, paranoid, antisocial, dramatic, obsessive-compulsive and passive-aggressive disorders (Caretti, La Barbera, 2009).

Comorbidity with ADHD has been investigated, in particular in relation to sexual aggressions, in comorbidity with paraphilia (Kafka, Hennen, 2006).

9.4. Pharmacotherapy of Sexual Addiction

As far as the conditions of sexual addiction are concerned, it is essential, preliminarily, to make a differentiated diagnosis between orgasmic reaction dependence and hypersexual ego-syntonic behaviour (HESB), which is connoted by an abnormal sexual instinct which is more easily pharmacologically controlled than the orgasmic reaction dependence. As well as being effectively treated with the use of an anti-androgenic therapy, neuroleptic therapy considerably curbs its characteristic symptomatology (Liggio, 2007b). Amongst neuroleptics, thiroridazine is widely used for its selectivity towards dopaminergic receptors at the level of the nuclei of the base and limbic-prosencephalic projections.

As in the other conditions of lack of control over drives, there is also wide use in sexual addiction of SSRI. Satisfactory results have been obtained in treatment with fluovoxamine (Pallanti et al., 2002) and fluoxetine (Levine et al., 2002).

Therapy with SSRI shows an ascertained efficacy of the thymic sphere and on the behavioural level, but also causes the unpleasant side effect of the reduction of libido. The optimal condition would therefore be that of curbing drives, without causing a suppression of the libido.

Other research (Wilson, Nicoll, 2002) has shown the role of endogenous cannabinoids in causing compulsivity. The disinhibiting action of exogenous Δ-9 tetrahydrocannabinol (THC), the specific receptors of which have been detected in the system of the reward system, is well known.

The endocannabinoid 2-AG hinders the production of GABA reducing, in turn, its inhibitory action.

In the near future, the development of drugs effective in blocking, at the level of specific brain circuits, the release of excess endocannabinoids, could be foreseen and they could therefore be useful in further improving the pharmacotherapeutic attempts proposed to control orgasmic reaction dependence.

10. COMPULSIVE SHOPPING. HAVING, BEING AND APPEARING

Having ,being and appearing are three dimensions that belong to every person, three autonomous but, at the same time, interdependent, spheres. Our time has peculiar characteristics which often mark a dangerous balance among the three dimensions. Having seems to prevail over the spheres of being and appearing and risks making one being identified with the others.

An individual's personality is expressed not only by class of belonging, birth, profession or activities, but also by the type of clothes worn, the type of home and furniture, musical tastes, diet etc.: consumption not only as an economic activity but above all as a social and symbolic-communicative activity. Consumption creeps into physical and mental space, and becomes a real occupation, at times forced to the point of exaggeration, which invades our collective cultural imagination. In its initial form, shopping is motivated by the needs of daily life: anthropologically, it can be seen as an evolution of the activities, in primitive tribes, of the ancient hunters-gatherers who spent much of the day in search of food and other gifts of the land, in order to guarantee satisfying the needs of the members of the tribe. Today, as well as buying what is necessary, shopping can have different superficial or profound, conscious or unconscious, balanced or pathological purposes. Exploring the territory and going in search of objects, shopping offers many people a sort of active power which, if in some cases makes up for deficiencies in some spheres of their lives, for others it acts as a defence against feelings of emptiness and a lack of significance. When we give into shopping and fantasize, look for and in the end obtain the object of our desires, we relive, in some way, that comforting experience linked to the privileged relationship of our past, that of child-mother when, after food, we felt relaxed, satisfied and protected (Oliverio Ferraris, 2002). When the object to be purchased becomes a narcissistic object, then signs of inner distress may come into play.

Shopping addiction describes a pathological case characterized by recurring concerns and impulses aimed at looking for and excessively buying goods, which are often superfluous or of a greater value than one's economic possibilities; it occupies the person for longer than the time intended, it entails a compromise of the social and professional functioning and is often associated with feelings of guilt, shame and negative emotive experiences (McElroy et al., 1994). The goods that are purchased, the preference for some shops or periods of the season (purchases are sometimes intensified at special occasions such as Christmas, family birthdays or during the sales) and the ways this activity is conducted are, generally, strictly subjective. Unlike other purchasing habits which can be experienced as a time of sharing, sociality, with relatives or friends, pathological shopping is mainly done alone, experienced as a sort of private pleasure, a desire that could however also conceal a certain embarrassment in showing others one's consumption habits, often above their financial possibilities and therefore, if shared with others could arouse criticism, reactions or questions.

Black (2007b) distinguishes four phases through which pathological behaviour is manifested. The first is called Anticipation and is the phase when the person develops a thought or an impulse, relative to the purchase of a specific object or, more in general, the desire to go shopping: this moment is often preceded by feelings of boredom, anxiety, depression or self-devaluation. The second is the phase of Preparation, which concerns the organization of the activity, the identification of the shop or the area where to go shopping, the choice of clothes, accessories and means of payment. This is followed by the third phase, Shopping, with the electrifying and gratifying experience of the purchase, to reach the last one, the Spending phase which usually culminates in the purchase and is also followed by feelings of depression, guilt and self-reproach.

Compulsive shopping was already known at the beginning of the last century (Kraepelin, 1915), under the term of oniomania, meaning the compulsive desire to shop and was classified as a reactive or pathological impulse, together with kleptomania and pyromania.

The compulsive element was then resumed and, although the DSM-IV does not consider this addiction in its diagnostic categories, (Mc Elroy et al., 1994), a diagnostic case of the addiction has been suggested fairly recently which respects the presence of some criteria such as: the presence of concerns and maladaptive drives to make purchases or, more in general, to buying, which are experienced as irresistible, unreasonable and often, with an economic cost superior to one's possibilities. The presence, after the purchase, of a feeling of stress; the considerable amount of time spent, to the detriment of other activities which are necessary such as work or family commitments and the onset of serious economic problems (which at times, as well as debts, often reach insolvency). Lastly, the uncontrolled habit of buying even in the absence of maniacal or hypo-maniacal episodes.

10.1. Etiopathogenetic Models and Therapeutic Approaches

Compulsive shopping is a pathology of which the etiopathogenesis has not been fully understood, also because elements which can be traced back to obsessive-compulsive disorders, but also depression and other themes, which more properly characterize the phenomena of addiction, converge. A recent scientific review on the subject (Pani, Biolcati, 2005) underlines how, in the sphere of psychodynamic comprehension, compulsive shopping is put into relation with feelings of impotence and loss of control deriving from precocious experiences of abuse. The compulsive purchase of gratifying material goods expresses the search for a sort of symbolic nourishment thanks to which the feelings of inner void can be annulled. The thoughts and fantasies linked to the action of the purchase often have characteristics of intrusiveness and repetitiveness which recall those of obsessions and shopping itself can be identified as a compulsion enacted in order to prevent the onset of anxiety and can be described as an attenuated form of the obsessive-compulsive disorder with which it appears to have high rates of comorbidity, especially in the cases where purchasing is associated with a pathological tendency to accumulate objects without value or use.

The choice of consumer goods, in particular clothes, shoes, bags and jewellery, can take on the value of a gesture to repair self-esteem and positively influence the mood; these objects, as well as technological articles or sports goods, allow bringing the image of the ideal Self closer to the real one, reinforcing an image of a weak and instable self and relieving the feelings of interior emptiness and depression. In research on a sample of compulsive shoppers (Faber, O'Guinn, 1992), it was observed that many of the purchasing behaviours are dictated more by the need to relieve negative emotions and raise self-esteem than from the concrete desire to possess that precise object. 85% of the population interviewed however, do not recognize that the purchase can have the function of improving the mood. On the other hand, the prevalence of mood disorders, particularly depressive disorders, amongst the subjects suffering from compulsive shopping and the members of their family, is significant (Lejoyeux et al., 1995).

A further interpretation is offered by McDougall (2004), who suggests that all addiction disorders could originate from an alteration of the development of transactional phenomena in early infancy which prevent the adult from being able to be on his own and cultivate his psychic resources to dominate negative emotions and tensions. The transactional object is effectively destined to give way to conscious and more mature coping strategies of affects, but when this does not occur, it may be replaced by a transitory object such as alcohol, physical exercise or shopping, instruments which are capable of relieving the feelings on anguish and depression.

There are not many contributions on the therapeutic approach to compulsive shopping. Correct information on the pathology which fosters compliance and increases the efficacy of the therapy is also essential in this case of addiction; the need to provide some information of a psycho-educational nature in order to prevent relapses, such as suggesting not paying by credit card or cheques, being accompanied to shops by relatives or friends who can watch over the patient's behaviour and identifying alternative activities should be considered (Kuzma, Black, 2006).

In relation to the psychotherapeutic treatment, cognitive-behavioural therapy has shown good efficacy and stable results, using a model inspired by the twelve-step Minnesota Model, i.e. a multi-disciplinary programme for the treatment of addictions, borrowed from the programme of Alcoholics Anonymous and which lasts ten or twelve weeks with weekly meetings. It uses different instruments which go from keeping a diary of purchases, to self-monitoring, cognitive restructuring and systemic desensitization (Mitchell et al., 2006).

The psychoanalytic approach can, in turn, be considered as elective in the treatment of this addiction. The patient must however decide to start out on treatment with some precise conditions. There must be insight, i.e. the subject must have introspective abilities which allow him to dialogue with himself; tolerance of frustrations; capacity of abstinence; capacity of tolerating the duo or group relationship; capacity to tolerate any sense of shame regarding the invitation, by the therapist to dialogue with the inner judging parts of the self, therefore considered hostile (Di Maria, Formica, 2004).

Psychodynamic therapy can also be recommended for those patients interested in understanding the profound value of their compulsive behaviour, the narcissistic vulnerability and affective deregulation. Through the therapeutic relationship and the analysis of narrations, it is possible to identify the meaning of the symptom and develop alternative coping strategies of the emotions (Pani, Biolcati, 2005).

10.2. Recent Phenomenology of Compulsive Shopping

The marked growth, in the commercial world, of instalment payment or payment by credit card makes the purchase easier, less visible and therefore riskier for compulsive shoppers. Virtual money or, in its concrete immediacy, money that is not visible, can go unobserved and the spending of money can be perceived as less real than when cash is used. It is ideal for pathological shoppers who try to hide as much as possible any shortfall of money to start to pay for an object some time after the real purchase and possibly in instalments, which allows better hiding the expenditure.

The formula of telephone or television sales also represents a non-negligible risk in the incidence of compulsive shopping. Buying objects of very different categories from home, being fascinated and protected by formulas that exclude costs of sale and return and buying at any time in the day certainly hide threats for compulsive shoppers. The development of the Web and its online purchases have also had a strong commercial impact: this opportunity is a resource but, at the same time, also a dangerous incentive for those who are addicted to shopping. Some characteristics of the Web satisfy the needs of the subject who finds immediate gratification of needs and a response to distress.

In the first place (as for the Internet Addiction Disorder), the anonymity which allows the person to express themselves, their dreams and desires, without being seen or known; in this sense there is room for all those behaviours which, if manifested in public, could be the object of criticism and the fear of being judged. The technical characteristics of the instruments must not be underestimated either: the sensory signals that are reproducible thanks to multimedia, evoke particular emotive strata that undermine the subject's capacity of self-observation. Examples of significant sensory stimuli are, for example, the seductive descriptions of the objects for sale, the possibility of enlarging details, the attention to detail and the colours of the photos, the fact that (only on some sites) information on the prices is not immediately available, the announcements of promotions and discounts, the use of a credit card: all these are strategies that stimulate the impulsivity of the purchase. The capacity of judgement and control over one's actions are invalidated on the Internet above all because there is no social or concrete confirmation, linked to the direct experience of the person but, at the most, compulsive shoppers can meet and discuss in chat rooms or on forums, vicariously reinforcing their compulsion.

The Internet also has an influence on the function of self-gratification which acts as a reinforcement for the reiteration of the behaviour. When an object is really purchased in a shop, the satisfaction experience and the pleasure of having it drives the individual to repeat the experience. In the virtual world, it would seem that this reinforcement is absent but, in actual fact, there is also a strong and immediate gratification in online buying which comes not so much from possessing the object but the from the act of purchase in itself. For example, in virtual auctions, the pleasure is that of being awarded the item and the sensation experienced is very similar to that of winning when gambling.

10.3. Comorbidity of Compulsive Shopping

Compulsive shopping is an under-diagnosed pathology thanks to the post-modern cultural atmosphere and the market of emotions that justify it and recognize its symbolic power linked to the sense of realization, success and power (Guerreschi, 2005).

The act of compulsive shopping has something in common with the act of filling oneself up by the bulimic individual, aimed at dispelling tensions through purchasing objects that are useless or of little value and comorbidity with the binge eating disorder and other eating disorders is not infrequent (Mitchell et al., 2002).

Comorbidity with disorders of the control of impulses, kleptomania, obsessive-compulsive disorders, anxiety and mood disorders, other addictions the abuse of benzodiazepine is also high. Depression can be a consequence due to the loss of control but also a cause and shopping thus takes on a consolatory and compensatory role (Black, 2007b).

Compulsive shopping can also appear together with borderline and narcissistic personality disorder (Rose, 2007). Other behavioural addictions are also often present, such as pathological gambling, substance addiction, in particular alcohol and Internet addiction. Lastly, it can be secondary to schizophrenia or dementia (Guerreschi, 2005).

10.4. Pharmacotherapy

Neurobiological correlates of compulsive shopping still have to be adequately examined but they are probably similar to those involved in other disorders of impulse control linked to a dysfunction of the serotonin activities. The disorders linked to this chemical cerebral alteration also cause an absence of control of impulsivity therefore there is a drive to immediately gratify every need. Some studies (Bullock, Koran, 2003) hypothesize that in subjects with an addiction for compulsive shopping, the same modifications in the blood flow at the level of the limbic regions and in particular in the anterior cingulated cortex, can be observed as in gamblers.

Many of the studies on pharmacological therapy in Compulsive Buying include the use of antidepressants. There is abundant literature on the role of selective serotonin re-uptake inhibitors although, to date, the results obtained from the various clinical trials are not conclusive (Lee, Mysk, 2004). Of all the SSRI used in the treatment, the molecule that has shown greatest efficacy and tolerability was citolopram. Koran et al. (2002) verified a marked improvement in the psychopathological picture of subjects affected by compulsive shopping, independently of the comorbidity with other mood disorders; they then demonstrated that maintenance therapy contributed to a significant reduction in relapses.

A more recent proposal (Guzman et al., 2007) is topiramate: the inhibition of the release of glutamate, associated with the boost of the GABAergic inhibiting activity induced by topiramate, is believed to cause an adequate control of compulsive behaviour.

11. SPORT ADDICTION. PAIN AND MUSCLES

Every single person establishes a complex and dialect relationship with their physical nature; the body represents the physical dimension of the identity and, if at some times, we can feel that the body is an ally, as an object of admiration and pleasure, at others it may be perceived as separate from us, independent and detached from our will. At other times, it betrays us and instead of complying with our expectations and needs, it seems to follow another direction.

The practice of regular exercise, i.e. the traditional daily activities that imply movement and entail a growth in the expenditure of energy, physical exercise with structured programmes and sport with its activities subject to rules, are all effective practices aimed at improving the health and therefore valid responses to the natural needs for well-being.

The desire to be fit, however, can be taken to exasperation and lead to the trap of fully-fledged forms of addiction: physical exercise and sport become real obsessions with training which, very often, is transformed into over-training. Sport is progressively transformed from a healthy and harmonious therapeutic instrument into an activity at risk of physical pathologies and psychosocial imbalance, due to the exclusive investment of interest that limits all balance in the other spheres of life of a sport addict who is continuously engaged unhealthy and unsafe forms of training (La Barbera et al., 2008).

One of the signals of alarm of sport addiction is the presence of problems of physical health and mood swings linked to excessive training which can generate a real syndrome of overtraining, a physiological condition of imbalance which derives from excessive or frequently repeated efforts, which do not allow the organism to recover energy and work of effort (Cascua, 2004). The presence of this overtraining generally indicates a quantitative excess of training which could also be linked to a poor management of physical exercise for reasons connected with a lack of information on the risks deriving from some incorrect behaviour in the training phase or also from a disproportionate effort to achieve competitive objectives. This is to say that abuse of sport, even when it entails psychophysical disorders, does not always represent a certain symptom of the real presence of addiction of physical exercise: like an exaggerated consumption of alcohol, for a limited period, which does not make a person dependent on alcohol.

The variables that allow a correct identification of the problem are represented by some qualitative signals that allow discriminating the positive falsities (Caretti, La Barbera, 2009).

The first signal of alarm is the inclination to train alone: many addicts prefer to do physical activity on their own because in this way they are neither observed nor judged. This habit is often associated with lying about their training habits, the time spent in the gym, the number of sets of exercises carried out, the use of particular apparatus etc. Another indicator of risk is the change in habits and behaviour in the social sphere, with a tendency to spend less time in friendly contexts, missing occasions of leisure in the family and with friends, forgetting study or work commitments or other recreational activities. An increase in the time spent in training also represents another element which distinguishes loss of control: physical activity gradually tends to grow until all other daily activities are compromised. One more psychological characteristic that could indicate addiction is the presence of emotional tensions in the absence of training: some sport addicts show increased frustration, anxiety or anger in the presence of factors which disturb or interrupt training.

A further factor of suspicion is represented by the inclination to train, even if injured or in a condition of generally poor health: it is on these occasions that real forms of overtraining are carried out since for the athlete the torment of succeeding in developing his muscles is so pervasive that he continues training without heeding pain and trauma deriving from excessive exercise (at times the muscles are so ruthlessly strained that blood blisters are formed that have to be emptied of the excess blood).

The obsession to improve the physical appearance of the body, which can be manifested with an obsessive search to control weight and therefore with eating disorders, or with an obsessive search for the ideal physique represents an important indicator of risk of sport addiction. The risk of transforming a healthy habit into an obsessive unhealthy activity appears closely linked to the reasons why sport is done, in turn fuelled by ways of conceiving physical exercise that are not always correct.

Addiction to physical exercise is developed when the motivation for sport is closely connected to the improvement of the physical appearance or the development of energies and, consequently, to feeling perfectly fit. The representation of sport as an instrument to positively transform the aesthetic aspect of the body is typical of the imagination of female sport addicts who are motivated to exercise and seek increasingly suitable methods to sculpt the body and who, very often, develop other disorders, such as eating disorders.

Men, on the other hand, manifest attention to physical exercise as it can increase the muscular mass, tone the body and increase the feeling of well-being.

The people who develop more easily an addiction to physical exercise are those who tend to channel all their energy into a single sport, restricting themselves to a single and exclusive physical activity, which tends to give them a great feeling of well-being.

The way in which sports are practised seems, at times, to encourage or support the onset of an addiction: some disciplines, such as body building, swimming, running etc. offer greater possibilities of training in isolation, compared to others which, due to their intrinsic characteristics, require interaction and confrontation with team members. In the same way, self-managed fitness programmes can fuel obsessive behaviour by the athlete, because he has no coach or personal trainer to offer a competent and balanced perspective with respect to the presence of quantitative abuse, excessive specific activities or attitudes that can show a disharmonious relationship with training.

11.1. Bigorexia

As a consequence, although the body is an essential constitutive part of our identity, we tend to objectivize it, making it become the recipient of a series of images and actions.

Amongst the possible distorted expressions of the body image, muscular dysmorphia or bigorexia appears as a strong feeling of dissatisfaction with one's muscles, associated with the obsessive tendency to constantly increase their mass. The origin of the name comes from the combination of the English prefix 'big' with the Latin term 'orexis' (appetite). This condition is also known as the Adonis Complex and tends to stress the presence of what is called a hunger for largeness.

The disorder consists of an unmotivated fear of becoming too weak and thin in relation to the muscular mass and generates dissatisfaction with respect to one's physical consistency, a feeling which is tackled by obsessive activities aimed at developing the muscular mass through physical exercise and, sometimes, dietary abuse or protein supplements (Stevani, 2007).

Until not very long ago, the desire to be identified with an ideal model was considered a prerogative of the feminine gender and therefore, for several decades, the focus of attention concerning body image disorders was concentrated on women, with little concern about how men also relate to their masculine ideal of physical appearance. As women were for a long time, men can also be strongly oriented to creating a series of destructive anxieties concerning their body and, as Pope et al. (2000) note, they often have in their past a history of anxiety, mood disorders and obsessive-compulsive traits.

Attention is paid, in particular, to three possible determinants of the disorder which do not operate totally independent of one another, therefore it would nevertheless be appropriate to prefer an etiology of the multifactor type.

In the first place there is a genetic factor, i.e. in this case too, a predisposing biological component whereby some subjects would appear to be particular inclined to develop symptoms of the obsessive-compulsive type. In bigorexia, the obsessive component is closely connected to the body image and, more precisely, to the development of muscles and the fear of appearing thin, whilst the compulsion is in the constant effort to reach the desired levels of muscular power, which is concretized in exasperatedly checking the body in the mirror, becoming dominant in the life of the addict: it is the blackboard on which to draw, in an obsessive and hallucinatory way, the corporality desired.

According to Choi et al. (2002), some men may be aware that their obsessive convictions are really inadequate and irrational, but this awareness does not restrain them from continuing with self-destructive behaviour for their health and psychological balance.

The second explanation as one of the causes of bigorexia is of a psychological nature and underlines the low self-esteem of sport addicts and the way they tend to judge themselves, i.e. appearance. By exaggeratedly concentrating on their physical appearance, they develop an altered perception of their body, becoming increasingly sensitive and attentive to anomalies or any defects. They live in the perennial comparison of their physique with those of other men and the result of the perception that derives from this is invariably to their disadvantage.

In actual fact, the suffering and anguish that the image reflected by the mirror provokes in bigorexics is a product of their mind, on which different elements such as mood or expectations act. An exaggerated investment in the image is typical of narcissists but a form of healthy narcissism, understood as adequate personal care aimed at improving the image (for example through healthy and balanced exercise, including of body building) must be distinguished from an unhealthy, pathological form, where the investment in the self-image is absolute and annuls all other personal awareness that is not based on the exterior appearance. Thus, for many sport addicts, non-stop physical exercise becomes a narcissistic activity where muscular strength is not a means to feel better with themselves and others but becomes a goal to reach to elude and make up for an inner emptiness.

The third explanation of the origin of bigorexia is cultural. Post-modern society is strongly concentrated on the image and how we appear to the external world is very often more important than what we really are. This may cause the sense of identity to vacillate, constantly solicited by messages that stress the value of strength and physical appearance. As the body image is intimately connected with self-esteem and the sense of self-efficacy, the messages spread by the culture risk laying the foundations for a generation of people dissatisfied with their bodies, not due to lack of attractiveness but due to the responsibility of society which sends the imperative that it is necessary to show oneself off at one's best. This observation introduces a further reflection and the need to face up to another serious danger, connected with bigorexia, i.e. that the subjects obsessed by the unrealistic ideal of transforming their bodies into masses of developed muscles, can easily fall into the trap of the abuse of anabolic steroids or other substances without which it would be even harder to achieve their aspirations.

Solving the problem of sport addiction is not a rapid process and requires several passages. The first step consists of recognizing the problem: this is a fundamental moment which must be followed by reaching a phase of psychological and emotional predisposition to change where the subject becomes willing to do everything necessary to solve the addition.

In a further passage, there is the possibility of having recourse to professional help, as the obsessive practice of sport is connected with deep personal dissatisfaction of which the subject is not always aware. This means that it is necessary to involve various professional figures such as doctors, dieticians and psychologists who can help regain balance and well-being on the physical side, in the diet, in behaviour and in the psychological sphere.

12. AESTHETIC ADDICTION. THE POWER OF THE SCALPEL

Every period and every culture has its own model of beauty to which, more or less consciously, each individual tends to relate. The body thus becomes the place where hopes and desires meet, and clash with pain and failure. Through the body today, one's self-esteem and recognition of one's identity can be constructed and fuelled: the dissatisfaction linked to the body image and the consequent non-acceptance of the self are the elements with which the possibility of success and achievement are measured. The image becomes the representative and interpretative criterion of reality. The cultural and existential challenge is therefore played out on the image of the body. In this way, a cultural collective imagination is endorsed and boosted that stakes everything on aesthetic standards in a real dictatorship of the body. The media industry transmits, almost imposing them, social models, lifestyles and ways of behaviour that combine aesthetic ideals, all to the advantage of the appearance. The current situation of crisis and doubt leaves rooms for few certainties where refuge and consolation can be sought. Feeling beautiful and in harmony with one's body is a dream as common as it is difficult to achieve. Our epoch is characterized as being increasingly linked to well-being and the physical aspect. After having adopted the benefits deriving from the enormous progress made in the medical field, which has directly influenced the lengthening of the average human lifespan, there is increasing concentration today on treatment that aims at aesthetic perfection. Surgery, scalpels and operating theatres are increasingly transformed into sanctuaries where perfection is sought.

Over the years, plastic surgery has refined its techniques and these have now become a habit: botulinum, liposuction, laser depilation and facelifts. It is not only women who are captivated by plastic surgery to be more beautiful; the number of men who go under the knife to reduce their mammary glands (especially after a certain age) or to reinvigorate weakened abdominals is growing. A study published by Eurisko and Q-Med in 2011, out of a sample of some ten thousand people aged between 18 and 55 in Italy, Germany, the USA, China and South Korea, showed that about 50% of the interviewees would have plastic surgery to feel more comfortable with their bodies. For Italians, there is no age group that is better than others to go to the plastic surgeon (it makes no difference from 15 to 44). To make their physical appearance more attractive, closely connected with improved well-being in general, more than half would take into consideration the hypothesis of having surgery, choosing the face for the operation and not disdaining the idea of operations on several parts of the body.

It is not only the extensive spread of interest in cosmetic surgery, independently of gender and social class, that is increasingly worthy of attention, but it is the attraction that it has for an increasingly younger population, with the result that in Italy legislation was introduced a short time ago prohibiting surgery solely for aesthetic reasons on minors under 18. This also emerges from the survey carried out by AICPE, the Italian Association of Aesthetic Plastic Surgeons, amongst Italian plastic surgeons (2012). Three hundred and forty-seven specialists from all over Italy (the most represented region is Emilia Romagna, followed by Lombardy and Veneto) answered the multi-answer questionnaire. The interviewees performed 52,878 operations in 2011 whilst the non-surgical operations, i.e. aesthetic medicine, numbered over 170,000.

The plastic surgery that was most practised in 2011 was additive mastoplasty: 11,300 operations to increase the size of the bust. This was followed by liposuction to remove excess fat (10,267 operations) and in the third place blepharoplasty to rejuvenate the eyes (8,121). Amongst the non-surgical operations, injection of hyaluronic acid was the most in demand (46,909), followed by botulinum (40,394) and in third place laser depilation (13,374).

As the Eurispes Report Italy (2012) shows, recourse to surgery for aesthetic purposes has become a non-negligible aspect of the hedonistic drift of our times over the past thirty years. The number of medical centres, mostly private, where a new appearance can be chosen, has multiplied. The affordability, the multiplication of the centres and above all the improvement in and standardization of the techniques have led to the spread of aesthetic surgery and have made it, if not a mass phenomenon, at least an option that is accessible to almost all. In addition, the idea that surgery can be available not only for adults who do not want to age, but also for those for whom the imperative of beauty is a must, including adolescents, is now widespread. The spread of the practices of modification and manipulation of the body also entails, as well as a reflection of a cultural type on social changes, the need to underline the possible risks for health and at a psychological level.

12.1. The Increasing Exhibition of Post-Modern Bodies

Culture determines the appearance of the body, defining its limits and meanings. Today, in this age of globalization, the body is increasingly controlled by others, by the techniques in which culture risks being reduced to a decorative aspect and we see the rise of a need for public space where points of view can be shared and where we can endeavour to understand this increasingly indecipherable world (Depetris, 2011). It is an instrument with infinite and also mysterious potential: it allows us to know, produce, work, create, establish affective relations and communicate, but sometimes it is also a heavy burden that is difficult to carry, an obstacle to relations and can be an unacceptable torment for the individual who does not recognize himself in it.

There are many variables that intervene in acquiring one's body image and its acceptance, from the biological ones to the social ones, psychological and cultural, philosophical, aesthetic and even economic.

Its knowledge thus comes into being and develops in a historically encoded cultural reality and in a developmental process that involves the biological aspect of the person but also, and above all, the emotive and affective aspect. When one learns to know one's body, an important goal has been reached, made up of a long journey of many sacrifices and much suffering.

If, from the 1980s, the representation of corporality offered by the media was varied and less anchored to the stereotypes of gender, in post-modern culture, there is a tendency to give value to only one physical model with the characteristics of slenderness, muscular tone and youthfulness. Both genders are invited not to age and to eliminate every sign of passing time. Disciplining the body with physical exercise, diets and the maniacal care of each individual part is ideally rewarded by success in every sphere of life, power, well-being and therefore with attaining happiness as greatly desired (Capecchi, Ruspini, 2009).

The increasing dramatization of the body by the media takes place, on the one hand, by giving great significance to the exterior physical aspect of the subjects that populate the different kinds of content (whether advertising, fiction, reality shows, etc.) and decreeing, with success or failure, the positive or negative aspects of certain looks and some bodies, and on the other hand, by offering to anyone who wishes the opportunity to show off their image with the physical exposure of their bodies which is facilitated by the new information and communication technologies (from video phones to the Web and social networks, etc.).

The careful construction and presentation of the exterior aspect becomes the main credential used by the social actor to relate to others: a phenomenon which can be defined as social display where the dominant model consists of putting on show what is private, from thoughts to the actions of the body, even the most intimate (Codeluppi, 2007).

This attention to appearance and the maniacal care of the body in its external and aesthetic expression become the domain of narcissism. For the narcissist, the Self is the object of love that must be nourished by the approval of others and the line of demarcation between a decision for a valid aesthetic operation and an illegitimate decision, according to Battista (2008), lies in the fact that it is required more to please others than to please oneself. If the operation is wanted because it is fashionable or is to make an impression, then the aesthetic surgeon must ask several questions, to the patient and himself, before operating. It is normal to have an optimal interior perception of the corporeal Ego, but different when an obsessive search for perfection is enacted, which leads to unnecessary and excessive aesthetic surgery.

It may seem paradoxical, but in some cases, the responsibility to stop unjustified operations should come from the aesthetic surgeon himself. It is his task to recognize excessive and unsuitable requests and refuse to perform multiple operations on unsuitable candidates. The typical signs of unsuitability are: difficulty by the patient to accurately describe the imperfection to be eliminated; concern for objectively non-existent defects; the desire to have the operation to please other people (partner, parents, friends etc.); the refusal to consider the risks; the presence of states of anxiety or depression; the inappropriateness of the operation with respect to the patient's age; dissatisfaction with previous procedures of aesthetic surgery (Di Maria, Formica, 2005).

12.2. Diagnostic Problems of Body Dysmorphic Disorder

Disorders related to body image are culturally normative and, often, are not manifestations of the individual pathology (Lemma, 2005). However, the awareness of social pressure and the simple exposure to it are not sufficient to explain this type of disorder and dependence: people generally pursue an ideal of beauty and look after their body, but not all of them enter into the vortex of beauty and become slaves to it, to the point of developing clinically significant levels of disorder.

Very often, the pursuit of aesthetic surgery conceals the Body Dysmorphic Disorder, classified by the main diagnostic manuals (DSM-IV-TR, 2004), as a Somatoform Disorder, a category which includes pathologies such as Hypochondria or the Somatization Disorder.

Body Dysmorphic Disorder has been known in Italy since 1886 when Morselli described it as a subjective sensation of deformity or physical defect, for which the patient thought he was noticed by others, although his appearance is within the norm. The patient's primary symptom is the conviction of not being attractive or of having exterior physical defects that are thought to be obvious for others but which, objectively, come within the parameters of normality (Andreasen, Bardach, 1977).

Patients with the disorder are obsessed by the characteristics of one or more parts of their body and this leads them to behaviour which is repetitive to the limit of obsession, such as constantly looking in the mirror, continuously asking friends and family to receive assurance about their appearance. Any type of consolation, however, only brings temporary relief and does not reduce the dissatisfaction or the distress that becomes the soundtrack of the existence of the aesthetic perfection addict. The feelings and attitudes associated with this disorder are shame and the paranoid conviction that everyone looks at and judges their appearance; shunning all those situations that require exposure to the gaze of others, from the work environment to sentimental relations and relations in general, to arrive at a voluntary estrangement from social life. If obliged to be with other people, they not infrequently cover themselves up with clothes or go out at the loneliest and darkest times of day and night.

For these people, the only solution is aesthetic surgery which however can turn out to be ineffective: the image reflected by the mirror is not the one that was imagined and therefore the operation ends up by worsening the disorder and aggravating the psychological distress.

The diagnosis of Body Dysmorphic Disorder is also not easy due to the lack of recognition by the patients that they feel distress, precisely of this type. They often complain of generalized pain or burning that orient clinicians towards pathologies of a physiological and not psychological type. Usually there are three criteria that have to be satisfied to diagnose Body Dysmorphic Disorder (DSM IV-TR, 2004). Criteria A requires that the patient is preoccupied with an imagined defect. If the anomaly is present, the concern is markedly excessive; criterion B requires a preoccupation that causes clinically significant distress or impairment in social or occupational functioning and criterion C when the preoccupation is not better accounted for by another mental disorder. The diagnosis is also more complicated due to the massive presence of recurrent thoughts and repetitive actions that lead to the need to differentiate between Body Dysmorphic Disorder and Obsessive-Compulsive Disorder. A clinician should be oriented towards the former in the case in which the obsessions or compulsions are limited to preoccupations concerning the physical appearance only. The difficult differential diagnosis has led to a distinction being made between primary and Secondary, or Symptomatic Body Dysmorphic Disorder: the former is equivalent to the Body Dysmorphic Disorder, in the absence of other pathologies, the latter is to be considered as a non-specific symptom of other disorders such as Anorexia Nervosa or Obsessive-Compulsive Disorder.

13. DIETARY ADDICTION. EATING HEALTHY FOOD AT ALL COSTS

The food alarms launched by the media in recent years have influenced a new attitude towards food, which is different from anorexia and bulimia: orthorexia nervosa, i.e. an obsession with eating healthy food. It is a sort of maniacal attention to nutrition, to pure food, but it conceals much more: the dependent subjects are obsessed by a diet that allows them to stay healthy or become healthier, that purifies them and leads them to a state of perfect health.

Bratman (2000), observing the spread of an increasingly neurotic relationship with the food we eat, in such a maniacal relationship as to completely condition existence, coined the term orthorexia, from the Greek 'ortho', or 'right', 'correct' and 'orexis', i.e. 'desire', 'appetite'. This disorder is comparable to anorexia and bulimia, with the difference that whilst these two pathologies are correlated to the quantity of food, orthorexia is correlated to the quality of food. In addition, unlike bulimia and anorexia, the fear of gaining weight is not present but rather there it is more of a phobia, which can be specific to varying degrees, for certain foods that are considered impure or toxic.

Orthorexia has a great deal in common with eating disorders: the obsessive preoccupation for food invades the whole life of the patient, fostering social isolation, perceptive distortion can be present with respect to body shapes or the negation of corporeal signs of illness and the tendency to negate or not recognize emotions, feelings and conflicts, typical of the deficit of affective regulation, can be observed. Its dramatic resemblance with the anxiety disorder characterized by the presence of excessive preoccupations which are involuntary but irrepressible, by obsessions and repeated and irrepressible obsessions and behaviour, which take on the form of real rituals, for the purpose of reducing anguish. In Western society, the relationship with food is taking on, in an increasingly significant way, connotations with a strongly neurotic value. The eating disorder, due to its links with body identity, today profoundly linked to security of the Self and the obsession of appearances, lends itself to express a set of fears and contradictions that characterize our time (Della Ragione, 2005).

13.1. Identikit of the Orthorexic

Typically the orthorexic, following a dietary philosophy or theory (for example starting a macrobiotic diet or a specific diet for a particular blood group etc.) progressively becomes so maniacal about the diet as to begin to develop increasingly specific food rules, from simply carefully reading labels to choosing organic and genuine foods, to using a gradually longer and longer time to plan meals that can be several days in advance. When he goes out, he tends to take with him a survival kit with his own foods, because he cannot tolerate eating dishes made by others due to a fear of swallowing contaminated foods.

Schematically, the commonest symptoms that characterize orthorexics are as follows: they feel a strong need to know every single ingredient in the food and to plan every meal and they have an intense fear of contaminating their body. They express disgust at filling their body with substances that are not natural and want to continue purifying themselves. They are very severe with themselves and have feelings of guilt when they stray from the diet, accompanied by a sense of repulsion for the people who eat normally, to the point of having difficulties in relating with those who do not agree with their ideas on food.

The impairment of social relations are clear because the subject could begin to avoid eating with other people: this is probably the immediate effect of greatest importance, but orthorexia can, in particularly serious cases, have important physical consequences linked to malnutrition, like anorexia nervosa, as well as, naturally, the psychological suffering which consists of guilt feelings, depression, anxiety and phobia. Subjects who are addicted to eating healthily are included in the Eating Disorders – Not Otherwise Specified.

With respect to personality traits, the orthorexic individual can also show, like the restrictive anorexic, obsessive traits, psychological rigidity, perfectionism and need for control. Healthy food addicts think continuously about what they can do to obtain the right and appropriate food; from the morning they plan their day according to looking for shops and the food that they will have for lunch and dinner. The obsessive compulsive disorder appears, in the orthorexic, in the diet. The cognitive style is also characteristic: extremely logical, rational, distinguished by rigidity, attention to detail, lack of flexibility and spontaneousness.

Orthorexics have ritualized eating behaviour: they cut up their food with great precision, chew it a specific number of times and often eat in total solitude.

Obliged by the obsessive-compulsive syndrome, they concentrate their methodical and strict ritual on the food plan. They have a perfect knowledge of the nutritional components of each product, they can list with absolute accuracy the percentages of unsaturated and saturated fats in a food, the number of calories it contains etc. Their fixation overturns the scale of values: food becomes more important than anything and, obsessed by food, the addict loses the pleasure of having other life experiences, including the capacity to love and have desires beyond that of food, including sexual desire, work and learning to socialize.

Concentrating on food is an obsession, self-discipline is transformed into self-punishment and dependence; depression, anxieties, phobias and stress make progress which lead to a deterioration in the quality of life. Their diet, marked by the steps of planning, identifying, cooking and eating food, goes beyond the physiological meaning of nutrition to reach other meanings full of symbols, many yet to be discovered (Di Maria, Formica, 2006).

This addiction is apparently generated by well-being which affects, before others, affluent individuals and with particular characteristics and social roles that they become sources of identification for people of all genders, ages and social conditions.

In Italy the disorder appears to affect in particular people belonging to medium-high classes because, economically, it is rather expensive to eat organically but, according to some studies, the phenomenon is on the increase.

There are not many studies on this subject in Italy. One of the most significant was carried out by Donini et al. (2004, 2005) at the La Sapienza University of Rome, in collaboration with the Institute of Food Science of the NR (National Research Council) of Avellino. This study, conducted over two years, was designed to identify the dimensions of the phenomenon of orthorexia in Italy and involved a sample of 404 subjects who were given a test for diagnosis called ORTO-15. The results showed a definitely alarming situation: at least 7% of the subjects examined suffered from orthorexia nervosa.

13.2. Approaches to the Treatment of Orthorexia

It is clear that this dependence is determined above all by anxiety and has numerous characteristics in common both with eating disorders and with the Obsessive Compulsive Disorder: the excessive fear of being contaminated, in orthorexic subjects, drives them to compulsive avoidant behaviour of multiple foods that has the sole aim of sedating the anxiety of contamination. The first step in treating a subject suffering from orthorexia, like the one who has an obsessive-compulsive disorder, is essentially that of attenuating the fears linked to the obsession and being able to make the subject aware that the compulsions of obtaining from abstaining from eating certain foods considered harmful, lead to a temporary well-being linked exclusively to the control of anxiety.

Behavioural cognitive therapy combined with some SSRI antidepressants can be useful in the treatment, in analogy with the obsessive-compulsive disorder. Unfortunately, the orthorexic patient is obsessed by purity or a natural diet and could be terrorized by the idea of taking drugs. At the same time, being so attentive to his health, he could favourably accept something that he recognizes can no longer be postponed for his physical and psychological well-being.

14. COMBINATIONS OF 21ST CENTURY ADDICTIONS

To conclude, a brief excursus on some of the new non-drug addictions which distinguish this 21st century of ours. They are only some of the many and possibly, in appearance, extravagant addictions but all of them can always be interpreted as strong signals of the condition of great fragility of the post-modern identity.

Amongst those linked both to the eating disorders and the Obsessive-Compulsive Disorder we can find: the Gourmet Syndrome which affects people suffering from a particular cumulative disorder linked to niche gastronomic products and who exclusively cook and eat high quality and very expensive food; Drunkorexia, today particularly fashionable amongst the very young and in particular young women. Those who do not want to give up alcohol and social occasions linked to this habit, make up the calories from alcohol by skipping meals, reaching the point where these are replaced by alcohol. Then there is the Sweet Tooth which is not only known, in its botanical meaning as a strain of cannabis but is the obsessive search for sweet food. Lastly, Chocaholics, those who are obsessed by chocolate in all its forms: it is debatable whether to treat this as a dependence as apparently it does not produce abstinence but certainly dependence due to its boosting the level of serotonin in the brain.

Amongst those linked with conflicts with their image, we can recall Tanorexia, which is the compulsion of exaggerated exposure to the sun, despite awareness of the damage to the skin. People who are dependent on a tanned appearance are never fully satisfied, just as anorexics perceive themselves as always too fat, tanorexics always see themselves as pale. If they cannot be exposed to the sun, they overdo the use of sun lamps or self-tanning products. The opposite of this is Tanaphobia: an irrational fear of the sun, its rays and in general of light. These people avoid sunlight and expose themselves to the outside world completely covered by clothes, hats and other protection. Their behaviour is not to be interpreted as prevention of the onset of melanoma but a real obsession for diaphanous skin. In the long term, this attitude can cause a deficit of Vitamin D in the body. Blondarexia, or the obsession for blonde hair, is, on the other hand, a dependence greatly linked to fashion and figures of reference belonging to the world of the media. The people who suffer from this, obsessed by the aesthetic indications of the media, bleach their hair in a maniacal way to the point of weakening their hair and skin. Then there is Tatoorexia, the obsession for tattoos on a body which becomes a canvas, but with the risk of representing an identity which is not always authentic and coherent.

Conclusion

In recent years, social psychology has contributed to studying subjective well-being in depth and the factors that influence it, so that we can go beyond the simple conceptualization of well-being as happiness and satisfaction for life, to propose more articulated definitions and highlight a variety of cognitive and psychosocial processes that are involved in the subjective experience of well-being.

As has been amply documented in the text, post-modern culture bases its construct and its dynamic in the impoverishment of value horizons and of the existential sense, with the consequent loss of strong and univocal references. Every single individual is at grips with unlimited freedom but also an unsustainable responsibility of having to define the limits between licit and illicit. Today, finding personal equilibrium in well-being means contrasting the sense of vacuity that characterizes the post-modern personality.

A passion for risky activities also becomes the expression of our contemporary world, suffocated by exaggerations. The lack of legitimacy of the parameters of the meanings and values, their homogeneity in a society where everything becomes provisional, upsets the social and cultural patterns that form the fabric of life.

In the present age, risk takes on multiple forms and meanings which, however, are related. Taking risks has become a significant psychological and sociological phenomenon: to go beyond oneself, cross one's limits, discover them, surpass them, show that it can be done, are attitudes used by our young people and by sensation seekers.

Facing a risk aims at symbolically enchanting death. It is always a question of exposing oneself, or taking risks and temporarily abandoning comfort and security, of pushing the body to the extreme of its resources, of going beyond and being symbolically, for a varying period of time, on the brink between living and dying.

Binge drinking, drug addiction, accidents, the various types of at-risk behaviour, running away, suicide attempts and anorexia reach significant statistics in adolescence. The common denominator of these social crystallizations lies in the symbolic contact with death, conquered through an intimate search for meanings.

The sensation seeker submits himself voluntarily to a dangerous ordeal. Risk is a way of verifying the personal power of the individual and testing his solidity. In parallel, it also procures an exaltation which leads to an intimate sense of control.

Amongst the risky attitudes, the excessive consumption of alcohol is a serious problem.

The consumption of alcohol amongst young and very young people is a problem of social importance that must call on everyone, and in particular the institutions, to realize that it is not a transitory phenomenon restricted to a minority of the youth population, but is assuming worrying characteristics for styles and habits, even in youngsters of 11 or 12. There are often reports in the press of young people who even risk their lives due to excessive consumption of alcohol.

They have recourse to alcohol as a facilitator of social relations with a consequent reduction of inhibitions. The effects on health are however devastating because an adolescent's organism is still developing and alcohol slows down mental development and alters emotions. If initially it offers sensations of euphoria and well-being, it then depresses and young people feel emptied and anxious, with continuous mood changes. Young people drink because this way they feel confident, become more talkative, less shy and before their group of friends they acquire visibility. Those who do not drink are considered outsiders, subjects who do not break the rules and are soon marginalized from the group.

It is essential to prevent this form of distress: primary prevention must be fostered and must start very early on, as soon as the cognitive capacities allow it.

There is not only alcohol: there is also the danger of behavioural dependences. According to Steinberg (2004), there are two factors potentially involved in the development of dependences: changes in the sensitivity to the reward, because the passage from childhood to adolescence entails the need for a greater stimulation to reach a state of pleasure and the development of self-regulatory functions. These functions entail the possibility of reflecting before acting and the capacity of interrupting at-risk behaviour, directing actions towards more adequate choices.

All the factors that encourage a good adaptation and an adequate psycho-relational development, during adolescence, represent powerful factors of protections with respect to the possibility of developing conditions of dependence. It is therefore fundamental to evaluate the personal resources, the relational capacities and the family, educational and social context. The best prevention must be based, as well as on early information, on strong and secure family bonds.

The influence of parents and adults in general are pre-eminent in the socialization processes during the years of childhood. In the adolescent years, on the other hand, educational messages are less effective because the influences of contemporaries and the drive to oppose the world of adults in general are stronger. At this age, it is very useful to continue educating about health at primary school and discuss with adolescents the risks to which dependences expose them in the life cycle.

There are countless dangers. Young people are susceptible to developing various forms of dependence such as, for example, gambling, technological dependences, mobile phone dependence, eating disorders, compulsive shopping, sport addiction or relational dependence, because they are seeking immediate saturation of their needs and have difficulty in forgoing desired and needs, following the characteristic tendency of acting impulsively. The speed and rapidity of experiences thus become greatly sought-after and desired elements and, in general, exercise great appeal for that particular section of the population.

Beyond the specific object of dependence, or of the adolescent as an emblematic example of a dependent subject, it has to be remembered that, due to the particular susceptibility of post-modern identity to develop a dysfunctional mode of relation with gratifying objects that have addictive potential, it appears fundamental to hypothesize actions of primary and secondary prevention, raising the awareness of the general population on the risks and possible harmful effects of some types of behaviour that enjoy wide social consensus and which risk becoming a public health problem with a high social and health impact difficult to solve.

To conclude, a reflection on the subject of seeking well-being as the search for a personal value.

Some suggestions. The first one: to aim for subjective well-being as personal equilibrium that no longer has the characteristics of going "beyond" well-being. The second one: to look at life and all experiences, relations and choices from a new perspective, to recover a value that is being lost forever, attention.

Seeking well-being as an expression of a personal value means using a simple instrument but one that has fallen into disuse in post-modern culture where everything, from the lifestyle to the style of education, seems to be oriented towards speed, superficiality and multitasking. It means asking a question: in our life, what do we really want to put the spotlight of our attention on?

Whatever action is being carried out, focusing oneself means concentrating on an objective, directing energy, choosing the most suitable strategies to achieve success and gaining in psychological and physiological well-being.

The ability to see things in the right perspective, the art of being able to understand the various alternatives existing to face up to situations, the capacity to adapt to unforeseen events and be able to react to change, are feasible only if there has been a very precise focus on our actions. Only if we lead balanced lives.

This allows reaching an optimal state in experiences, because life, work and actions in general can be interpreted as a healthy challenge to our competences. The conscious and intelligent control of our attention could become the *conditio sine qua non* for a serene and well-balanced but energetic existence and the key to improve many aspects of our lives and therefore our personal well-being (Tappatà, 2011).

We can have exceptional experiences, whilst living our normal lives, if only we concentrate our attention on very precise goals or if we direct it towards ourselves or towards the sensations and emotions that we feel: if only we choose to live a focused life.

Concentrating on thoughts, people and events is by no means the only way to gain in personal awareness but it is certainly a good way, a healthy opportunity to reach well-being, understood in this sense as a form of equilibrium.

Attention controls our awareness. Even in everyday life, a high or low level of concentration for what we are doing, boosts or compromises the quality of our actions and our relations.

We can decide to lead a life focused on objectives, sensations, emotions and actions to reach optimal experiences or not.

Our mindfulness, i.e. that aware attention, which allows us to concentrate on ourselves and on life, in a deliberate way, linked to the present and in the absence of judgement is something that has to be practised and earned with commitment and balance.

Through mindfulness, each one of us learns something about ourselves: we observe our sensations and perceptions, we perceive the physical nature of our body, the breadth of our emotions, we learn the power of concentration and the curiosity of exploration. Promoting openness of the mind and mindfulness allows enjoying new ways of knowing and being, listening more carefully to our personal experience, moment after moment.

By being captured by the action of attention, whether it is for reading a novel, conceiving a major project, a prayer or reflection, and boosting our capacity for concentration, we extend the borders of our mind, raise our spirit and allow ourselves to perceive and relish everyday life in a more complete way and we achieve the healthy value of well-being and personal equilibrium.

REFERENCES

A.A. V.V. (2010). Guida ai social network. Facebook, Youtube e gli altri. *Altroconsumo*, 233, Supplemento n. 2, gennaio 2010.

Aicpe - Associazione Italiana di Chirurghi Plastici Estetici. (2012). Rapporto ANW - Agenzia News World. www.aicpe/org.

Albano, T., Gulimanoska, L. (2006). In-dipendenza: un percorso verso l'autonomia. In *Manuale sugli aspetti eziopatogenetici, clinici e psicologici delle dipendenze*. Volume 1, Franco Angeli: Milano.

Altieri, E. (1991). *Tracce di libertà. Gli adolescenti tra autonomia e dipendenza. Nuove modalità di relazioni familiari*. Angeli: Milano.

Anderson, P., Baumberg, B. (2006). Alcohol in Europe. Public Health Perspective: Report summary, *Drug: Education, Prevention e Polity,* 13, (6), 483-8.

Ania, Associazione Nazionale fra le Imprese Assicuratrici. (2010). www.ania.it/.

Andreasen, N.C., Bardach, J. (1977). Dysmorphophobia: Simpton or disease?. *American Journal of Psychiatry*, 134, 673-675.

Andrews, F. M., Withey, S. B. (1976). *Social Indicators of Well-being: America's Perception of Life Quality*. Plenum: New York.

Andrews, F. M., Robinson, J. P. (1991). Measures of Subjective Well-being. In Robinson, J., Shaver, P. and Wrightsman (eds). *Measures of Personality and Social Psychological Attitudes*. vol. 1, Academic Press: New York.

Anolli, L. (2002). *La psicologia della comunicazione*. Il Mulino: Bologna.

Antonovsky, A. (1980). *Health, Stress and Coping*. Jossey Bass: San Francisco.

Apa, (2000). *Diagnostic and Statistical Manual of Mental Disorders, 4th ed., Text Revision*. American Psychiatric Association: Washington, DC.

Apa, (2004). *DSM IV-TR, Manuale diagnostico e statistico dei disturbi mentali. Text Revision*. Masson: Milano.

Apa, (2007). *APA Dictionary of Psychology*. American Psychiatric Association: Washington, DC.

Argyle, M. (1987). *The Psychology of Happiness*. Metuen: London (trad. it. Psicologia della felicità, Cortina Editore: Milano).

Argyle, M., Martin, M. (1991). The Psychological Causes of Happiness. In Strack, F., Argyle, M, Schwarz, N. (eds). *Subjective Well-being*. Pergamon Press: Oxford.

Armeli, S. (2004). Stress and Alcohol Use: A Daily Process Examination of the Stressor-vulnerability Model. *Journal of Personality and Social Psychology,* 78, 5, 979-994.

Arnett, J. (1992). Reckless Behaviour in Adolescents: a Developmental Perspective. *Development Review*, 12, 339-373.

Arnett, J., Balle-Jensen, L. (1993). Cultural Bases of Risk Behaviour: Danish Adolescents. *Child Development*, 64, 1842-1855.

Avenia, F., Pistuddi, A. (2007). *Manuale sulla sex addiction*. Franco Angeli: Milano.

Bacchini, D. (2004). Rappresentazioni di sé, rappresentazioni genitoriali e rischio psicosociale in adolescenza. *Psicologia clinica dello sviluppo*, 8, 2, 239-268.

Baer, J. S. (2002). Student Factors: Understanding Individual Variation in College Drinking. *Journal of Studies on Alcohol*, 14, 40-53.

Baiocco, R., Couyoumdjian, A., Del Miglio, C. (2005). Le dipendenze in adolescenza. Aspetti epidemiologici, differenze di genere e aspetti psicologici. In Caretti, V., La Barbera, D. (a cura di). *Le dipendenze patologiche. Clinica e psicopatologia*. Cortina: Milano.

Baiocco, R., D'Alessio, M., Laghi, F. (2008). *I giovani e l'alcol. Il fenomeno del binge drinking*. Carocci: Roma.

Bandura, A. (2000). *Autoefficacia*. Erickson: Trento.

Barnes, G. M., Farrell, M. P., Banerjee, S. (1994). Family Influences on Alcohol Abuse and Other Problem Behaviors among Black and White Adolescents in a General Population Sample. *Journal of Research on Adolescence*, 4, 183-201.

Barnes, G. M. (1999). Influences of Demographic, Socialization, and Individual Factors. *Addictive Behaviors*, 24, 749-69.

Battista, I. (2008). *Specchio delle mie brame. Psicologia della chirurgia estetica*. Nuova Ipsa Editore: Palermo.

Bauman, Z. (1999). La società della gratificazione istantanea in culture differenti: Europa e Nord America. *Concilium*, 4/1999, 22.

Bauman, Z. (2003). *La società sotto assedio*. Laterza: Roma, Bari.

Bauman, Z. (2006). *Vita liquida*. Laterza: Roma, Bari.

Beccaria, F. (2004). (a cura di). *Sul filo del rischio. Percezione del rischio tra i giovani e prevenzione dei traumi cranici*. Franco Angeli: Milano.

Beck, U. (1986). *Risikogesellschaft. Auf dem Weg in eine andere Moderne*. Suhrkamp: Frankfurt (trad. it. 2000). *La società del rischio. Verso una seconda modernità*. Carocci: Roma.

Beck, U. (1994). *Reflexive Modernization. Politics, Tradition and Aesthetics in the modern Social Order*. Polity Press: Cambridge, (trad. it. 1999*). In *Modernizzazione riflessiva. Politica, tradizione ed estetica nell'ordine sociale della modernità*. Asterios: Trieste.

Beck, U. (1996). World risk society as cosmopolitan society? Ecological questions in a framework of manufactured uncertainties. *Theory, Culture and Society*, 13, (4), 1-32.

Becker, M. H., Maiman S. (1975). Sociobehavioral determinants of compliance with health and medical care recommendations. *Medical Care*, 13, 10-24.

Bell, N. J., Bell, R. W. (1993). *Adolescent Risk Taking*. Sage: London.

Benasayag, M., Schmit, G. (2003). *L'epoca delle passioni tristi*. Feltrinelli: Milano.

Benthin, A., Slovic, P., Severson, H. (1993). A Psychometric Study of Adolescent Risk Perception. *Journal of Adolescence*, 16, (2), 153-168.

Bertini, M. (1988). *Psicologia e salute*. NIS: Roma.

Bishop, D. (2005). Identity Development and Alcohol Consumption: Current and Retrospective Self-reports by College Students. *Journal of Adolescence*, 28, 523-33.

Black, D.W., et. al. (2007a). A Open-label Trial of Escitalopram in Treatment of Pathological Gambling. *Clinical Neuropharmacology,* 30, 206-212.

Black, D.W. (2007b). A Review of Compulsive Buying Disorder. *World Psychiatry*, 6, (1), 14-18.

Blanco, C., et. al. (2000). A Pilot Placebo-controlled Study of Fluvoxamine for Pathological gambling. *Annals of Clinical Psychiatry*, 14, 9-15.

Bloch, A. (1990). *Il terzo libro di Murphy*. Longanesi: Milano.

Bloomfield, K. (1999). *Alcohol Consumption and Alcohol Problems among Women in European Countries.* Institute for Medical Informatics, Biostatistics and Epidemiology. Fɪcc University of Berlin: Berlin

Bird, M.H. (2006). Sexual Addiction and Marriage and Family Therapy: Facilitating Individual and Relationship Healing through Couple Therapy. *Journal Family Marital Therapy*, 32, 297-311.

Bonino, S. (2004). Famiglie e rischio in adolescenza. *Psicologia clinica e dello sviluppo,* 8, (2), 235-320.

Bonino, S., Cattelino, E., Ciariano, S. (2003). *Adolescenti e rischio. Comportamenti, funzioni e fattori di protezione.* Giunti: Firenze.

Bosma, H. A., Kunnen, E. S., Saskia, E. (2001). Determinants and Mechanisms, Ego-Identity Development: A Review and Synthesis. *Developmental Review*, 21, (1), 39-66.

Bostwick, J. M., Bucci, J. A. (2008). Internet Sex Addiction Treated with Naltrexone. *Mayo Clinic Proceedings*, 83, pp. 226-230.

Bowlby, J. (1983) *Attaccamento e perdita*. Bollati Boringhieri: Torino.

Bradley, C., Brewin, C., Gamsu, D., Moses, J. (1984). Development of scale to measure perceived control of diabetes mellitus and diabetes related health beliefs. *Diabetic Medicine,* 1, 213-218.

Bradley, C., Lewis, K., Jennings, A., Ward, S. (1990). Scales to measure perceived control developed specifically for people with tablet treated diabetes. *Diabetic Medicine,* 7, 685-694.

Bradburn, N. M. (1969). *The Structure of Psychological Well-being.* Aldine: Chicago.

Bratman, S. (2000). *Health food junkies. Overcoming the obsession with healthful eating.* Broadway Books: New York.

Browne, B.R. (1991). The Selective Adaptation of the Alcoholics Anonymous Program by Gamblers Anonymous. *Journal of Gambling Studies*, 7, (3), 187-205.

Bullock, K., Koran, L. (2003). Psychopharmacology of Compulsive Buying. *Drugs Today,* 39, 695-700.

Buzzi, C., Cavalli, A., De, Lillo A. (1997). *Giovani verso il Duemila. Quarto rapporto Iard sulla condizione giovanile in Italia.* Il Mulino: Bologna.

Buzzi, C., Cavalli, A., De Lillo, A. (2002). *Giovani del nuovo secolo. Quinto rapporto Iard sulla condizione giovanile in Italia.* Il Mulino: Bologna.

Calandri, E. (2004). Relazioni familiari e rischio: un'analisi della circolarità. *Psicologia clinica dello sviluppo*, 2, 289-306.

Campanile, A. (1960). *Se la luna mi porta fortuna*. BUR: Milano.

Campbell, A., Converse, P. E., Rodgers, W. L. (1976). *The Quality of American Life*. Russel Sage Foundation: New York.

Cannizzaro, S., La Barbera, N., La Barbera, D. (2009). La dipendenza da tecnologie della comunicazione. In Caretti, V., La Barbera, D. (a cura di.) *Le nuove dipendenze: diagnosi e clinica*. Carocci: Roma.

Cantelmi, T. (2001). Psicopatologia delle condotte on-line. In Caretti, V., La Barbera, D. (a cura di). *Psicopatologia delle realtà virtuali*. Masson: Milano.

Cantelmi, T., D'andrea, A. (2000). Fenomeni psicopatologici Internet-correlati: osservazioni cliniche. In Cantelmi, T., Del Miglio, C., Talli, M., D'Andrea, A. (a cura di). *La mente in internet. Psicopatologia delle condotte on-line*. Piccin: Padova.

Cantelmi, T., Lambiase, E, Sessa, A. (2004). Le dipendenze comportamentali. *Psicobiettivo*, 2, 13-28.

Cantelmi, T., Talli, M. (2007). Anatomia di un problema, una review sui fenomeni psicopatologici Internet-correlati. *Psicotech*, 5, (2), 7-31.

Cantelmi, T., Toro, M. B., Talli, M. (2010). *Avatar: Dislocazioni mentali, personalità tecno-mediate, derive autistiche e condotte fuori controllo*. Edizioni Magi: Roma.

Cantor, N., Harlow, R. E. (1994). Social Intelligence and Personality: Flexible Life Task Pursuit. In Sternberg, R. J., Ruzgis, P. (a cura di). *Personality and Intelligence*. Cambridge University Press: New York.

Cantril, H. (1965). *The Patterns of Human Concerns*. Rutgers University Press: New Brunswick (NJ).

Capecchi, S., Ruspini, E. (2009). *Media, corpi, sessualità. Dai corpi esibiti al cyber sex*. Franco Angeli: Milano.

Carrà, E., Marta, E. (1996). *Relazioni familiari e adolescenza. Sfide e risorse nella transizione dell'età adulta.* Franco Angeli: Milano.

Carbone, P. (2003). *Le ali di Icaro*. Bollati Boringhieri: Torino.

Caretti, V., La Barbera, D. (2005). (a cura di). *Le dipendenze psicologiche. Clinica e psicopatologia*. Raffaello Cortina: Milano.

Caretti, V., La Barbera, D. (2009). (a cura di). *Le nuove dipendenze: diagnosi e clinica*. Carocci: Roma.

Carnes, P. (1982). *Contrary to Love. Helping the Sexual Addiction*. Comp-care: Minneapolis.

Carnes, P. (1991). *Don't call it love: Recovery for sexual addiction*. Bantam Books: New York.

Cascua, S. (2004). *Lo sport fa davvero bene alla salute? Quali sport scegliere: benefici e rischi*. Red: Milano.

Castiello d'Antonio, A. (2010a). Ubriachi di lavoro. Il workaholism. *Psicologia Contemporanea*, 221, 21-25.

Castiello d'Antonio, A. (2010b). *Malati di lavoro. Cos'è e come si manifesta il Workaholism*. Cooper: Roma.

Cavalli, A., De Lillo, A. (1993). *Giovani anni '90. Terzo rapporto Iard sulla condizione giovanile in Italia*. Il Mulino: Bologna.

Choi, P., et. al. (2002). Muscle Dysmorphia: A New Syndrome in Weightlifters. *British Journal of Sport Medicine*, 36, 375-377.

Christiansen, M., Vik, P. W., Jarchow, A. (2002). College Student Heavy Drinking in Social Contexts versus Alone. *Addictive Behaviors,* 27, (3), 393-404.

Cipresso, P., Villamira, M., Mauri, M., Balgera, A., Riva, G. (2012). Altruistic Behavior in Facebook Improves Emotional Experience: An Eye-tracking and Psychophysiological Research. *Cyberpsychology, Behavior and Social Networks*, (in press).

Cloninger, C.R. (2004). *Feeling Good. The Science of well being*. Oxford University Press:New York.

Cloninger, C.R. (2006). The Science of well being: An Integrated Approach to Mental Health and its Disorders. *World Psychiatry*, 5, 71-76.

Cicognani, E., Zani, B. (1999). La salute a rischio in adolescenza: il fenomeno dell'ottimismo irrealistico. *Psicologia clinica dello sviluppo*, 1, 81-100.

Cocci, V., et. al. (2006). Gioco d'azzardo patologico, funzionamento borderline e tratti antisociali. Un'indagine preliminare sugli aspetti di personalità dei giocatori d'azzardo attraverso l'utilizzo del test MMPI-2. *Personalità/Dipendenze*, 11, (1), 1-13.

Codeluppi, V. (2007). *La vetrinizzazione sociale. Il processo di spettacolarizzazione dell'individuo e della società*. Bollati Boringhieri:Torino.

Cohen, S. (1988). Perceived Stress in a Probability Sample of the United States. In Spacapan, S., Oskamp, S. (a cura di). *The Social Psychology of Health*. Sage: Newbury Park, CA.

Cohen, S., Taylor, L. (1992). *Escape Attempts. The Theory and Practice of Resistance to Everyday Life*. Routledge: London.

Coker, B. L. (2009). Freedom to Surf: The Productive Benefits of Workplace Internet Leisure Browsing. *News-The University of Melbourne*, (2 April 2009).

Coleman, E. (1992). Is Your Patient Suffering from Compulsive Sexual Behavior?. *Psychiatric Annals*, 22, 320-325.

Coleman, J., Roker, D. (1998). *Teenage sexuality: health, risk and education*. Harwood Academic Press: London.

Confalonieri, E., Grazzani, G. I. (2002). *Adolescenza e compiti di sviluppo*. Unicopli: Milano.

Cooper, A., et. al. (2000). Cybersex Users, Abusers, and Compulsives: New Findings and Implications. *Sexual Addiction and Compulsivity*, 7, 5-29.

Cooper, A., et. al. (2004). Sex and Internet: Furthering Our Understanding of Men with Online Sexual Problems. *Psychology of Addictive Behaviors*, 18, (3), 223-230.

Costa, A. S. (2007). Alcohol and Psychiatric Co-morbidity. *European Psychiatry*, 22, (1), 187-188.

Cottino, A., Prina, F. (1997). *Il bere giovane. Saggi su giovani e alcol*. Franco Angeli: Milano.

Couyoumdjian, A., Baiocco, R., Del Miglio, C. (2006). *Adolescenti e nuove dipendenze. Le basi teoriche, i fattori di rischio, la prevenzione*. Laterza: Roma-Bari.

Cox, W. M., Klinger, E. (2004). A Motivational Model of Alcohol Use: Determinants of Use and Change. In Cox, W. M., Klinger, E. (eds.). *Handbook of Motivational Counseling: Concepts, Approaches, and Assessment*. Wiley: Chichester.

Croce, M. (2001). Il caso del gioco d'azzardo: una droga che non esiste, dei danni che esistono, *Personalità e Dipendenze*. 11, 225-242.

Crockett, L. J. (1997). Cultural, Historical and Subcultural Contexts of Adolescence: Implication for Health and Development. In Schulenberg, J., Maggs, L., Hurrelmann, K. (eds.). *Health Risks and Developmental Transitions During Adolescence*. Cambridge University Press: New York.

Crum, R. M., Pratt, L. A. (2001). Risk of Heavy Drinking And Alcohol Use Disorders in Social Phobia: A Prospective Analysis. *American Journal of Psychiatry*, 158, (10), 1693-1700.

Csikszentmihalyi, M. (1975). *Beyond Boredom and Anxiety*. Jossey Bass: San Francisco.

Custe,r R.L. (1984). Profile of the Pathological Gambler. *Journal of Clinical Psychiatry*, 45, 35-38.

D'Alessio, M., Laghi, F. (2007). *La preadolescenza: identità in transizione tra rischi e risorse*. Piccin: Padova.

Dannon, P., et. al. (2005). Topiramate versus Fluvoxamine in the Treatment of Pathological Gambling: A Randomized Blind-rater, Comparison Study. *Clinical neuropharmachology*, 28, 6-10.

Della Ragione, L. (2005). *La casa delle bambine che non mangiano*. Il Pensiero Scientifico: Roma.

Depetris, P. G. (2011). *Rappresentazioni sociali del corpo*. Franco Angeli: Milano

Dell'Osso, B., Hadley, S., Allen, A., Bake,r B., Chaplin, W. F., Hollander, E. (2006). An Open Label Trial of Escitalopram in the Treatment of Compulsive-impulsive Internet Usage Disorder. *European Neuropsychopharmacology*, 16, pp. 82-83.

Del Miglio, C., Gamba, A., Cantelmi, T. (2001). Costruzione e validazione preliminare di uno strumento (UADI) per la rilevazione delle variabili psicologiche e psicopatologiche correlate all'uso di Internet. *Giornale Italiano di Psicopatologia*, 7, (3), 293-306.

DeNeve, K. M., Cooper, H. (1998). The Happy Personality: a Meta-analysis of 137 Personality Traits and Subjective Well-being. *Psychological Bulletin*, 124, n. 2, 197-229.

Di Benedetto. A. (2003). *Psiche. Rivista di cultura psicoanalitica: la scomparsa del purgatorio*. Il Saggiatore: Milano.

Di Clemente, R. J. (1996). Sexually Transmitted Diseases and Human Immunodeficiency Virus Infection among Adolescents. In Di Clemente, R. J., Hansen, W., Ponton, L. (eds.). *Handbook of Adolescent Risk Behavior*. Plenum: New York.

Di Chiara, G. (2002). Nucleus Accumbens Shell And Core Dopamine: Differential Role in Behavior and Addiction. *Behavioral Brain Research*, 2, (137), 75-114.

Diener, E. (1984). Subjective Well-being. *Psychology and Health*, 95, 542-575.

Diener, E., Fujita, F. (1997). Social Comparison and Subjective Well-being. In Buunk, B., Gibbon, R. (eds). *Health, Coping and Social Comparison*. Erlbaum: Mahwah, NJ.

Diener, E. (1999). Subjective well-being: Three decades of progress. *Psychological Bulletin*, 125, 276-303.

Di Grande, L. (2000). Alcohol Use and Correlates of Binge Drinking among University Students on the Island of Sardinia, Italy. *Substance Use and Misuse*, 35, 1471-83.

Di Gregorio, L. (2003). *Psicopatologia del cellulare. Dipendenza e possesso del telefonino*. Franco Angeli: Milano.

Di Maria, F., Formica, I. (2003). Hikikomori. Il male oscuro dei figli del Sol Levante. *Psicologia Contemporanea*, 179, 18-25.

Di Maria, F., Falgares, G. (2004). Il sesso compulsivo. *Psicologia Contemporanea*,185,22-28.

Di Maria, F., Formica, I. (2004). Lo Shopping compulsivo. *Psicologia Contemporanea*, 184, 12-17.

Di Maria, F., Formica, I. (2005). Rifatti e insoddisfatti. *Psicologia Contemporanea*, 191, 1-5.

Di Maria, F., Formica, I. (2006). Ortoressia nervosa. L'ossessione di mangiar sano. *Psicologia Contemporanea*, 194, 48-55.

Diskin, K.M., Hodgins, D.C. (1997). Narrowing of Attention and Dissociation in Pathological Video Lottery Gamblers. *Journal of Gambling Sudies*, 15, (1), 17-28.

Dogana, F. (2002). *Uguali e diversi. Teorie e strumenti per conoscere se stessi e gli altri*. Giunti: Firenze.

Donati, P. (1990). Famiglia e infanzia in una società rischiosa: come leggere e affrontare il senso del rischio. In Ferracuti, F. (a cura di). *Aspetti criminologici e forensi dell'età minorile*. Giuffrè: Milano.

Donini, L.M., et. al. (2004). Orthorexia Nervosa: A Preliminary Study with a Proposal for Diagnosis and an Attempt to Measure the Dimension of the Phenomenon. *Eating and Weight Disorders*, 9.

Donini, L.M., et. al. (2005). Orthorexia Nervosa: Validation of Diagnosis Questionnaire. *Eating and Weight Disorders*, 10.

Doxa- Osservatorio Permanente sui Giovani e l'Alcool, (2011). Sesta Indagine, Gli Italiani e l'Alcool. Consumi, tendenze e atteggiamenti in Italia. www.alcol.net/

Douglas, M. (1985). *Risk Acceptability to the Social Sciences*. Russell Sage Foundation: New York, (trad. it. 1991). *Come percepiamo il pericolo. Antropologia del rischio*. Feltrinelli: Milano.

Douglas, M. (1992). *Risk and Blame. Essays in Cultural Theory*. Routledge: London. (trad. it. 1996). *Rischio e colpa*. Il Mulino: Bologna.

Dryfoos, J. G. (1990). *Adolescence at Risk. Prevalence and Prevention*. Oxford University Press: New York.

Durkheim, E. (1912). *Les formes èlèmentaires de la vie religieuse*. Alcan: Paris.

Emler, N., Reichers, A. E. (1995). *Adolescence and Deelinquence*. Blackwell Publishers: Oxford, (trad. it., 2000). *Adolescenza e devianza*. Il Mulino: Bologna.

Emmons, R. A. (1986). Personal Strivings: An Approach to Personality and Subjective Well-being. *Journal of Personality and Social Psychology*, 51, 1058-1068.

Emmons, R. A. (1992). Abstract versus Concrete Goals: Personal Striving Level, Phisical Illness, an Psychological Well-being. *Journal of Personality and Social Psychology*, 62, (2), 292-300.

Engel, G.L. (1977). The Need for a New Medical Model: A Challenge for Biomedicine. *Science,* 196, (4286), 129-136.

Esposito, C. (2003). Adolescenza, tra conservazione e rivoluzione. In Mangini, E., *Lezioni sul pensiero post-freudiano. Maestri, idee, suggerimenti e fermento della psicoanalisi del Novecento*. Led: Milano.

Eurisko, Q-Red (2011). Rapporto XXXII Congresso nazionale della Società Italiana di medicina Estetica. 6-7-8- Maggio, Roma. www.lamedicinaestetica.it/congressosime/2011/14_2011.

Eurispes Rapporto Italia, (2012). Sintesi 24° Rapporto Italia. www.eurispes.it/.

Esposito, M. (2002). *Prevenzione dell'alcolismo o prevenzione dei rischi da Alcol? Una rivisitazione critica di concetti e programmi della Prevenzione*. Comunicazione personale.

Esposito, C. (2003). Adolescenza, tra conservazione e rivoluzione. In Mangini E. *Lezioni sul pensiero post-freudiano. Maestri, idee, suggerimenti e fermento della psicoanalisi del Novecento*. Led: Milano.

Ewald, F. (1993). Two infinities of risk. In Massum,i B. (a cura di). *The Politics Of Everyday Fear*. University of Minnesota Press: Minneapolis, Minn.

Faber, R.J., O'Guinn, T.C. (1992). A Clinical Screener for Compulsive Buying. *Journal of Consumer Research*, 19, 459-469.

Featherstone, M. (1995). *Undoing Culture. Globalization, Postmodernism and Identity.* Sage: London, (trad. it. 1998). *La cultura dislocata. Globalizzazione, postmodernismo, identità.* Seam:Formello.

Fenichel, O. (1951). *Trattato di psicoanalisi delle nevrosi e delle psicosi.* Astrolabio: Roma.

Ferenczi, S. (1933). *Confusione delle lingue tra adulti e bambini.* Mondadori: Milano.

Fernandez Montalvo, J., Echeburua, E. (2006). Pathological Gambling and Personality Disorders: A Pilot-study with the MCMI-II. *Psicothema*, 18, (3), 453-458.

Finn, P., Bragg, B. W. (1986). Perception of the Risk of the Risk an Accident by Young and Older Drivers. *Accident Analysis and Prevention,* 18, (4), 289-298.

Finzi, S. V. (2009). Viviamo nella società del rischio. In Francesconi, M., Zanetti, M. A. *Adolescenti: cultura del rischio ed etica dei limiti.* Franco Angeli: Milano.

Fishbein, M., Ajzein, I. (1975). *Beliefs, attitude, intention and behavior.* Reading, Mass: Addison-Wesley.

Fishbein, M. (1980). A Theory of Reasoned Action: Some Applications and Implications. In Howe, H. E., Page, M. (eds.). *Nebraska Symposium on Motivation 1979.* University of Nebraska Press: Lincoln (NE).

Fisher, S. (1999). A Prevalence Study of Gambling in British Adolescences. *Addiction Research*, 7, 509-538.

Flynn, J. (1994). Gender, race, and perception of environmental health risks. *Risk Analysis,* 14, (6), 1101-1108.

Francesconi, M., Zanetti, M. A. (2009). *Adolescenti: cultura del rischio ed etica dei limiti.* Franco Angeli: Milano.

Gatti Pertegato, E., (1987). *Dietro la maschera. Sulla formazione del sé e del falso sé.* Franco Angeli: Milano.

Gardini, S., Venneri A. (2011). Il benessere psicologico. *Psicologia Contemporanea*, 226, 76-80.

Giddens, A. (1990). *The Consequences of Modernity.* Polity Press: Cambrige. (trad. it. 1994). *Le conseguenze della modernità.* Il Mulino: Bologna.

Giddens, A. (1991). *Modernity and Self-Identity.* Polity Press: Cambrige, UK.

Giddens, A. (1992). *Transformation of Intimacy: Sexuality, Love and Eroticism in Modern Society.* Polity Press: Cambridge, UK.

Giddens, A. (1994). *Living in a post-traditional society, in Reflexive Modernization. Politics, Tradition and Aesthetics in the Modern Social Order.* Stanford University Press: California.

Gold, J. (1987). Eating Disorders and Cocaine Abuse: A Survey of 259 Cocaine Abusers. *Journal of Clinical Psychiatry,* 48, 47-50.

Goleman, D.(1996). *Intelligenza emotiva. Cos'è e perché può renderci felici.* RCS: Milano.

Gomà-i-Freixanet, M. (2004). Sensation seeking and participation in physical risk sports. In Stelmack, R. M. (a cura di). *On the psychobiology of personality.* Pergamon: Amsterdam.

Gonzales, R. A., Job, M. O. Doyon, W. M. (2004). The Role of Mesolimbic Dopamine in the Development and Maintenance of Ethanol Reinforcement. *Pharmacology and Therapeutic,* 103, 121-46.

Gonzalo Miranda, L.C. (2008). Precauzione e prudenza. In Marini, L., Palazzoni, L., (a cura di). *Il principio di precauzione tra biodiritto e biopolitica.* Studium: Roma.

Goodman, A. (1998). *La dipendenza sessuale. Un approccio integrato.* Astrolabio: Roma.

Goodman, A. (2008). Neurobiology of Addiction. An integrative Review. *Biochemical Pharmachology,* 75, 266-322.

Gossop, M. (2001). Health Care Professionals Referred for Treatment of Alcohol and Drug Problems. *Alcohol and Alcoholism,* 36, 2, pp. 160-164.

Graham, J., Clemente, K. (1996). Hazards in the news. Who believes what?. *Risk in Perspective,.* 4, (4), 1-4.

Grant, J.E., Brewer, J.A., Potenza, M. (2006). The Neurobiology of Substance and Behavioral Addictions. *CNS Spectrums*, 11, 924.930.

Griffin, C., Bengry-Howell, A., Hackley, C. Mistral, W., Szmigin, I. (2009). Every Time I Do It I Absolutely Annihilate Myself: Loss of (Self) Consciousness and Loss of Memory in Young People's Drinking Narratives. *Sociology,* 43, (3), 457-476.

Griffiths, M.D., Wood, R.T. (2000). A Risk factors in Adolescence: The Case of Gambling, Videogame Playing, and the Internet. *Journal of Gambling Studies*, 16, 199-225.

Grob, A. (1995). Subjective Well-being and Significant Life-events across the Life Span. *Swiss Journal of Psychology*, 54, 3-18.

Guerreschi, C. (1998). *Le frontiere del gioco d'azzardo. Conferenza sul gioco d'azzardo patologico.* (29 Giugno 1998). Kolpinghaus, Bolzano, Italia.

Guerreschi, C. (2005). *New addictions. Le nuove dipendenze.* San Paolo: Cinisello Balsamo, Milano.

Guerreschi, C. (2011). *La dipendenza sessuale. Quando il sesso può uccidere.* San Paolo: Cinisello Balsamo, Milano.

Guzman, C.S., et. al. (2007). Compulsive Buying Treatment with Topiramate. A Case Report. *Revista Brasileira de Psiquitria*, 29, 383-384.

Hansen, W. B., Raynor, A. E., Wolkenstein, B. H. (1991). Perceived Personal Immunity to the Consequences of Drinking Alcohol: The Relationship between Behavior and Perception. *Journal of Behavioral Medicine,* 14, (3), 205-224.

Havighurst, R. J. (1953). *Human Development and Education.* Longmans Green New York.

Headey, B., Wearing, A. (1991). Subjective Well-being: a Stocks and Flows Framework. In Strack, F., Argyle, M, Schwarz,. N., (eds). *Subjective Well-being.* Pergamon Press: Oxford.

Hollander, E., et. al. (1998). Short-term Single-blind Fluvoxamine Treatment of Pathological Gambling. *American Journal of Psychiatry*, 155, 1781-1783.

Hollander, E., et. al. (2000). A Randomized Double-blind Fluvoxamine/ placebo Crossover Trial in the Pathological Gambling.*Biological Psychiatry*, 47, 813-817.

Holmes, T. H., Rahe, R. M. (1967). The Social Adjustment Rating Scale. *Journal of Psychosomatic Research*, 11, 213-218.

Ingram, R. E., Price, J. M. (2001). *Vulnerability to Psychopathology. Risk across the Lifespan.* Guildford Press: New York.

Ingrosso, M. (2003). Pluralizzazione delle droghe e immaginario iperprestativo. In Di, Blasi M. (a cura di). *Sud-Ecstasy. Un contributo alla comprensione dei nuovi stili di consumo giovanile.* Franco Angeli: Milano.

International Center for Alcohol Policies (ICAP), (1999). *Blue Book Practical Guides for Alcohol Policy and Prevention Approaches.* Author Washington: Washington (DC).

Irwin, C. E., Millstein, S. G. (1986). Biopsychosocial Correlates of Risk Taking Behaviors during Adolescence: Can The Physician Intervene?,.*Journal of Adolescence Health Care,* 7. (6), 82-96.

Istat-Aci, (2011).Incidenti Stradali 2010: Rapporto Istat- Aci. www.istat.it/it/archivio/44063.

Jack, M. S. (1989). Personal fable: A potential explanation for risk-taking behavior in adolescent. *Journal of Pediatric Nursing*, 4, 334-333.

Jahoda, M. (1958). *Current Concepts of Positive Mental Health*. Basic Books: New York.

Janiri, L., et. al. (2006). *Impulsività e compulsività: psicopatologia emergente*. Astrolabio: Roma.

Jessor, S. L., Jessor, R. (1975). Transition from Virginity to Non-Virginity among Youth: A Social-Psychological Study over Time. *Developmental Psychology*, 11, (4), 473-484.

Jodice, F. (2005). Malessere sociale: la reclusione volontaria. I ragazzi dell'autoclausura, http://archivio.panorama.it/home/articolo/idA020001030479.

Jourard, S. M., Landsman, T. (1980). *Health Personality: an Approach from the Viewpoint of Humanistic Psychology*. Macmillan: New York.

Kafka, M.P., Hennen, J. (2006). A DSM-IV Axis I Comorbidity Study of Males (n=120) with Paraphilias and Paraphilia-related Disorders. *Sex Abuse*, 14, (4), 349-366.

Kalmuss, D. (1986). Contraceptive use: A comparison of ever and never pregnant adolescents. *Journal of Adolescent Health Care,* 7, 332-337.

Keyes, C. L. M. (1998). Social Well-being. *Social Psychology Quarterly*, 2, (1), 156-165.

Kets de Vries, M.F.R., Miller, D. (1984). *Psicopatologia del management. La valutazione psicologica della personalità nei ruoli di responsabilità organizzata*. Raffaello Cortina: Milano.

Kim, K., et. al. (2001). Double-blind Naltrexone and Placebo Comparison Study in the Treatment of Pathological Gambling. *Biological Psychiatry*, 49, 914-921.

Kim, K., et. al. (2007). Internet Addiction in Korean Adolescents and Its Relation to Depression and Suicidal Ideation: A Questionnaire Survey. *International Journal of Nursing Studies*, 44, (1), 157.

Ko, C.H., et.al., (2008), Psychiatric Comorbidity of Internet Addiction in College Students: An Interview Study.*CNS Spectrums*, 13, (2), 147-153.

Koob, G.K., Bloom, F.E. (1998). Cellular and Molecular Mechanisms of Drug Dependence. *Science*, 242, 715-723.

Koran, M., et. al. (2002). Citalopram Treatment of Compulsive Shopping: An Open-label Study. *Journal of Clinical Psychiatry*, 63, 704-708.

Kraepelin, E. (1915). *Psichiatrie*. Verlag von Johann Ambrosius: Barth, Leipzig.

Kroker, A., Kroker, M. (1988). Panic sex in America. In Kroker, A. , Kroker, M. (a cura di). *Body Invaders, Sexuality and the Postmodern Condition.* Macmillan: Toronto.

Kruedelbach, N., et. al. (2006) Comorbidity on Disorders with Loss of Impulse-control: Pathological Gambling, Addictions and Personality Disorders. *Actas Españolas de Psiquiatria*, 34, (2), 76-82.

Kumar, K., Makarova, E. (2008). Portable Home: The Domestication of Public Space. *Sociological Theory*, 26, (4), 324-343.

Kuzma, J., Black, D.W. (2006). Compulsive Shopping-When Spending Begins to Consume the Consumer. *Current Psychiatry*, 7, 27-40.

Ingoglia, S. (2004). Percezione della relazione con i genitori: differenze individuali nella connessione e nell'autonomia in adolescenza. *Psicologia clinica dello sviluppo*, 8, (2), 341-354.

Ingrosso, M. (2003). Pluralizzazione delle droghe e immaginario iperprestativo. In Di Blasi, M. (a cura di). *Sud-Ecstasy. Un contributo alla comprensione dei nuovi stili di consumo giovanile.* Franco Angeli: Milano.

La Barbera, D. (2005). Le dipendenze tecnologiche: la mente nei nuovi scenari dell'Addiction Tecnomediata. In Caretti, V., La Barbera, D. (a cura di). *Le dipendenze patologiche. Clinica e psicopatologia.* Raffaello Cortina: Milano.

La Barbera, D., et. al. (2006). Uno strumento di indagine per valutare i nuovi stili di comportamento adolescenziale: TSB (Tech Style Behavior). *Psicotech,* 1, 160-203.

La Barbera, et. al., (2008), La dipendenza dallo sport. In *Nuove dipendenze. Eziologia, Clinica e Trattamento delle dipendenze senza droga.* Il Pensiero Scientifico: Roma.

Ladoucer, R., et. al. (2000). *Il gioco d'azzardo eccessivo. Vincere il gambling.* Centro Scientifico Torinese: Torino.

Lambiase, E. (2001). *La dipendenza sessuale, modelli clinici e proposte di intervento terapeutico.* LAS: Roma.

Larsen, R. J., Diener, E. ,Cropanzano, R. S. (1987). Cognitive Operations Associated with Individual Differences in Affect Intensity. *Journal of Personality and Social Psychology,* 53, 767-774.

Larson, J. S. (1993). The Measurement of Social Well-being. *Social Indicators Research,* 28, 285-296.

Lasch, C. (1984). *L'io minimo.* Feltrinelli: Milano.

Lash, S., Urry, J. (1994). *Economies of Signs and Space.* Sage: London.

Lash, S. (2000). *Modernismo e postmodernismo: i mutamenti culturali delle società postmoderne.* Armando Editore: Roma.

Laukkannen, E. R. (2001). Heavy Drinking Is Associated with More Severe Psychosocial Disfunction among Girls than Boys in Finland. *Journal of Adolescent Health,* 28, (4), 270-277.

Lee, S., Mysk, A. (2004). The Medicalization of Compulsive Buying. *Social Science and Medicine,* 58, 1709-1718.

Lejoyeux, M., et. al. (1995). Compulsive Buying and Depression. *Journal of Clinical Psychiatry,* 56, 38.

Lejoyeux, M., et. al. (2005). Study of Compulsive Buying in Patients Presenting Obsessive-compulsive Disorder. *Comprehensive Psychiatry,* 46, (2), 105-110.

Lemma, A. (2005). *Sotto la pelle. Psicoanalisi delle modificazioni corporee.* Raffaello Cortina: Milano.

Lesieur, H.R., Blume, S.B. (1987). The South Oaks Gambling Screen (SOGS): A New Instrument for the Identification of Pathological Gamblers. *American Journal of Psychiatry,* 144, 1184-1188.

Lesieur, H.R., Blume, S.B. (1992). Modifying the Addiction Severity Index for Use with Pathological Gambling. *American Journal on Addiction,* 1, (3), 240-247.

Leventhal, H. (1992). *Illness cognition: The study of the representation and coping with current and future health threats over the life span.* Annual Pieter de la Court Readings: Leiden, The Netherlands.

Leventhal, H., Meyer, D., Nerenz, D. R. (1980). The common sense representation of illness danger. In Rachaman, S. (a cura di). *Contributions to medical psychology.* Pergamon Press: New York.

Leventhal, H., Cameron, L. (1987). Behavioural teorie and the problem of compliance. *Patient Education and Counseling,* 10, 117-138.

Leventhal, H., Diefenbach, M. (1991). The active side of illness cognition. In Skelton, J. A., Croyle, R. T. (a cura di). *Mental representation in health and illness.* Springer: New York.

Levine, R., Hoffman, J.S., et. al. (2002). Long-term Fluoxetine Treatment of a Large Number of Obsessive-Compulsive Patients. *Journal of Clinical Pharmacology,* 9, 281-283.

Liggio, F. (2007a). Dipendenza e compulsività e dipendenza da reazione orgasmica. In Avenia, F., Pistuddi, A. *Manuale sulla sex addiction.* Franco Angeli: Milano.

Liggio, F. (2007b). La terapia farmacologica della dipendenza da reazione orgasmica. In Avenia, F., Pistuddi, A.,*Manuale sulla sex addiction.* Franco Angeli: Milano.

Lyng, S. (1990). Edgework. A social psychological analysis of voluntary risk taking. *American Journal of Sociology,* 95, (4), 851-886.

Luhmann, N. (1993). *Risk. A Sociological Theory.* Aldine de Gruyter: New York.

Lukassen, J., Beaudet, M. P. (2005). Alcohol Dependence and Depression among Heavy Drinkers in Canada. *Social Science and Medicine,* 61, 1658-67.

Lipovetsky, G. (1995). *L'era del vuoto, saggi sull'individualismo contemporaneo.* Feltrinelli: Milano.

Lupton, D. (1998). *The Emotional Self. A Sociocultural Exploration.* Sage: London.

Maffesoli, M. (1988). *Le temps des tribus. Le dèclin de l'individualisme dans les sociètès de masse.* Mèridiens klincksieck: Paris, (trad. it., 1988). *Tempo delle tribù. Il declino dell'individuo.* Armando: Roma.

Marcia, J. E. (1993). The Ego Identity Status Approach to Ego Identity. In Id. (eds.). *Ego Identity: A Handbook for Psychosocial Research.* Springer-Verlag: New York.

Matarazzo, J. D. (1980). Behavioural health and behavioural medicine: frontiers for a new health psychology. *American Psychologist,* 35, 807-817.

Macken, D. (1998). Life on the edge, *Sydney Morning Herald.* Fairfax Media: Sydney.

McDougall, J. (1990). *Teatri del corpo.* Raffaello Cortina: Milano.

McDougall, J. (2004). L'economia psichica della dipendenza patologica. *Psicobiettivo,* 22, 55-71.

McDowell, I. ,Newell, C. (1987). *Measuring Health: a Guide to Rating Scales and Questionnaires.* Oxford University Press: New York.

McElroy, S.L., et. al. (1994). Compulsive Buying: A Report of 20 Cases. *Journal of Clinical Psychiatry,* 55, 242-248.

McMillan, D. W. ,Chavis, D. M. (1986). Sense of Community: a Definition and Theory. *Journal of Community Psychology,* 14, 6-23.

Magrin, M.E. (1999). *Ecologia del rischio e della responsabilità.* ISU, Università Cattolica: Milano.

Maldonado, T. (1997). *Critica della ragione informatica.* Feltrinelli: Milano.

Mangiarotti, A. (2009). I giovani che si autorecludono: il mondo esterno è solo sul computer. http://www.corriere.it/.

Marinelli, A. (1993). *La costruzione del rischio.* Angeli: Milano.

Marlatt, G.A., Gordon, J.R. (1985). *Relapse Prevention: Maintenance Strategies in the Treatment of Addiction Behaviors.* Guilford Press: New York.

Marrazzo, G., Rumeo, M. V., Mulè, A. (2009). Dipendenze patologiche e nuova adolescenza. In Caretti, V., La Barbera, D. (a cura di). *Le nuove dipendenze: diagnosi e clinica.* Carocci: Roma.

Marta, E. (2004). La relazione genitori-adolescenti: un predittore della devianza?. *Psicologia clinica dello sviluppo,* 2, 269-288.

Martini, C. (1998). Adolescenza e assunzione di rischi. *Animazione sociale,* 2, 12-24.

Massumi, B. (1993). Everywhere you want to be. Introduction to fear. In Massumi, B. (a cura di). *The Politics of Everyday Fear.* University of Minnesota Press: Minneapolis.

Mauri, M., Villamira, M., Cipresso, P., Balgera, A., Riva, G. (2012). Why is Facebook so Successful? Psychophysiological Measures Describe a Flow State During Facebook Use. *Cyberpsychology, Behavior and Social Networks,* (in press).

Measham, F., Brain, K. (2006). Binge Drinking, British Alcohol Policy and the New Culture of Intoxication. *Crime, Media, Culture,* 1, (3),.262-83.

Mellor, P., Shilling, C. (1997). *Re-forming the Body. Religion, Community and Modernity.* Sage: London.

Michalos, A. (1985). Multiple Discrepancies Theory (MDT). *Social Indicators Research,* 16, (4), 347-414.

Mick, T.M., Hollander, E. (2006). Impulsive-compulsive Sexual Behavior. *CNS Spectrums,* 11, 944-955.

Miller, D. (1997). *Donne che si fanno male.* Feltrinelli: Milano.

Mitchell, K., Welling, K. (1998). First Sexual Intercourse: Anticipation and Communication. Interview with Young People in England. *Journal of Adolescence,* 21, 717-726.

Mitchell, D., et. al. (2002). The Relationship between Compulsive Buying and Eating Disorders. *International Journal of Eating Disorders,* 32, (1), 107-111.

Mitchell, J.E., et. al. (2006). Cognitive Behavioral Therapy for Compulsive Buying Disorder. *Behavioral Research Therapy,* 44, 1859-1865.

Morawska, A., Oei, T. P.S. (2005). Binge Drinking in University Students: A Test of the Cognitive Model. *Addictive Behaviors,* 30, 203-18.

Morrongiello, B. A., Dawber, D. (2004). Identifying Factors That Relate to Children's Risk Taking Decisions. *Canadian Journal of Behavioral Science,* 36, 255-266.

Morselli, E. (1886). Sulla dismorfofobia e sulla talefobia. *Bollettino dell'Accademia delle Scienze Mediche di Genova,* 4, 100-119.

Myers, D. G. e Diener, E. (1995). Who Is Happy?. *Psychological Science,* 6, (1), 10-19.

Nava, F.(2004). *Manuale di neurobiologia e clinica delle dipendenze.* Franco Angeli: Milano.

Nerenberg, A. (2000). The Value of Group Psychotherapy for Sexual Addictis in Residential Setting. *Sexual Addiction and Compulsivity,* 7, 197-209.

Nizzoli, U. (2004). L'utilizzo di sostanze psicotrope. In Nizzoli, U., Colli, C. (a cura di). *Giovani che rischiano la vita.* McGraw-Hill: Milano.

Noventa, A. (2004). L'alcol e i giovani: fattori di rischio, caratteristiche e nuovi consumi, in Nizzoli U., Colli C. (a cura di). *Giovani che rischiano la vita. Capire e trattare i comportamenti a rischio negli adolescenti.* McGraw-Hill: Milano.

Nuvolati, G., Zajczyck, F. (1997). L'origine del concetto di qualità della vita e l'articolazione dei filoni di studio nella prospettiva europea. In Altieri, L., Luison, L. (a cura di). *Qualità della vita e strumenti sociologici.* Franco Angeli: Milano.

Oates, W.E. (1971). *Confessions of a Work-aholic: The facts About Work Addiction.* World Publishing: New York.

Oei, T. P. S., Morawska, A. (2004). A Cognitive Model of Binge Drinking: The Influence of Alcohol Expectancies and Drinking Refusal Self-efficacy. *Addictive Behaviors*, 29, 159-179.

Olievenstein, C. (1984). *Il destino del tossicomane*. Borla: Bologna.

Oliverio Ferraris, A. (2002). Shopping. Compro, dunque esisto. *Psicologia Contemporanea*, 169, 18-24.

Oliverio Ferraris, A. (2004). AAA genitore cercasi. *Psicologia contemporanea*, 184, 56-57.

OMS, (1949). *Manual of the International Statistical Classification of Diseases, Injuries, and Causes of Death*. Sixth Revision. OMS: Genéve.

OMS, (1980). *Classificazione Internazionale delle menomazioni, disabilità e degli handicap* (ICIDH), Cles: Trento.

OMS, (1986). *The Ottawa charter for health promotion*. OMS: Genève.

OMS, (1992). *Decima Revisione della Classificazione Internazionale delle Sindromi e dei Disturbi Psichici e Comportamentali* (ICD-10). Masson: Milano.

OMS, (1999). *Classificazione Internazionale del funzionamento e delle disabilità, ICIDH-2, Bozza Beta-2*. versione integrale. Erickson: Trento.

OMS, (2001). *Classificazione internazionale del Funzionamento, della Disabilità e della Salute* (ICF). Erickson: Trento.

Pallanti, S., et. al. (2002). Lithium and Valproate Treatment of Pathological Gambling: A Randomized Single-blind Study. *Journal of Clinical Psychiatry*, 63, 559-564.

Pallanti, S., et. al. (2006). Serotonin Dysfunction in Pathological Gamblers: Increased Prolactin Response to Oral m-CPP versus Placebo. *CNS Spectrums*, 11, 956-964.

Palmonari, A. (1997). *Psicologia dell'adolescenza*. Il Mulino: Bologna.

Palmonari, A., Cavazza, N., Rubini, M. (2002). *Psicologia sociale*. Il Mulino: Bologna.

Pan,i R., Biolcati, R. (2005). Compulsività e dipendenza da shopping. In Caretti, V., La Barbera, D. (a cura di). *Le dipendenze psicologiche. Clinica e psicopatologia*. Raffaello Cortina: Milano.

Park, C. L., Levinson, M. R. (2002). Drinking to Cope among College Students: Prevalence, Problems, and Coping Processes. *Journal of Studies on Alcohol*, 63, 486-97.

Park, C. L., Armeli, S., Tennen, H. (2004). The Daily Stress and Coping Process and Alcohol Use among College Students. *Journal of Studies on Alcohol*, 65, 126-37.

Parsi, M. R., Cantelmi, T., Orlando, F. (2009). *L'immaginario prigioniero. Come educare i nostri figli a un uso creativo e responsabile delle nuove tecnologie*. Mondadori: Milano.

Pellai, A., Boncinelli, S. (a cura di). (2002). *Just do it! I comportamenti a rischio in adolescenza. Manuale di prevenzione per scuola e famiglia*. Franco Angeli: Milano.

Peluso, T., Ricciardelli, L. A., Williams, R. J. (1999). Self-control in Relation to Problem Drinking and Symptoms of Disorder Eating. *Addictive Behaviors*, 24, 439-442.

Pinamonti, H., Rossin, M. R. (2004). *L'assunzione multipla di sostanze in una prospettiva interdisciplinare di clinica integrata*. Franco Angeli: Milano.

Pietropolli, C. G. (1999). *Segnali d'allarme. Disagio durante la crescita*. Mondadori: Milano.

Pietropolli, C. G., Riva, E. (1995). *Adolescenti in crisi, genitori in difficoltà*. Franco Angeli: Milano.

Pope, H.G. jr., et. al. (2000). *The Adonis Complex: the Secret Crisis of Male Body Obsession*. The Free Press: New York.

Presley, C. A., Leichliter, M. A., Meilman, P. W. (1998). *Alcohol and Drugs on American College Campuses: A Report to College Presidents: Third in a Series, 1995,1996, 1997.* Core Institute, Southern Illinois University: Carbondale (IL).

Prochaska, J. O., DiClemente, C. C. (1982). Self change and therapy change of smoking behavior: A comparison of process of change in cessation and maintenance. *Addictive Behaviors,* 7, 133-142.

Prochaska, J. O., Velicier, W. F., DiClemente, C. C., Fava, J. (1988). Measuring process of change: Application to the cessation of smoking. *Journal of Consulting and Clinical Psychology,* 56, 520-525.

Prochaska, J. O., Redding, C. A., Harlow, L. L., Rossi, J. S. e Velicer, W. F. (1994). The Transtheoretical model of change and HIV prevention: A review. *Health Education Quarterly,* 21, (4), 471-486.

Pruyn, J., van der Borne, H., de Reuver, R., de Boer, M., Ter Pelkwijk, M., de Jong, P. (1988). The Locus of Control Scale for cancer patients. *Tijdsscrift vour Sociale Gezondherdszong,* 56, 404-408.

Ptnam, D.E. (2000). Initiation and Maintenance of Online Sexual Compulsivity: Implications for Assessment and Treatment. *Cyberpsychology and Behavior,* 3, (4).

Pulcini, E. (1996). Tra Prometeo e Narciso. Le ambivalenze dell'identità moderna. In Cerutti, F. *Identità e Politica.* Laterza: Roma.

Raylu, N., Oei, T.P.S. (2002). Pathological Gambling. A Comprehensive Review. *Clinical Psychology Review,* 22, 1009-1061.

Rampazi, M. (2009). *Storie di normale incertezza.* LED: Milano.

Reddy, S. (1996). Claims to expert knowledge and the subversion of democracy: the triumph of risk over uncertainty. *Economy and Society,* 25, (2), 222-254.

Reid, R.C., et. al. (2008). Alexithymia. Emotional Instability and Vulnerability to Stress Proneness in Patients Seeking Help for Hypersexual Behavior. *Journal Sex Marital Therapy,* 34, 133-149.

Rheingold, H., (1993). *La realtà virtuale.* Baskerville: Bologna.

Rheingold, H. (1994). *Comunità virtuali. Parlare, incontrarsi, vivere nel ciberspazio.* Sperling and Kupfer: Milano.

Riboldi, F., Magni, E. (2010). *Droghe ricreative. Le life skills per crescere in-dipendenti.* Franco Angeli: Milano.

Ricci, C., (2008). *Hikikomori: adolescenti in volontaria reclusione.* Franco Angeli: Milano.

Ryff, C. D. (1989). Happiness is Everything, or Is It? Exploration on the Meaning of Psychological Well-being. *Journal of Personality and Social Psychology,* 47, (6), 1069-1081.

Rigliano, P. (1998). *Indipendenze. Alcol e cibo, farmaci e droghe, comportamenti di rischi e d'azzardo: le relazioni di dipendenza.* Edizioni Gruppo Abele: Torino.

Riva, G. (2004). *Psicologia dei nuovi media.* Il Mulino: Bologna.

Robinson, B.E. (1998a). *Chained to the Desk: a Guidebook for Workaholics, their Partners and Children and the Clinicians who Treat Them.* NYU Press: New York.

Robinson, B.E, Kelly, L. (1998). Adult Children of Alcoholics: Self-concept, Anxiety, Depression and locus of Control. *American Journal of Family Therapy,* 26, (3), 223-238.

Robinson, T.E., Berridge, K.C. (1993). The Neural Basis of Drug Craving: An Incentive Sensitization Theory of Addiction. *Brain Research Review,* 18, 247-291.

Rodgers, K. A. E. (2000). Risk Factors for Depression and Anxiety in Abstainers, Moderate Drinkers. *Addiction,* 95, (12), 1833-1845.

Romano, R.G. (2004). *Ciclo di vita e dinamiche educative nella società postmoderna.* Franco Angeli: Milano.

Rook, K. S. (1990). Social relationships as a source of companionship: Implications for older adults' psychological well-being. In Sarason, B. R., Sarason, I. G. and G. R. Pierce (Eds.). *Social support: An interactional* view. Wiley: New York.

Rosci, E. (2004). Adolescenza e sostanze psicoattive. In Maggiolini, A., Pietropolli, C. G. (a cura di). *Manuale di psicologia dell'adolescenza: compiti e conflitti.* Franco Angeli: Milano.

Rose, P. (2007). Mediators of the Association between Narcissism and Compulsive Buying: The Roles of Materialism and Control. *Psychology of Addictive Behaviors*, 21, (4), 576-581.

Rosenstock, I. M. (1966). Why people use health services. *Milbank Memorial Fund Quarterly,* 44, 94-124.

Rotter, J. B. (1966). Generalised expectancies for internal versus external control of reinforcement. *Psychological Monographs,* 80, 1-28.

Roversi, A. (2004). *Introduzione alla comunicazione mediata dal computer.* Il Mulino: Bologna.

Ryff, C. D. (1989). Happiness is Everything, or Is It? Exploration on the Meaning of Psychological Well-being. *Journal of Personality and Social Psychology*, 47, (6),1069-1081.

Sacco, P., et. al. (2008). The Association between Gambling Pathology and Personality Disorders. *Journal of Psychiatry Research*, Feb. 21, 1-8.

Salvadori, L., Rumiati, R. (1996). Percezione del rischio negli adolescenti italiani. *Giornale Italiano di Psicologia, XXIII, 1,* 85-105.

Salvadori, L., Rumiati, R. (1998). *Percezione del rischio:esperti vs non esperti.* Vita e Pensiero: Milano.

Savron, G., Pitti, P., De Luca, R., Guerreschi, C. (2001). Psychopathology and gambling: a preliminary study in a sample of Pathological Gamblers. *Rivista di psichiatria,* 36, (1), 14-20.

Scafato, E. (2004). *L'alcol in Italia. Analisi dei consumi e delle tendenze, in Alcol Prevention Day. L'analisi dell'OSSFAD sui consumi alcolici in Italia.* Istituto superiore di sanità: Roma

Schwartz, M.F. (1989). Effective Treatment for Sex offenders. *Psychiatric Annals*, 22, 315-319.

Schwarzer, R. (1994). Optimus, vulnerability, and self- belief as health-related cognition: A systematic overview. *Psychology and Health,* 9, 161-180.

Sciolla, L. (1993). Identità e trasmissione dei valori. Un problema di generazioni. In Ansaloni, S., Borsari, M. (a cura di). *Adolescenti in gruppo. Costruzione dell'identità e trasmissione dei valori,.* Angeli: Milano.

Seligman, M. (1995). *The Optimistic Child.* Random House: Australia.

Seligman, M. (1996). *Imparare l'ottimismo: come cambiare la vita cambiando il pensiero.* Giunti: Firenze.

Sennet, R. (1998). *The Corrosion of Character. The Personal Consequences of Work in the New Capitalism.* Norton and Co: N.Y, London.

Sereni, C. (2005). Qualcosa da aspettare, D. La Repubblica delle donne. 10 settembre. www.d.repubblica.it.

Shaffer, H.J., et. al. (1994). Pathological Gambling among Adolescents: Massachusetts Gambling Screen (MAGS). *Journal of Gambling Studies*, 10, (4), 339-362.

Shapira, N.A., et. al. (2003). Problematic Internet Use: Proposed Classification and Diagnostic Criteria. *Depression and Anxiety*, 17, 207-216.

Sharpe, L., Tarrier, N. (1993). Toward a Cognition-behavioural Theory of Problem Gambling. *British Journal of Psychiatry*, 162, 407-412,

Siracusano, A., Peccarisi, C. (1997). Internet addiction disorder: note critiche. *Bollettino di Aggiornamento in Neuropsicofarmacologia*, n.62, Anno XIII.

Slovic, P. (1987). Perception of Risk. *Science,* 236, 280-285.

Slovic, P., Fischhoff, B., Lichtenstein, S. (1980). Risky Assumptions. *Psychology Today,* 14, (1), 44-48.

Skinner, E. A. (1995). *Perceived Control, Motivation and Coping*. Thousand Oaks: London.

Smart, R.G., Ferris, J. (1996). Alcohol, Drugs, and Gambling in the Ontario Adult Population, 1994. *Canadian Journal of Psychiatry*, 41, 36-45.

Stanton, A. (1987). Determinance of adherence to medical regimens by hypertensive patients. *Journal oh Behavioral Medicine,* 10, 377-394.

Steinberg, L. (2004). Risk Taking in Adolescence. What Changes and Why?. *Annals of the New York Academy of Science*, 1021, 51-58.

Steiner, J. (1996). *I rifugi della mente. Organizzazioni patologiche della personalità nei pazienti psicotici, nevrotici e borderline*. Bollati Boringhieri: Torino.

Stevani, J. (2007). Muscoli e lacrime. *Psicologia Contemporanea*, 199, 18-25.

Stevani, J. (2008). Pornodipendenza da Internet. *Psicologia Contemporanea*, 207, 26-31.

Taylor, S. E. (1983). Adjustment to threatening events: A theory of cognitive adaptation. *American Psychologist*, 38, 1161-1173.

Taylor, S. E., Brown, J. D. (1988). Illusion and well-being: A social psychological perspective on mental health. *Psychological Bulletin*, 102-103, 193-210.

Taylor, G.J., Bagby, R.M., Parker, J.D.A (2000). *I disturbi della regolazione affettiva*. Giovanni Fioriti Editore: Roma.

Talarico, A., (2010). Internet Addiction Disorder: aumenta il numero di giovani dipendenti da internet. http://www.key4biz.it/

Tappatà, L. (2011). *Stay Focused*. Lupetti: Milano.

Tappatà, L. (2012). Benessere è attenzione ed equilibrio. Io Come Docente. Junes 2012, 16-19. htpp//issue.com/io come/docs/io_come_docente_03.

Tenzer, E. (2010). Sempre connessi. *Psicologia Contemporanea*, 221, pp. 38-42.

Trincas, R. (2008). Parental monitoring e comportamenti a rischio in adolescenza. *Psicologia clinica dello sviluppo*,3, 401-435.

Tubman, J. G., Windle, M., Windle, R. C. (1996). Cumulative Sexual Intercourse Patterns among Middle Adolescents: Problem Behavior Precursors and Concurrent Health Risk Behaviors. *Journal of Adolescent Health,* 18, 182-191.

Turchi, G.P., Della Torre, C. (a cura di). (2007). *Psicologia della salute. Dal modello bio-psico-sociale al modello dialogico*. Armando Editore: Roma.

Valence, G., D'Astous, A., Fortier, L. (1988). Compulsive Buying: Concept and Measurement. *Journal of Consumer Policy*, 11, 419-433.

Volkow, N.D., Fowler, J.S., Wang, G.J. (2004). The Addicted Human Brain Viewed in the Light of Imaging Studies: Brain Circuits and Treatment Strategies. *Neuropharmachology,* 47, 3-13.

Wallstone, K. A., Wallstone, B. S., De Vellis, R. (1978). Development of the Multidimensional Health Locus of Control (MHLC) Scales. *Health Education Monograph,* 6, 161-170.

Wallstone, B. S., Wallstone, K. A. (1984). Social psychological models of health behavior: An examination and integration. In Baum, A., Taylor, S. E., Singer, J. E. (a cura di). *Handbook of psychology and health: volume 4. Social psychological aspects of health.* Lawrence Erlbaum: Hillsdale, NJ.

Waterman, A. S. (1993). Two Conceptions of Happiness: Contrasts of Personal Expressiveness (Eudamonia) and Hedonic Enjoyment. *Journal of Personality and Social Psychology,* 64, (4), 678-691.

Watts, J. (2002). Public Health Experts Concerned About "Hikikomori". *The Lancet,* 359.

Watzlawick ,P., Beavin, J.H., Jakson, D. (1971). *Pragmatica della comunicazione umana.* Astrolabio: Roma.

Wechsler, H., Isaac, N. (1992). Binge Drinkers at Massachusetts Colleges. Prevalence, Drinking Style, Time Trends, and Associated Problems. *Journal of the American Medical Association,* 267, (21), 2929-31.

Weinstein, N. D. (1980). Unrealistic Optimism about Future Life Events. *Journal of Personality and Social Psychology,* 39, 806-820.

Weinstein, N. D. (1982). Unrealistic optimism about susceptibility in health problems. *Journal of Behavioral Medicine,* 5, 441-460.

Wilson, R.I., Nicoll, R.A. (2002). Endocannabinoid Signaling in the Brian. *Science,* 296, 678-682.

World Health Organization, (WHO) (1946). *Constitution.* Wold Health Organization: New York.

World Health Organization. (1992). The ICD-10. International Classification of Diseases. Geneve.

Young, K.S. (2000). Internet Addiction: The Emergence of a New Clinical Disorder. *Cyber-Psychology and Behavior,* 1, 337-244.

Young, K.S, (2000). *Presi nella rete. Intossicazione e dipendenza da Internet.* Calderini Edagricole: Bologna.

Zani, B., Cicognani, E. (2000). *Psicologia della salute.* Il Mulino: Bologna.

Zanon, I., et. al. (2002). Trance Dissociativa e Internet dipendenza: studio su un campione di utenti della rete. *Giornale Italiano di Psicopatologia,* 8, (4), 381-390.

Zimmermann, M., et. al. (2002). An Open-label Study of Citalopram in the Treatment of Pathological Gambling. *Journal of Clinical Psychiatry,* 63, 44-8.

Zimmermann, P. (2004). Attachment Representations and Characteristics of Friendships Relations During Adolescence. *Journal of Experimental Child Psychology,* 88, 83-101.

Zuckerman, M. (1971). Dimension of Sensation Seeking. *Journal of Consulting and Clinical Psychology,* 36, 1, 42-45.

Zuckerman, M. (1979). *Sensation Seeking: Beyond The Optimal Level of Arousal.* Lawrence Erlbaum: Hillsdale, NJ.

Zuckerman, M. (1983). La ricerca delle sensazioni. *Psicologia contemporanea,* 59, 26-33.

Zuckerman, M. (1983). Sensation seeking and sports. *Personality and Individual Differences,* 4, 285-292.

Zuckerman, M. (1999). *Vulnerability to Psychopathology: A biosocial model.* American Psychological Association: Washington DC.

Zuckerman, M. (2000). Personality and risk-taking: Common biosocial factors. *Journal of Personality,* 68, 999-1029.

Zuckerman, M. (2002). *Sensation Seeking and Risky Behavior.* American Psychological Association: Washington DC.

INDEX

D

miniature, 37
Minneapolis, 132, 135, 141
minors, 117
mission, 74
misunderstanding, 34
mobile phone, 89, 93, 94, 126
modelling, 12, 44
models, 2, 3, 9, 11, 12, 16, 21, 26, 33, 39, 49, 52,
    64, 71, 73, 79, 80, 93, 94, 105, 116, 146
modern society, 23, 25, 27, 28, 50, 116
modernism, 48
modernity, 1, 24, 26, 27, 29, 31, 48, 49, 84
modernization, 26, 48
modifications, 68, 77, 112
mood change, 126
mood disorder, 88, 101, 103, 107, 110, 112, 113,
    115
mood swings, 113
moral reasoning, 45
moral standards, 45
morale, 15
morbidity, 133
mortality, 63
Moses, 131
motivation, vii, 11, 14, 16, 40, 61, 66, 76, 100,
    106, 114
multidimensional, 52
multimedia, 104, 111
multiplication, 49, 117
murder, 3
muscles, 114, 115, 116
muscular mass, 114, 115
music, 27, 35, 38, 54, 90
mutual respect, 67
MySpace, 86

N

narcissism, 1, 41, 49, 50, 56, 115, 118
narcissistic personality disorder, 98, 112
National Research Council, 122
negative affectivity, 5
negative consequences, 35, 55, 56, 70, 80, 85, 95,
    99
negative effects, 106
negative emotions, 3, 5, 16, 63, 65, 81, 97, 110
negative experiences, 55, 79
negative mood, 63
negative reinforcement, 101
neglect, 78

nerve, 68
Netherlands, 139
neuroleptics, 108
neurons, 28
neuroses, 32
neurotransmitter, 69, 76
neurotransmitters, 68, 69, 77
new media, 91
nicotine, 75
NMDA receptors, 69
nuclei, 108
nucleus, 6, 15, 36, 76, 95, 97
nutrition, 120, 121

O

obesity, 98
obsessive-compulsive disorder, 97, 103, 105, 110,
    112, 122
obstacles, 10, 12
offenders, 144
openness, 20, 36, 127
operations, 25, 75, 117, 118
opioids, 78, 102
opportunities, 38, 42, 63, 87
optimism, 14, 15, 19, 51, 53, 54, 55, 85, 146
oral stage, 78
organic disease, 106
organism, 3, 6, 8, 9, 68, 69, 75, 113, 126
organized fluidly, 10
otherness, 49
outpatient, 91
outpatients, 101
overtraining, 113, 114

P

pain, 3, 10, 32, 106, 114, 116, 119
parallel, 21, 73, 79, 125
paraphilia, 105, 106, 107
parental control, 65, 91
parenthood, 25, 56
parents, 1, 10, 34, 36, 37, 41, 43, 64, 65, 67, 71,
    90, 91, 93, 96, 100, 106, 119, 126
passive-aggressive, 107
pathology, 6, 7, 10, 92, 95, 110, 112, 119
pathways, 8, 69
peace, 38, 95, 97
peer group, 2, 35, 37, 43, 51, 58, 64, 65, 66, 72
penalties, 43, 52

Q